RECOVERING DAMAGES FOR PSYCHIATRIC INJURY

RECOVERING DAMAGES FOR PSYCHIATRIC INJURY

Michael Napier, LLB, Solicitor

and

Kay Wheat, BA, Solicitor

BLACKSTONE PRESS LIMITED

First published in Great Britain 1995 by Blackstone Press Limited, 9-15 Aldine Street, London W12 8AW. Telephone: 0181-740 1173

© M. Napier and K. Wheat, 1995

ISBN: 1 85431 352 5

British Library Cataloguing in Publication Data
A CIP catalogue record for this book is available from the British Library.

Typeset by Montage Studios Ltd, Tonbridge, Kent
Printed by Livesey Ltd, Shrewsbury, Shropshire

Foreword
by The Honourable Mr Justice Wright

The law on the recoverability of damages for psychiatric injury — 'nervous shock' in lawyers' language — is currently in a state of considerable flux. It has rightly been described by the Master of the Rolls as being 'one of the most vexed and tantalising topics in the modern law of tort'. Two conflicting policy considerations can clearly be seen at work in the judgments in the various actions which have emerged from the Piper Alpha and Hillsborough disasters. On the one hand, there is the natural desire to compensate those who, as a result of the fault of another, have been exposed to horrific experiences or images, and have suffered psychiatric injury, often of a life-shattering nature, as a result. On the other hand there is the equally understandable perception of a need to contain such claims, so easily made and so difficult to verify, within clearly identifiable and if necessary even arbitrary bounds. Only in such a way, it is said, can the courts and the public, in the form of tax — and premium — payers be protected from a rising flood of increasingly remote and suspect claims by opportunist plaintiffs. The degree of public interest in the topic is underlined by the recent publication of Law Commission Consultation Paper No. 137 on Liability for Psychiatric Illness, as recently as March of this year.

In such circumstances it is clear that this book comes pat upon its moment. As is to be expected from its authors, they argue the case for a liberal approach to the whole question in a cogent and forthright manner, and this book will unquestionably be regarded as a major asset by those who seek to push back the boundaries within which claims for damages in cases of this nature can be entertained.

But quite apart from this particularly topical aspect of their work, the authors have in this book provided practitioners in the field, whether legal or medical, with a work of reference which will provide them with valuable guidance over the whole extent of a topic which is, understandably, regarded by many as daunting in the extreme. They are to be congratulated for reducing the technicalities, both legal and medical, into manageable scope in language which is not merely approachable but indeed very readable. As such, I am sure that this book will find its way onto the shelves, certainly of all those who are concerned in any way with the advancement of claims for compensation for psychiatric injury before our courts, and of many others besides. I am very happy to commend it to its readers.

Michael Wright
April 1995

Contents

physical injuries — Use of questionnaires for assessment — Genuineness of
symptoms — The child victim

The once-and-for-all rule — Provisional damages — Effect of illness or
accident supervening before assessment of damages (*novus actus* or *nova
causa*) — Damages where there is a pre-existing condition — Certainty of
loss — Damages claimed must not be too remote — General damages —
Special damages for pecuniary loss — Other damages — Mitigation of loss
— Level of damages — the main cases — The *Herald of Free Enterprise*
arbitration awards

Limitation — Delay after issue of proceedings — Discovery — Interim
payments — Disclosure of medical history — Medical evidence — Pleadings
— Trial — Costs — Arbitration

The physical/psychiatric distinction — Proximity — Floodgates — A flexible
approach in negligence — Ordinary fortitude and egg shell skulls —
Psychiatric injury in the workplace — Legislation — Law Commission
Consultation Paper No. 137

Preface

The intention of this book is to combine a number of different aspects of this developing medico-legal area: an outline of the relevant law; an excursion into the field of classification of psychiatric disorders and their diagnosis; practical advice for professionals involved in psychiatric injury cases and comment on what we believe to be salient and often worrying features of the law. Selected further reading is contained within the text and in Appendix 5.

We have referred, where appropriate, to criminal injuries compensation for psychiatric injury, but it has not been possible to take into account the recent House of Lords decision upholding the Court of Appeal's finding (*R* v *Secretary of State for the Home Department, ex parte Fire Brigades Union* [1995] 2 WLR 1) that the Tariff Scheme introduced in April 1994 pursuant to the Home Secretary's executive powers, is invalid. The old scheme will therefore apply unless, or until, the Government fulfils its stated intention of legislating to introduce the Tariff Scheme.

We are indebted to Surgeon Commander Morgan O'Connell, Consultant Psychiatrist, of the Royal Naval Hospital, Haslar for his assistance and for kindly agreeing to read chapter two. Our thanks are also due to Professor John Gunn, Professor William Yule, both of the Institute of Psychiatry, University of London, Marian Preston, Clinical Psychologist, all of whom made material available to us, and to Adelene Greenburgh, trainee solicitor, for help in the preparation of Appendix 4. Any errors, however, remain our responsibility, and the views expressed are our own. We are also grateful to the staff at Blackstone Press for their guidance and encouragement. Finally, we thank our immediate professional colleagues, families and friends for their support.

The law is as stated at 1 March 1995.

M. Napier and K. Wheat

Acknowledgments

The authors and publishers would like to thank the following for permission to reproduce copyright material:

Legal Studies & Services: the *Herald of Free Enterprise* arbitrations which first appeared in the *Personal and Medical Injuries Law Letter* in June 1989.

Bruno Press (New Orleans LA): C. B. Scrignar, *Post-Traumatic Stress Disorder: Diagnosis* (1988).

American Psychiatric Association (Washington DC): *American Psychiatric Association's Diagnostic and Statistical Manual* (DSM IV) (1994).

Table of Cases

Introduction

Canst thou not minister to a mind diseas'd,
Pluck from the memory a rooted sorrow,
Raze out the written troubles of the brain,
And with some sweet oblivious antidote
Cleanse the stuff'd bosom of that perilous stuff
Which weighs upon the heart?

(*Macbeth*, act V, scene iii)

When Macbeth asked this question after embarking on the traumatic experience of multiple murder, he was probably exhibiting the despair of someone suffering the classic symptoms of post-traumatic stress disorder. Whilst we will be cautious about having sympathy for Macbeth, we may be more sympathetic to, say, Samuel Pepys, who was greatly disturbed by his experience during the Great Fire of London, writing diary entries such as 'much terrified in the nights nowadays with dreams of fire and falling down of houses' (15 September 1666). The term 'the piercing of the mental skin' is a vivid metaphor to describe the effect of trauma on the human psyche. It is so well-known that frightening experiences can have damaging and sometimes long-term effects upon the mind that it is surprising there should ever have been any doubt whether the courts should order compensation for those effects in the same way as physical injury to the person has been compensated. However, such injury has been treated with a great deal of circumspection by the courts, particularly in the case of *negligently* inflicted psychiatric injury.

There has been considerable development in this area of the law over recent years, due mainly to two factors. The first is the increasing recognition by lawyers and judges of psychiatric injury as a genuine and non-trivial form of damage, and the second is, tragically, the spate of disasters which occurred during the 1980s such as the Bradford football stadium fire in 1985; the capsize of the *Herald of Free Enterprise* ferry in 1987, which was the same year as the King's Cross Underground fire; the sinking, near Athens, of the ship *Jupiter*, carrying holidaying schoolchildren, and the Piper Alpha oil rig blaze, both of which took place in 1988; and the 1989 disasters at Hillsborough football ground and on the River Thames when the dredger *Bowbelle* sank the *Marchioness* riverboat.

The horrific nature of these events resulted not only in physical injuries, but also, in numerous cases, the suffering of psychiatric illnesses by victims, their loved ones and witnesses to the events. As litigation ensued, much was learnt by lawyers and judges alike of the awful psychiatric consequences which can result from experiences such as these. The law developed on two important fronts. Firstly, the seminal House of Lords review of the area in *Alcock* v *Chief Constable of the South Yorkshire Police* [1992] 1 AC 310, and secondly, at grassroots level there was much learnt about the handling and evaluation of the claims of individual victims.

It is important to stress that psychiatric injury can result from situations far less catastrophic than events such as the above. Every day, small-scale horrific happenings occur which affect perhaps only one or two people and do not even merit a mention in a local newspaper, but can have devastating consequences on those affected. Sometimes one of those consequences will be a psychiatric illness.

This book is about compensation for psychiatric injury, including what lawyers call 'nervous shock' claims. 'Nervous shock' is the expression used to describe a claim for psychiatric injury in the tort of negligence. Although the terminology is archaic and has no medical meaning, it is a useful form of shorthand to differentiate such claims from psychiatric injury claims in, say, intentional torts such as assault or in claims in contract.

Throughout the book we use the term 'psychiatric injury'. In other contexts the term 'psychological' as opposed to 'psychiatric' may be encountered. The terms are not mutually exclusive, nor are they precise; it is merely that we prefer the higher terminology of 'psychiatric'.

The purpose of this book is to outline the present state of the law in this area, and to provide some practical assistance to lawyers who may be dealing with such claims. It is also hoped that it may be of interest to doctors and other health care professionals working in the field.[1]

Although we deal primarily with 'nervous shock' claims, some consideration is given to other torts where psychiatric damage results and also to such claims which may arise in a claim in contract.

It is worth summarising here the essential requirements of a nervous shock claim. First, the claim must be for damages for a *recognised* psychiatric injury.

---

[1] For an excellent and very detailed analysis of claims for psychiatric injury in tort see N. Mullany and P. Handford, *Tort Liability for Psychiatric Damage* (London: Sweet & Maxwell, 1993).

What is often described as 'ordinary shock' will not do, and neither will frightening and distressing emotions such as fear and grief.

A nervous shock claim may also arise in one of the following circumstances: (a) the plaintiff has also suffered physical injury, or has had a reasonable fear of being physically injured; (b) the plaintiff has suffered because of injury to another or has had a reasonable fear of injury to another person when that person stands in a special relationship to the plaintiff, and when the plaintiff has witnessed, through his or her unaided senses, the causative event or its immediate aftermath. The event itself must be sufficiently upsetting to cause distress to the person of ordinary fortitude (the reason why a 'mere' bystander cannot usually recover damages for psychiatric injury), but the principle that one must take one's victim as one finds him applies equally in nervous shock claims.

Apart from evidential and causation problems, there is less room for contention about a claim when the plaintiff has also suffered physical injury, but difficulties arise in the other cases, particularly when the plaintiff has suffered through concern for a third party. The main cases are considered in relation to these areas.

Although nervous shock claims are probably those which cause most problems, it must not be forgotten that other torts can result in psychiatric injury, e.g., the intentional infliction of mental distress as in *Wilkinson* v *Downton* [1897] 2 QB 57, and assault, and, of course, damages can be awarded in contract if the resulting injury was within the contemplation of the parties to the contract. Chapter 1 sets the claim in its legal context, looking at the general principles of negligence, other areas of tort, and contract.

Chapter 2 is concerned with the sorts of psychiatric injury which may occur, and also provides a brief history of the development of the recognition of general 'reactive' psychiatric disorders, such as post-traumatic stress disorder (PTSD). It must be stressed that PTSD is by no means the only disorder which can result from trauma, and, given the courts' demand for a properly diagnosed psychiatric illness to be established, it is dangerous to assume that because PTSD has not been diagnosed then the plaintiff is not able to establish a claim. However, PTSD is described in some detail because, by its very nature, it is *only* caused by trauma.

Chapter 3 considers the causative event itself. Whilst the majority of cases will concern 'sudden trauma', e.g., domestic, industrial or transportation accidents, 'silent trauma' can also cause the psychiatric injury in nervous shock claims as well as in other areas. For example, professional negligence can cause psychiatric damage.

Chapter 4 looks at the mechanism by which the injury may be caused. It is not every causal chain that will result in a compensatable claim. Consideration is given here to the position of witnesses to traumatic events and how they must satisfy certain conditions to avoid any subsequent injury being too remote.

Chapter 5 looks at the practical problems which can arise in identifying the sufferer. It is worth stressing that, however distressing the experience, some people will not suffer any psychiatric injury. We would not wish it to be thought that we are encouraging lawyers to find psychiatric problems where there are none. However, it must also be said that those who do suffer may not realise it, or may feel embarrassed about admitting it as many people see this as a sign of weakness, and need to be dealt with in a sensitive and sympathetic way. This chapter also considers some of the more common forms of questionnaire used by psychologists to make initial assessments of potential sufferers.

Chapter 6 examines the principles of assessing damages and looks at quantum in detail in a number of cases, whilst chapter 7 is concerned with civil procedural matters which may be particularly pertinent to psychiatric injury.

Finally, in chapter 8 we examine shortcomings in the present law and consider ways in which it may be reformed, and possible future developments. Whilst not of specific value to the practitioner we feel it is important to stress the fact that the present state of the law in relation to nervous shock claims is in need of reform and to consider ways in which this may be carried out.

ONE

The legal context

This chapter outlines the legal framework in which a claim in respect of psychiatric injury may arise. The various elements of a claim will be examined in more detail in subsequent chapters.

Claims for damages for psychiatric injury can arise in both contract and tort. They can arise with or without physical injury. The majority of claims will arise from situations of sudden trauma, such as industrial or transportation accidents, where the claim will usually be in tort. This book deals largely with claims of that kind. However, claims for psychiatric injury need to be understood in the context of the legal framework which allows or disallows a claim for such damage.

In the law of negligence, claims for damages for psychiatric injury have for many years been described as claims for 'nervous shock', but this has no medical meaning, and has been largely superseded by the term 'psychiatric injury'. However, it is still convenient shorthand to describe psychiatric injury caused by negligence and is a useful reminder of the rule that damages will be awarded only if the illness was caused by shock, i.e., the causal event must be of a type generally thought of as 'shocking'.

Generally in tort it must be established that the plaintiff has suffered some recognisable psychiatric injury as opposed to, what we will call, ordinary mental distress. Certainly this is the case in negligence, but not, for example, in intentional torts or in nuisance.[1] In breach of contract cases, damages can be awarded for both a recognised psychiatric illness and for ordinary mental distress depending on the terms of the contract and the circumstances of its breach.

---

[1] See *Bone* v *Seale* [1975] 1 WLR 797, CA, and *Campbelltown City Council* v *Mackay* (1989) 15 NSWLR 501.

NEGLIGENCE

Before looking at the special problems which arise when claiming for
psychiatric injury, it is essential to see the claim in the general context of the
concepts of foreseeability, remoteness and proximity.[2]

Duty of care

It is worth stating the legal truism that in order to establish an action in
negligence, the plaintiff must show that the defendant owes the plaintiff a
duty of care, that the defendant is in breach of that duty, and that the
plaintiff has suffered damage as a result. Again, returning to basic legal
principles, the duty of care has been said to be owed to the defendant's
neighbours, who are 'persons who are so closely and directly affected by my
act that I ought reasonably to have them in contemplation as being so
affected'.[3] Is saying that a duty of care is owed to a person because that
person may suffer harm if the defendant is negligent the same as saying that
the possibility of the person suffering harm is foreseeable? If it is not
foreseeable then they are not neighbours: the defendant does not owe the
person a duty of care. But *if* harm is foreseeable it will not necessarily follow
that the person will recover damages for injury or loss caused (in the factual
sense of 'caused') by the defendant's action. There will be cases when the
damage is said to be too remote (that is, there is no legal causation): although
the action factually caused the injury or loss, there is no legal causation. See,
for example, the seminal case on this point — *Overseas Tankship (UK) Ltd* v
Morts Dock & Engineering Co., The Wagon Mound (No. 1) [1961] AC 388,
in which a careless oil spillage which was ignited by a spark in open water and
destroyed a wharf by fire, undoubtedly satisfied the test of factual causation
but failed the legal causation test of remoteness of damage. 'A defender is
not liable for a consequence of a kind which is not foreseeable. But it does
not follow that he is liable for every consequence which a reasonable man
could foresee.'[4] In other words, foreseeability is a necessary condition for
liability in the tort of negligence, but it is not a sufficient condition if the
damage caused is too remote.

The language can be perplexing and there is no doubt that the concepts of
foreseeability and remoteness can be used to mean exactly the same thing.
Certainly the cases show the interchangeable use of these concepts;

---

[2] For a full analysis of these concepts see H. L. A. Hart and T. Honoré, *Causation in the Law*,
2nd ed. (Oxford: Clarendon Press, 1985). See in particular *Hughes* v *Lord Advocate* [1963] AC
837, HL; *Overseas Tankship (UK) Ltd* v *Morts Dock & Engineering Co. Ltd* [1961] AC 388, PC;
Overseas Tankship (UK) Ltd v *Miller Steamship Co. Pty* [1967] 1 AC 617, PC.
[3] *Donoghue* v *Stevenson* [1932] AC 562 per Lord Atkin at p. 580.
[4] *McKew* v *Holland & Hannen & Cubitts (Scotland) Ltd* [1969] 3 All ER 1621 per Lord Reid at
p. 1623.

sometimes confusingly; sometimes in a more straightforward fashion, as per Lord Denning MR:

> The more I think about these cases, the more difficult I find it to put each into its proper pigeon-hole. Sometimes I say: 'There was no duty'. In others I say: 'The damage was too remote'.[5]

So, in order to establish the existence of a duty of care foreseeability is a requirement. In other words, in order to establish a claim at all one has to show that a duty of care was owed to *this* plaintiff whose presence should have been foreseen by the defendant. In a road traffic accident, another user of the highway would be said to be owed a duty of care, as the likelihood of his or her presence on the highway is reasonably foreseeable, and personal injury or physical damage to his or her vehicle are foreseeable types of damage.[6] However, psychiatric injury is not regarded by the courts as 'physical' damage and hence the separate criteria (to be considered in detail in due course) which have to be satisfied in order to establish a claim for such injury. Perhaps, for the avoidance of doubt, we should stress that psychiatric injury is regarded as *personal* injury for the purposes of litigation.

Was the alleged damage too remote? To establish that the damage, of whatever kind, was not too remote, either (a) it has to be a direct physical consequence of the accident; or (b) it is a foreseeable consequence, even though it arises indirectly. An example of the latter is the case of the rescuer. A person who comes along to the scene of an accident and helps to rescue the injured and thereby also suffers injury could not say that his or her injuries are a direct physical consequence of the negligent behaviour of the person who caused the accident, but the likelihood of a rescuer being involved was foreseeable.[7]

To return to the specific issue of psychiatric injury, the practical application of these concepts can be seen in the case of *King* v *Phillips* [1953] 1 QB 429, CA. The facts were that a taxi driver had backed his vehicle into a small boy on a tricycle. The injury to the boy and damage to his tricycle were slight but his mother heard him scream and, looking out of an upstairs window some 70 to 80 yards away, saw the tricycle under the taxicab but could not see the boy. She ran downstairs and into the road, and she met the boy running towards her. She suffered psychiatric injury attributable to the shock of that incident. It was held that no legal wrong had been done to the mother (as opposed to the child). This was because no 'hypothetical

---

[5] *Spartan Steel & Alloys Ltd* v *Martin & Co. (Contractors) Ltd* [1972] QB 27; and see also below on the issue of public policy.
[6] General principle established in *Donoghue* v *Stevenson* [1932] AC 562.
[7] See chapter 4 for further discussion of the position of rescuers.

reasonable observer'[8] could reasonably or probably have anticipated that injury, either physical or nervous, could have been caused to her by the backing of the taxi without due attention. Accordingly, the driver owed no duty to the plaintiff mother and was not liable to her for negligence. Denning LJ said (at pp. 439–40):

> What is the reasoning which admits a cause of action for negligence if the injured person is actually struck, but declines it if he only suffers from shock? I cannot see why the duty of a driver should differ according to the nature of the injury.... If he drives negligently with the result that a bystander is injured, then his breach of duty is the same, no matter whether the injury is a wound or is emotional shock.... If you view the duty of care in this way, and yet refuse to allow a bystander to recover for shock, it is not because there was no duty owed to him, nor because it was not caused by the negligence of the driver, but simply because it was too remote to be admitted as a head of damage.
>
> A different result is reached by viewing the driver's duty differently. Instead of saying simply that his duty is to drive with reasonable care, you say that his duty is to avoid injury which he can reasonably foresee.... Then you draw a distinction between physical and emotional injury, and impose a different duty on him in regard to each kind of injury, with the inevitable result that you are driven to say there are two different torts — one tort when he can foresee physical injury, and another tort when he can foresee emotional injury. I do not think that that is right. There is one wrong only, the wrong of negligence.

One may be forgiven for thinking at this stage that the unfortunate Mrs King was going to recover damages, but Denning LJ (who was supported by both other members of the Court of Appeal) went on to say (at p. 442):

> ... I think that the shock in this case is too remote to be a head of damage. It seems to me that the slow backing of the taxicab was very different from the terrifying descent of the runaway lorry.[9] The taxicab driver cannot reasonably be expected to have foreseen that his backing would terrify a mother 70 yards away, whereas the lorry driver ought to have foreseen that a runaway lorry might seriously shock the mother of children in the danger area.

It can only be a matter of speculation whether this case would be decided differently today; suffice to say that there is an uncomfortable element of

[8] Applying the test laid down in *Bourhill* v *Young* [1943] AC 92, HL, see page 25.
[9] Here reference was being made to the case of *Hambrook* v *Stokes Brothers* [1925] 1 KB 141, where a woman recovered damages following the shock she received when she saw a lorry run away downhill towards an area where she had just left her children. See below, page 24.

subjectivity in the notion that the slow inexorable backing of a motor vehicle towards a child is less shocking than the swift progress of a larger motor vehicle towards an area where children are likely to be. It must also be remembered that the case was decided in the days when the psychiatric injuries complained of were always described as 'nervous shock', and it may have influenced the sort of events that the courts would regard as capable of causing shock that was not too remote. However, it does illustrate the conceptual acrobatics which judges are apt to indulge in when considering the wider effects of an initial negligent event by employing the filtering devices of foreseeability or remoteness to avoid liability 'in an indeterminate amount for an indeterminate time to an indeterminate class',[10] or avoid cases presenting enormous evidential difficulties. This may be linked to the question of public policy which features significantly in claims for psychiatric injury. Put simply the courts have seen it as their duty to envisage floodgates[11] and to keep them firmly locked.

We do not subscribe to the public policy justification for imposition of otherwise unjustifiable restrictions on claims for psychiatric injury. However, there are several possible reasons for the public policy arguments. For example, it could be said to be unfair (i.e., as a matter of general morality) to extend the potential liability for, say, a momentary lapse of concentration to a vast and possibly ruinous extent; or it could be said that its effect upon the liability of insurers with the inevitable and dire consequences for everyone in terms of availability and cost of insurance would be disastrous. It is instructive, however, to consider the speech of Lord Edmund-Davies in *McLoughlin* v *O'Brian* [1983] 1 AC 410 at p. 425:

> My lords, the experiences of a long life in the law have made me very familiar with this 'floodgates' argument. I do not, of course, suggest that it can invariably be dismissed as lacking cogency; on the contrary, it has to be weighed carefully, but I have often seen it disproved by later events. It was urged when abolition of the doctrine of common employment was being canvassed, and it raised its head again when the abolition of contributory negligence as a total bar to a claim in negligence was being urged.
>
> ... I remain unconvinced that the number and area of claims in 'shock' cases would be substantially increased or enlarged were the respondents here held liable.

---

[10] Per Cardozo CJ in *Ultramares Corporation* v *Touche* (1931) 174 NE 441 at p. 444.
[11] See *McLoughlin* v *O'Brian* [1983] 1 AC 410, HL, especially at pp. 430 and 438.

The proximity test

All important is the related concept of 'proximity'.[12] It was used by Lord
Atkin to explain the 'neighbour principle', i.e., my neighbour is someone to
whom I stand in a particular relationship of 'proximity'.[13]

The proximity test — in relation to economic loss

A comparable area where the proximity issue defeats claims in negligence is
in the area of economic loss and it is worth a short digression to consider
such cases as being illustrations of the way in which the proximity test has
been considered by the courts.

It is an established general principle that a claim in negligence for pure
financial loss is not allowable,[14] and that it would only follow on the heels of
physical damage, e.g., if the electricity suppliers damage a cable on a
manufacturer's property then the manufacturer will be able to claim
pecuniary loss following upon this physical damage; the manufacturer will
have no such claim if the electricity supply is interrupted by a power cut
unaccompanied by physical damage. However, the tort of negligence has
been widened to include some cases of pure economic loss, where some
special relationship exists between the parties.[15] In the well-known negligent
misstatement case of *Hedley Byrne & Co. Ltd* v *Heller & Partners Ltd* [1964]
AC 465 the House of Lords held that in principle there was no difference
between physical loss and financial loss, and that a duty to take care in the
making of statements existed whenever there was a special relationship, i.e.,
where the inquirer was trusting the other to exercise a reasonable degree of
care, and when the other knew or ought to have known that the statement
would be relied on by the inquirer.

This issue is illustrated by *Caparo Industries plc* v *Dickman* [1990] 2 AC
605 in which shareholders who purchased more shares and implemented a
company takeover in reliance on an inaccurate and misleading auditor's
report brought an action against the auditors alleging that they had been
negligent in auditing the accounts, that the respondents had relied upon the
accounts, and that the auditors owed them a duty of care either as potential
bidders for the company or as existing shareholders. It was held that there
were three criteria for the imposition of a duty of care — foreseeability of
damage, proximity of relationship and the reasonableness or otherwise of

---

[12] The term appears to have been first used in *Thomas* v *Quartermaine* (1887) 18 QBD 685 at
p. 688.
[13] See *Donoghue* v *Stevenson* [1932] AC 562, HL, and also *Home Office* v *Dorset Yacht Co. Ltd*
[1970] AC 1004.
[14] See *Spartan Steel & Alloys Ltd* v *Martin & Co. (Contractors) Ltd* [1972] QB 27.
[15] See *Weller & Co.* v *Foot & Mouth Disease Research Institute* [1966] 1 QB 569 and *Spartan Steel
and Alloys Ltd* v *Martin & Co. (Contractors) Ltd* [1972] QB 27.

imposing a duty.[16] Their lordships went on to state that when a statement was put into general circulation, there was no general relationship of proximity with those who may read it, and so no duty of care was owed by the auditors to the public at large, or to shareholders who read accounts for the purpose of buying shares with a view to a profit.

The proximity requirement is well-illustrated by the House of Lords case of *Murphy* v *Brentwood District Council* [1991] 1 AC 398. The case concerned the liability of a local authority for the approval of plans for a defective foundation to the plaintiff's house. Lord Bridge of Harwich said (at p. 475):

> If a builder erects a structure containing a latent defect which renders it dangerous to persons or property, he will be liable in tort for injury to persons or damage to property resulting from that dangerous defect. But if the defect becomes apparent before any injury or damage has been caused, the loss sustained by the building owner is purely economic.... These economic losses are recoverable if they flow from breach of a relevant contractual duty, but, here again, they are not recoverable in tort in the absence of a special relationship of proximity ....

The proximity test — in relation to psychiatric injury
What effect does the proximity issue have on a claim for psychiatric injury? Such a claim can either be ancillary to another claim, e.g., physical damage to either property or person, or it can stand on its own. If there is physical damage then the claim for associated psychiatric injury is an allowable claim provided the psychiatric injury was actually caused by the tortious event, and, of course, that the defendant is liable in tort for the event. Proximity should not, therefore, be an issue in cases where physical injury has also been caused to the plaintiff.

In what kind of case can psychiatric injury arise in the absence of physical injury? Let us take first of all the case of a bereavement. There are no damages available in negligence for 'ordinary' grief.[17] (In certain cases, of course, bereavement damages can be claimed under the Fatal Accidents Act 1976, but these relate to financial loss and not personal injury.) This is because grief is a normal human emotion and therefore there is no damage of any sort. However great the distress, a widow, for example, will not recover damages for her grief upon the loss of her husband. If, however, she

---

[16] The use of the concept of 'the reasonableness or otherwise of imposing a duty' is another way of allowing a number of considerations (usually of policy) to influence whether there is a duty of care.
[17] See *Hinz* v *Berry* [1970] 2 QB 40, CA.

suffers from a recognised psychiatric illness,[18] she still cannot recover, unless a number of conditions pertained at the time of the event that killed him, i.e., she can show the required degree of proximity to the event.

What are the conditions at the time of the event? She must have either been involved in the event itself, e.g., in the same motor vehicle as her husband (if she suffers physical injury then she can claim regardless of the proximity issue), or she must have witnessed the event or its *immediate aftermath*. In chapter 4 we will look at precisely what the immediate aftermath may mean, but it is a way of saying that she must have been sufficiently proximate to the event.

Let us look at another example. A motorist is travelling down the motorway when he comes upon speed restrictions, and police warning signs. Eventually in a queue of traffic he travels past the scene of a dreadful accident which has obviously only just happened because the fire and ambulance crews are still there attending the injured. He continues on his journey, but the incident he has just seen, which was also seen by many other motorists who have driven past it, has an extremely distressing effect upon him, so much so that he is later diagnosed as suffering from a recognised psychiatric illness directly attributable to the scene he witnessed. Can he claim damages in respect of this illness and how will the proximity issue affect his claim? He will be able to say that he witnessed the immediate aftermath of the event, but he will have to satisfy the second limb of the proximity test (satisfied by the widow in the first example): he will have to show that his relationship to one or more of the injured or killed is sufficiently close, i.e., sufficiently proximate. If he had recognised his wife's car as one of the damaged vehicles then that would suffice. If he had recognised his fiancée's car in the same way, then that *may* suffice. If he had recognised his next-door neighbour's car then that probably would not suffice. Since, in the example, there was no 'relationship proximity', he will almost certainly not be successful.

It must always be remembered that 'relationship proximity' is not confined to intimate, emotional relationships. The required degree of proximity can arise when someone becomes involved in a traumatic event as a rescuer, for example, or when the relationship is commercial, as in the case of a relationship between worker and worker.

Suppose the accident happens rather differently. Our motorist was waiting in a queue of traffic on a bridge, say, over the motorway, upon which there is heavy traffic in both directions. He sees a petrol tanker travelling along the motorway, away from the bridge. The tanker careers across on to the opposite carriageway and bursts into flames. Vehicles become out of

---

[18] Of course, the cause of her illness must relate to the trauma of the event and not just to the loss of her husband: *Hinz* v *Berry* [1970] 2 QB 40, CA.

control, themselves bursting into flames, overturning, colliding with others. There is general mayhem. It is some distance away from the bridge so he is in no danger himself nor does he perceive himself to be. He is horrified by what he sees and, as a result, suffers psychiatric injury. He has no reason to believe that anyone close to him is anywhere near the accident, nor indeed are they. The question here is whether there are circumstances which are sufficiently horrific to cause psychiatric injury to one who witnesses them even if they have no relationship to any one of the participants. In the context of this type of claim, this motorist would be classified as a 'mere bystander'. Atkin LJ in *Hambrook* v *Stokes Brothers* [1925] 1 KB 141, CA, suggested that there was no reason why such a person should not be able to claim, and in *Alcock* v *Chief Constable of South Yorkshire Police* [1992] 1 AC 310 there was speculation about the type of event which would be sufficiently horrifying to justify the mere bystander recovering damages. However, this possibility has recently received a setback in the Court of Appeal in the case of *McFarlane* v *E. E. Caledonia Ltd* [1994] 2 All ER 1 when it overturned the first-instance decision to award damages to a worker who witnessed the explosions and fire on the Piper Alpha oil rig from a support vessel approximately 550 yards away. Stuart-Smith LJ said (at p. 14):

> In my judgment both as a matter of principle and policy the court should not extend the duty to those who are mere bystanders or witnesses of horrific events unless there is a sufficient degree of proximity, which requires both nearness in time and place and a close relationship of love and affection between plaintiff and victim.

Whether or not on the facts of this particular case, the Court of Appeal was entitled to reject the claim, this statement of general policy which is clearly contrary to the House of Lords decision in *Alcock* v *Chief Constable of the South Yorkshire Police* was not justified.

It is surely no coincidence that the early cases of claims for psychiatric injury concern pregnant women who, as a result of shock, have miscarried or given birth to brain-damaged children.[19] In such cases physical damage is present. No doubt the distress would have been just as great if the plaintiffs concerned had not been pregnant, or if they had been fortunate enough to have had healthy babies, but their distress would not have been perceived to be physically measurable. There is interesting research being undertaken which may show that psychiatric injury can actually be identifiable in the chemical composition of the nervous system (see page 56). If this is scientifically established and then accepted by the courts then, by showing physical injury, the need for proximity to time and place, and to a relationship, will disappear.

---

[19] *Dulieu* v *White & Sons* [1901] 2 KB 669; *Bourhill* v *Young* [1943] AC 92; *Hambrook* v *Stokes Brothers* [1925] 1 KB 141.

Causation

Once it has been established that there is a breach of the duty of care in negligence, it still has to be shown that there has been damage caused by this breach. Generally it is said that causation is a question of fact and remoteness of damage is a question of law, but the issues are often very closely related. The simple test of causation is the 'but for' test,[20] i.e., would the damage have occurred but for the defendant's negligence. However, this is complicated by factors such as intervening causes, competing causes, third-party acts and unreasonable acts of the plaintiff. These issues are explored further in chapter 6. The issue of causation in a psychiatric injury was considered by the Court of Appeal in *Page* v *Smith* [1994] 4 All ER 522. This concerned a plaintiff who had previously suffered from the condition known as myalgic encephalomyelitis (ME) and was subsequently involved in a fairly minor road accident. He suffered no physical injury but the judge at first instance accepted that the accident had caused the plaintiff's ME to recur. In the Court of Appeal, Ralph Gibson LJ said:

> The point at which, for my part, the reasoning and conclusion of the judge on the issue of causation appear to be unsatisfactory is in his application of his finding about the degree of severity of the collision to the reasoning and opinions of the doctors. . . . It seems to me that the submissions for the defendant must be accepted, namely that there was no clear evidence from any witness to the effect that other cases had been observed or reported in which an accident causing no physical injury, and no more 'nervous shock' than some immediate fright, had caused either the onset or serious or permanent worsening of symptoms of ME. I am unable to accept that the evidence before the court is sufficient to justify a holding that the accident in probablity caused or materially contributed to the plaintiff's condition.

It is interesting to speculate whether the judgment would have been the same if the disorder suffered by the plaintiff had been a reactive depression or post-traumatic stress disorder, or whether the scepticism which surrounds the condition of ME was a factor which influenced the court.

The eggshell-skull rule

The Court of Appeal in *Page* v *Smith* [1994] 4 All ER 522 also looked at the application of what is variously known as the 'eggshell-skull' or *'talem qualem'* rule, that one takes one's victim as one finds him: 'If a man is

---

[20] See *Barnett* v *Chelsea & Kensington Hospital Management Committee* [1969] 1 QB 428.

negligently run over or otherwise negligently injured in his body, it is no answer to the sufferer's claim for damages that he would have suffered less injury, or no injury at all, if he had not had an unusually thin skull or an unusually weak heart.'[21] This applies as much to psychiatric injury claims as it does to claims for physical injury, i.e., once some psychiatric injury is foreseeable then, even if the plaintiff is suffering from some pre-existing susceptibility which results in much more severe illness than in the 'normal' person, there can be recovery for *all* psychiatric injury because it is damage of the same *kind*. What is *not* the case, however, is that if the plaintiff is of a psychologically vulnerable disposition then, no matter how trivial the event, if it produces the necessary psychiatric illness, the plaintiff can recover. In order for the claim to succeed at all, the event itself must be such that a person of normally phlegmatic disposition would be likely to be affected. This was established in *Bourhill* v *Young* [1943] AC 92. Lord Wright said (at pp. 109–10):

> No doubt it has long ago been stated and often restated that if the wrong is established the wrongdoer must take the victim as he finds him. That, however, is only true ... on the condition that the wrong has been established or admitted. The question of liablity is anterior to the question of the measure of the consequences which go with the liability.

There is no contradiction with the *talem qualem* rule. It is simply that injury of that type must be foreseeable. An example given in that case of unforeseeable *physical* injury illustrates the position. Lord Wright said (at p. 109):

> One who suffers from the terrible tendency to bleed on slight contact, which is denoted by the term 'a bleeder', cannot complain if he mixes with the crowd and suffers severely, perhaps fatally, from being merely brushed against. There is no wrong done there.

Unfortunately for Mr Page, the Court of Appeal found in *Page* v *Smith*, that it was not foreseeable that a plaintiff would suffer psychiatric injury in an accident which did not injure him physically, and where there was no evidence that the frightening experience included fear of the plaintiff's own death or fear for the death of a passenger. This decision sits uneasily with *Brice* v *Brown* [1984] 1 All ER 997 (see page 120) which concerned a woman who suffered minor injuries in a road accident, and whose daughter suffered a very bad laceration to her forehead. Clearly it was a much more distressing accident than the one in which Mr Page was involved, but nevertheless it was

---

[21] *Dulieu* v *White & Sons* [1901] 2 KB 669 per Kennedy J at p. 679.

a relatively minor accident, though Mrs Brice developed a most severe psychiatric condition as a result of it. Although this decision is quoted with approval in *Page* v *Smith*, consideration of the two cases does point up the unsatisfactorily subjective nature of the requirement that the event must be such that a person of ordinary fortitude would be likely to be distressed by it.

However, the law at present is that the person vulnerable to injury of this type will recover nothing if the event itself would not be distressing or shocking to the person of average mental resilience because it would not have been foreseeable that distress or shock would have been experienced. Once it has been established that the event is distressing or shocking then, by application of the egg-shell skull rule, the vulnerable plaintiff will recover for the injury caused, however severe. This is assuming, of course, that factual causation can be proved. A pre-existing condition can have an effect upon the level of damages awarded in certain circumstances. This will be further considered in chapter 6.

Prior to *Page* v *Smith*, one may have been forgiven for thinking that the 'ordinary fortitude' rule applied only to the mere bystander, but the Court of Appeal have confirmed in this case that it also applies to participants in the 'shocking' event. This case is considered further in chapter 8.

OTHER AREAS OF TORT

Although a psychiatric injury claim will usually arise in negligence, it may arise in a number of other tortious areas. It is essential to remember that the restrictions which we have been considering above apply only to *negligence* and if it is possible to plead another cause of action this may have enormous advantages for the plaintiff. The tort of deceit for example, could result in psychiatric injury. One of the earliest cases where damages were awarded was *Wilkinson* v *Downton* [1897] 2 QB 57, where, as a practical joke, the defendant had falsely represented to a married woman that her husband had met with a serious accident whereby both his legs were broken, as a result of which the woman suffered serious shock.

Other torts where psychiatric injury may result include false imprisonment, malicious prosecution, defamation and intimidation (see *Godwin* v *Uziogwe* (1992) *The Times*, 18 June, CA). The tort of breach of statutory duty may also give rise to a claim for psychiatric injury if, upon a construction of the relevant legislation, it is appropriate to infer a private action for damages. There has been much judicial dispute as to the relationship of common law negligence and breach of statutory duty, but what is certainly different is the standard of care, which can be the same as the standard at common law or can be strict, so that the defendant will be responsible regardless of steps taken to avoid breach. (See Jones, *Textbook on*

Torts, 4th edition, Blackstone Press, 1993.) If an action in breach of statutory duty is possible therefore, it may have considerable advantages over an action in common law negligence. In the case of *M (A Minor) and Another* v *Newham London Borough Council and Others* [1994] 2 WLR 554 the Court of Appeal considered whether an action could be founded for breach of statutory duty when a local authority may be in breach of its statutory child care duties. The plaintiffs were mother and child who had been separated due to a mistaken diagnosis of child abuse, as a result of which they both suffered from an anxiety neurosis. The court held that, having regard to the general terms in which the duties imposed on local authorities in respect of child care were framed, and to the alternative remedies available to an aggrieved party, there was no indication that the legislature intended those duties to be directly enforceable by private law action. Both mother and child also failed in negligence: the mother because she was neither a client nor patient so there was no duty of care owed to her; the child because imposition of a duty would be detrimental to the functioning of local authorities (Sir Thomas Bingham MR dissenting).

Generally speaking, where the tort allows for recovery of damages for physical injury then, in principle, recovery for psychiatric injury should be also possible. Subject to foreseeability this would include public nuisance, and probably private nuisance, although there is no English authority for the latter and would probably include an action such as in *Rylands* v *Fletcher* (1868) LR 3 HL 330,[22] which, since the decision in *Cambridge Water Co.* v *Eastern Counties Leather plc* [1994] 2 WLR 53 is no longer a separate strict liability action, but a species of nuisance and is subject to the damage being foreseeable.

CONTRACT

Put simply, the purpose of damages for breach of contract is to put the injured party in the position which would have obtained if the contract had been properly performed. Damages are awarded to compensate for loss caused by the breach which the parties, at the time of entering into the contract, would expect to arise from a breach. The rule is well-known and was first formulated in *Hadley* v *Baxendale* (1854) 9 Ex 341, in which Alderson B said (at p. 354):

> Where two parties have made a contract which one of them has broken, the damages which the other party ought to receive in respect of such breach of contract should be such as may fairly and reasonably be

---

[22] See also *Shiffman* v *Order of the Hospital of St John of Jerusalem* [1936] 1 All ER 557.

considered either arising naturally, i.e., according to the usual course of things, from such breach of contract itself, or such as may reasonably be supposed to have been in the contemplation of both parties, at the time they made the contract, as the probable result of the breach of it.

Injury of a psychiatric nature, therefore, would have to be a natural consequence of the breach, i.e., what reasonable persons entering into the contract would believe to be a likely consequence of the breach, or it would have to be a consequence of the breach given what the parties knew or should have known at the time the contract was made. However, in a personal injury case (including psychiatric injury this rule does not apply. For an injured railway passenger, for example, any claim for physical or psychiatric injury would be founded in tort and so the rule in *Hadley* v *Baxendale* would not apply.[23] Similarly for cases of medical negligence when the plaintiff is a private paying patient the claim would be in contract, whereas in NHS cases, it would be founded in tort.[24] Specific issues relating to professional negligence cases will be considered in chapter 3.

However unforeseeable the damage may have been in tort, as long as the special circumstances can be shown to exist in *this* contract, the claim is allowable. Nonetheless, as in tort, once this has been established, it does not matter if the extent of the psychiatric injury is far greater than either party could have anticipated. The distinction is that once the *type* of damage is accepted as being within the contemplation of the parties then it does not matter that the *extent* of the damage was not so contemplated.[25] However, arguments do arise over the difference between type and extent of damage, and sometimes the distinction is not made out. It is always important to remember that regardless of whether one is pursuing a claim in contract or in tort, one will be facing limitations which, in both cases, have been devised by the courts to avoid extending the area of liability to an unacceptable extent.

ORDINARY MENTAL DISTRESS

Often when psychiatric injury is considered, reference will also be made to 'shock' in its colloquial and non-medical sense. Most people involved in, say, a road traffic accident, would say they felt shocked by it. Anyone who

---

[23] See *Phillips* v *London & South Western Railway Co.* (1879) 4 QBD 406.
[24] It was held in *Pfizer Corporation* v *Ministry of Health* [1965] AC 512 that where services are provided pursuant to a statutory obligation there is no contractual relationship.
[25] *H. Parsons (Livestock) Ltd* v *Uttley Ingham & Co. Ltd* [1978] QB 791, CA; *Victoria Laundry (Windsor) Ltd* v *Newman Industries Ltd* [1949] 2 KB 528; *Koufos* v *C. Czarnikow Ltd* [1969] 1 AC 350.

receives news of the injury of a loved one will be distressed; a close bereavement will cause grief. All these are examples of non-medical distress. Is it possible to claim damages for such conditions?

Ordinary mental distress in tort

Ordinary mental distress is not generally compensatable in tort. However, there are a number of torts where, by their very nature, mental distress is an esential component, such as defamation (injury to feelings), malicious prosecution, false imprisonment, deceit, injurious falsehood and assault. In *Bone v Seale* [1975] 1 WLR 797, the Court of Appeal considered the appropriateness of awarding damages for distress in nuisance. The nuisance concerned was a noxious odour which had been present for some 12 years or so, but in respect of which there had been no provable diminution in the value of the plaintiff's property. The trial judge had awarded £6,000 in damages, but this was reduced by the Court of Appeal to £1,000. Drawing a parallel between such a case and personal injury cases, Stephenson LJ said (at pp. 803–4):

> Is it possible to equate loss of sense of smell as a result of the negligence of a defendant motor driver with having to put up with positive smells as a result of a nuisance created by a negligent neighbour? There is, as it seems to me, some parallel between the loss of amenity which is caused by personal injury and the loss of amenity which is caused by a nuisance of this kind.

It may be that other torts such as trespass to property, trespass to goods etc. are capable of giving rise to damages for mental distress if the appropriate set of circumstances prevailed. Statutory torts such as breaches of the Sex Discrimination Act 1975 or the Race Relations Act 1976 have, as an allowable head of damages, compensation in respect of injury to feelings.[26] In *Racz v Home Office* [1994] 2 AC 45 damages for mental distress were awarded for misfeasance in public office.

What of damages for ordinary mental distress in negligence? In one sense damages are always awarded for mental distress if there is some physical injury because in such a case there are damages for pain and suffering, both of which are forms of mental distress. If, however, we look for a separate head of damage to cover mental distress or shock or grief or anger, or any other similar aspect of non-medical distress, then we look in vain. It has been held by the Court of Appeal in the case of *Nicholls v Rushton* (1992) *The Times*, 19 June that a plaintiff involved in a motor accident who had suffered

[26] See the Sex Discrimination Act 1975, s. 66(4), and the Race Relations Act 1976, s. 57(4).

no physical injury, but had suffered a nervous reaction falling short of an identifiable psychiatric illness, could not recover damages: unless there was physical injury no question of damages for mental suffering, fear, anxiety and the like arose.

The House of Lords considered damages for fear in *Hicks* v *Chief Constable of the South Yorkshire Police* [1992] 2 All ER 65. The case concerned two victims of the Hillsborough football stadium disaster, who had died of traumatic asphyxia. Their personal representatives brought actions for damages for pre-death injuries. The post-mortems showed no evidence of any physical injuries attributable to anything other than the fatal crushing that had caused the asphyxia, which, it was said, would have caused loss of consciousness within seconds and death within five minutes. It was held therefore that it could not be proved on the balance of probabilities that they had sustained any pre-death physical injuries. There was also argument as to whether damages for physical injuries should be increased on the account of the terrifying circumstances in which they were inflicted. Lord Bridge of Harwich said that it was perfectly clear law that fear by itself, of whatever degree, was a normal emotion for which no damages could be awarded. This is the same principle which denies the sufferer from 'ordinary' grief any damages for this normal emotion, which principle has a long and continuing history.[27] Similarly, it was held in *Reilly and another* v *Merseyside Regional Health Authority* (1994) *Independent*, 29 April, that claustrophobia and fear, even when they produced physical reactions such as sweating and vomiting, were within the normal human emotional experience and would only be compensatable if they amounted to a recognised psychiatric condition. However, it should be noted that there is a recognised psychiatric condition known as 'acute distress reaction' (see page 41), which is of short duration, and there appears no reason why damages should not be awarded for this, albeit in a modest sum. In other words, if so-called 'ordinary shock' is definable medically, then on the present law damages must surely be allowable. We regard this as an important point for practitioners to note. If the appropriate diagnosis had been made in *Nicholls* v *Rushton* then the plaintiff should have recovered damages.

Ordinary mental distress in contract

Where breach of contract has caused mental distress the crucial questions are whether the mental distress was a natural consequence of the breach of contract or whether it was within the contemplation of the parties that the breach would result in such distress. The history of damages claims shows a

---

[27] See, for example, *Alcock* v *Chief Constable of the South Yorkshire Police* [1992] 1 AC 310 per Lord Ackner at p. 401.

robust approach by the courts. In *Addis* v *Gramophone Co. Ltd* [1909] AC 488, HL, it was held that damages for the wrongful dismissal of a servant could not include compensation for his injured feelings, however harsh and humiliating his dismissal had been. In a professional negligence case (see chapter 3 for a further discussion of this type of case), Lord Denning MR said:

It can be foreseen that there will be injured feelings; mental distress; anger; and annoyance; but for none of these damages can be recovered.[28]

This view remained paramount until 1971 when a Scottish case[29] awarded damages for distress and disappointment to a bride who had no photographs of her wedding day following the breach of contract of the photographer commissioned to attend. In the important decision of *Jarvis* v *Swans Tours* [1973] QB 233, the well-known case of the solicitor disappointed with his holiday, it was held that damages could be recovered for disappointment, distress, annoyance and frustration. As Mcgregor points out, 'the predominant object of the contract was the provision of some mental satisfaction ... by the giving of pleasure',[30] and in the subsequent case of *Heywood* v *Wellers* [1976] QB 446, CA, 'some mental satisfaction ... by the removal of distress'. The *Heywood* case concerned an action against a solicitor by his former client, who had asked him to bring proceedings for a non-molestation order, and it was held that both solicitor and client would have contemplated that a failure by the solicitor to perform the contract would result in vexation, frustration or distress.

There is limited scope, however, in contract cases for a claim for non-medical distress. In 1975 Lawton J awarded damages to a former employee who claimed damages in respect of mental distress following breach of the contract of employment since it would have been in the contemplation of the parties that the breach, without reasonable notice, would expose the plaintiff to vexation, frustration and distress.[31] However, in the later case of *Bliss* v *South East Thames Regional Health Authority* [1987] ICR 700, the Court of Appeal overruled that decision stating that no such damages could be awarded in contract. It may be argued, with some ingenuity on the part of lawyers, that all successfully and properly completed contracts will contain some element of mental satisfaction, and no doubt this is something the courts would not wish to encourage, and would explain the reason for the decision in *Bliss*.

[28] *Cook* v *Swinfen* [1967] 1 WLR 457, CA at p. 461.
[29] *Diesen* v *Samson* 1971 (Sh Ct) 49.
[30] *McGregor on Damages*, 15th ed. (London: Sweet & Maxwell, 1988).
[31] *Cox* v *Philips Industries Ltd* [1976] 1 WLR 638.

In *McConville and Others* v *Barclays Bank and Others* (1993) *The Times*, 30 June, it was held that damages were not recoverable for worry and distress caused to bank customers arising from allegedly unauthorised debits from their accounts through automatic telling machines.

DEFENCES

Contributory negligence

Damages for psychiatric injury may be reduced, in precisely the same way as for any other kind of injury, because of the plaintiff's contributory negligence, according to the facts of the accident that caused the injury. There is nothing particularly special in this. However, an interesting point arises when the plaintiff is not the *primary* victim of the accident. An example was given in *Alcock* v *Chief Constable of the South Yorkshire Police* [1992] 1 AC 310 of a mother who suffers psychiatric injury through witnessing the death of her son when he negligently walks in front of an oncoming motor car. If, say, the son is 75 per cent to blame for the accident, should the mother be able to recover 100 per cent damages from the motorist, who is only 25 per cent to blame? Lord Oliver of Aylmerton said it would be a curious and wholly unfair situation if the mother could so recover, pointing out that the son and the motorist could not be joint tortfeasors, as the son would not have acted tortiously. Mullany and Handford seem to think that this sits uneasily with the principle that the person psychiatrically injured has a claim independent of any other party involved, not least because they contend that in that case the son negligently injuring himself would give rise to a claim in tort.[32] Another objection is that the so-called secondary victim, i.e., the mother (the son being the primary victim), has an independent claim which does not derive from any claim that the primary victim may have. Litigation to clarify this point is awaited, but it seems to us wholly arbitrary that a claim should fail for this reason. There is no logical difference between the claim of the mother in this situation and the claim of her son against the motorist when the son is too young to be contributorily negligent and therefore recovers 100 per cent damages from the motorist, albeit that the motorist is only 25 per cent to blame. In connection with this, again speaking in *Alcock*, Lord Oliver also questioned the dictum in *Jaensch* v *Coffey* (1984) 155 CLR 549 at p. 604 which ruled out a claim which arises when the plaintiff witnesses the victim's self-inflicted injury (see page 86).

Volenti non fit injuria

Again, there is no authority to assist on whether this defence would be appropriate, save to say that it is well-established that a bona fide rescuer will

---

[32] N. Mullany and P. Handford, *Tort Liability for Psychiatric Damage* (London: Sweet & Maxwell 1993), p. 254.

not be denied relief on this ground.[33] However, it is likely that this defence would defeat a psychiatric injury claim by someone participating in or observing a dangerous entertainment such as stunt-riding.

NERVOUS SHOCK IN ENGLISH LAW — A BRIEF HISTORY

Having looked at the legal framework in which the claim for psychiatric injury sits, we now propose to give such claims their historical setting, with a brief look at the major English cases which have established psychiatric injury as a valid head of damage, and the way in which the legal concepts discussed above have been employed in these cases.

Two early non-English cases merit a mention not least because of their contrasting decisions on the same point. The first is a Privy Council case, *Victorian Railways Commissioners* v *Coultas* (1888) 13 App Cas 222, in which it was held that there are no damages for nervous shock that is unaccompanied by physical injury. The second is the Irish case of *Bell* v *Great Northern Railway Co. of Ireland* (1890) 26 LR Ir 428, in which damages were awarded for nervous shock despite the absence of physical injury.

Dulieu v *White & Sons* [1901] 2 KB 669, CA

This Court of Appeal case is one of the earliest English cases to consider the claim in some detail. The facts concerned a publican's wife, Mrs Dulieu, who was standing behind the bar of the public house, when a horse van was driven into the public house by the defendant's servant. Mrs Dulieu was pregnant at the time, and following this incident she was prematurely delivered of a brain-damaged child. She recovered damages, not for the birth of the brain-damaged child, but for her own 'illness' brought about by the shock sustained from the incident. The negligent driving of the defendant's servant was not doubted; the issue was whether damages could be recovered for shock, and, if so, under what circumstances. First, it is interesting to note the reason given for preferring the term 'nervous' as opposed to 'mental' shock. Kennedy J said (at pp. 672–3):

... I venture to think 'nervous' is probably the more correct epithet where terror operates through parts of the physical organism to produce bodily illness.... The use of the epithet 'mental' requires caution, in view of the undoubted rule that merely mental pain unaccompanied by any injury to the person cannot sustain an action of this kind.

[33] *Baker* v *T. E. Hopkins & Sons Ltd* [1958] 1 WLR 993, CA.

It can be seen that this is a long way off from the concept of purely psychiatric injury. His lordship went on to say (at p. 675) that if the fear, as opposed to impact:

> is proved to have naturally and directly produced physical effects . . . why should not an action for those damages lie just as well as it lies where there has been an actual impact? It is not, however, to be taken that . . . every nervous shock . . . gives a cause of action. . . . The shock, where it operates through the mind, must be a shock which arises from a reasonable fear of immediate personal injury to oneself.

So there is a great deal of emphasis on the shock having produced physical injury and the restriction imposed that fear for *oneself* is essential (this is no longer good law). The case contains a good statement from Kennedy J (at p. 681) on the policy question:

> . . . I should be sorry to adopt a rule which would bar all such claims on grounds of policy alone, and in order to prevent the possible success of unrighteous or groundless actions.

Hambrook v *Stokes Brothers* [1925] 1 KB 141, CA

The defendants' lorry was left at the top of a steep and narrow street unattended, with the engine running. The lorry, being inadequately secured, ran down the hill at great speed. Mrs Hambrook was walking up the hill when she saw the lorry running away towards the spot where she had just left her children. She was immediately afterwards informed by a bystander that a child answering the description of one of her children had been injured, and that the child was in a state of some distress. She later discovered that one of her children had indeed suffered serious injury. She was pregnant at the time, and the shock was said to have caused a severe haemorrhage and she died some two and a half months after the incident. Damages were recovered on the basis that the shock received was caused by *what she saw with her own eyes* and not by what she was told by the bystander. *Dulieu* v *White & Sons* was disapproved on the basis that the fear did not have to be for oneself. The legal argument as to why Mrs Hambrook's estate should recover damages went as follows. A duty of care is owed to all those using the highway; the breach of duty does not necessarily take place when a user is struck or injured, it can take place before then, i.e., when the lorry was left in such a condition that it could run away. The fact that the particular injury which Mrs Hambrook suffered was not contemplated is irrelevant: if the act might cause damage, then it is immaterial that it was not damage of the exact kind caused. As a matter of policy, it was decided that it would not be right that a mother frightened only for herself would recover, whereas a selfless mother concerned only for her child would not. Hence the disapproval of *Dulieu* v *White & Sons*. Atkin LJ went on to say (at p. 157):

> Personally I see no reason for excluding the bystander in the highway who receives injury in the same way from apprehension of or the actual sight of injury to a third party.

The law has still to catch up with this generous dictum (see page 87).

Bourhill v *Young* [1943] AC 92, HL

The 'pregnant fishwife' case. Mrs Bourhill was a passenger on a tram and had alighted at a stop. She was about to collect her fish basket from the driver's platform, when she heard the noise of the impact between a motor cycle which had been travelling in the same direction as the tram and a motor vehicle which was turning into the road occupied by the tram. She was some 50 feet away from the collision. She subsequently saw the blood of the cyclist on the road. Her child was stillborn a month later owing to the shock sustained. The House of Lords held that she was not entitled to recover damages. The example of the 'hypothetical reasonable driver' was cited and it was held that such a driver would not have foreseen that in this case the plaintiff would suffer shock. The duty of the road user to avoid inflicting injury by shock was maintained, this being to such persons as he may reasonably foresee, but as she was not within the area of potential danger, there was no duty owed to her. In other words, she was not in fear for herself being physically injured, and, of course, she was not in fear for a loved one. When Lord Porter spoke of the 'customary phlegm' he said (at p. 117):

> It is not every emotional disturbance or every shock which should have been foreseen. The driver of a car or vehicle, even though careless, is entitled to assume that the ordinary frequenter of the streets has sufficient fortitude to endure such incidents as may from time to time be expected to occur in them, including the noise of a collision and the sight of injury to others, and is not to be considered negligent towards one who does not possess the customary phlegm.

McLoughlin v *O'Brian* [1983] 1 AC 410, HL

This House of Lords decision examined the tort of nervous shock in some depth and will be looked at in detail in chapter 4. The plaintiff was a woman who claimed damages for psychiatric injury following an accident involving her husband and children. She did not witness the accident itself, but, on arriving at the hospital, was confronted with a distressing scene of physical suffering. The two main areas considered by their lordships were, first the issue of proximity in space and time to the accident itself, and secondly whether policy issues were such as to defeat such a claim. The plaintiff had failed in her claim at first instance, and the Court of Appeal had dismissed her appeal on the basis that although it was foreseeable that a wife and mother in her position would suffer injury by shock, policy considerations were such that the duty of care was limited to those at the scene of the accident. The House of Lords allowed the plaintiff's appeal. On the issue of proximity in space and time, it was held that it was sufficient if the plaintiff witnessed the event itself *or its immediate aftermath*. Whichever is experienced, however, the experience must be through the unaided senses of the plaintiff, although some speculation was made as to whether experience through simultaneous television broadcast would suffice.

On the policy question, their lordships did not see that this would defeat a claim, largely because the risk of the floodgates opening was not regarded as a serious one: 'However liberally the criterion of reasonable foreseeability is interpreted, both the number of successful claims in this field and the quantum of damages they will attract are likely to be moderate' (per Lord Bridge at p. 441).

Alcock v Chief Constable of the South Yorkshire Police [1992] 1 AC 310

On 15 April 1989 a football match was due to be played at the Sheffield Wednesday football stadium at Hillsborough, Sheffield. It was the semi-final of the FA Cup between Liverpool and Nottingham Forest. The Leppings Lane end of the ground had been reserved for Liverpool supporters. South Yorkshire police were organising the crowds of supporters and negligently allowed too many into the Leppings Lane end. The result is well-known. After only about six minutes, the match was abandoned due to the mayhem caused by the overcrowding on the terraces. Over 400 people were injured in the resulting crush, and 95 people were killed. The match was due to be broadcast live. Instead, the live broadcast showed the scenes of panic and chaos as supporters desperately tried to disengage themselves from a terrifying, volatile mass of people tragically confined in the 'pens' on the terraces. The broadcast appeared to have complied with the standards imposed by the requirements of broadcasting guidelines not to show pictures of suffering by recognisable individuals. The broadcast was recorded for later transmission on news programmes. Many of the television viewers that afternoon and evening had friends and relatives at the match.

Action was brought by a number of plaintiffs against the Chief Constable of South Yorkshire who admitted negligence in respect of the deaths and physical injuries. The psychiatrically injured plaintiffs included people, both with and without physical injuries, who had been present at the match, and people who had witnessed the televised scenes both live and on news bulletins subsequently transmitted. The controversial cases were (a) where the plaintiffs were present at the match, received no physical injury and did not claim that they received psychiatric injury as a result of being involved in distressing scenes, but that their psychiatric injuries were a result of losing a relative in the disaster, and (b) those who were not present at the match but claimed psychiatric injury as a result of seeing the television broadcast in the full knowledge that their relative was present at the match. In other words, the cases which caused the Court of Appeal and House of Lords such concern were those which raised the tortuous problems of both proximity to the event and proximity in terms of relationship to a killed or injured person.

It will be recalled that it was established by the House of Lords in *McLoughlin* v *O'Brian* that a person who had witnessed 'the immediate aftermath' of a distressing event could recover damages and, in that case, Lord Wilberforce suggested that 'whether some equivalent of sight or hearing, e.g., through simultaneous television, would suffice may have to be considered' (at 423).

Due consideration came in *Alcock*, but it was decided that, given the television broadcasting guidelines, those who saw a disaster on television could not be considered to have suffered nervous shock induced by seeing or hearing the event since they were not in sufficient proximity to the event and would not have suffered shock in the sense of a sudden assault upon the nervous system. Lords Ackner and Oliver did, however, admit the possibility of television placing the spectator in the required degree of proximity, using the example given by Nolan LJ, when the case had been before the Court of Appeal, of live television pictures of a hot-air balloon containing a number of children, floating across the sky and suddenly bursting into flames. It was suggested by Lord Ackner (at p. 405) that the impact of this image upon the television spectators could be as great, if not greater, than if they had been present at the scene of the accident. This image and the reason for choosing it have caused some bemusement although it is accepted that a very similar situation occurred in real life when the *Challenger* space shuttle burst into flames shortly after its launch on 28 January 1986, and this event was broadcast simultaneously. The assertion that seeing this image on television would be more horrific than being present at the event itself is, of course, based upon the purely subjective assessment of the judges concerned, and it is odd that such speculation should have been made. A less subjective reason for the alleged potency of such an image may well be that it would leave no doubt in the minds of the spectators that the occupants of the balloon would perish. Yet it is somewhat ironic when one considers that this would be a situation where this conclusion would be reached by *reasoning* as opposed to an instinctive reaction, and it is clear the impact of an event is not necessarily governed by the witness's rational response. It may be that their lordships did not want to reject absolutely and unequivocally all possibility of liability for an experience through an audiovisual medium, and this speculation was

their way of saying the door was still slightly ajar. Even so Lord Oliver was
cautionary (at p. 417):

> ... any further widening of the area of potential liability to cater for the
> expanded and expanding range of the media of communication ought, in my
> view, to be undertaken rather by Parliament, with full opportunity for public
> debate and representation, than by the process of judicial extrapolation.

However, see the speech of Brennan J in *Sutherland Shire Council* v *Heyman*
(1985) 157 CLR 424 discussed below.

So what did *Alcock* say about the proximity of relationship to the dead,
injured or, indeed, almost-injured person? In England and Wales no remoter
relative than a parent or a spouse has successfully claimed for psychiatric
injury, save for rescuers and others who fall into categories of special, but
non-intimate relationship (see pages 84–86). It was accepted that cases
involving more distant relatives may be admitted, albeit after being
subjected to careful scrutiny. Lord Jauncey of Tullichettle stated (at p. 422):

> I do not consider that it would be profitable to try and define who such
> others might be or to draw any dividing line between one degree of
> relationship and another.... the proper approach is to examine each case
> on its own facts in order to see whether the claimant has established so
> close a relationship of love and affection to the victim as might reasonably
> be expected in the case of spouses or parents and children.

Since the *Alcock* decision there have been a number of other significant cases
on nervous shock. In *Nicholls* v *Rushton* (1992) *The Times*, 19 June, the Court
of Appeal confirmed that damages were not payable for ordinary shock
which falls short of an identifiable psychiatric illness. There are earlier cases
where plaintiffs have recovered, see, for example, *Whitmore* v *Euroways
Express Coaches Ltd* (1984) *The Times*, 4 May.

The Court of Appeal considered both the position of the rescuer and the
mere bystander in *McFarlane* v *EE Caledonia Ltd* [1994] 2 All ER 1. The
plaintiff was employed as a painter on an oil rig in the North Sea and on the
night of the massive Piper Alpha oil rig explosions he was on a support vessel
550 metres away. As a result of what he saw he suffered psychiatric injury.
His position as a rescuer was considered and rejected on the basis that he was
not involved in the rescue operation beyond helping to move blankets and
assisting two walking injured. He also claimed, that, regardless of his
involvement in the rescue, he should recover as a mere bystander because
the event was exceptionally horrific. The Court of Appeal rejected this
argument stating that a 'close' relationship was necessary for a witness to
recover. As we have said (see page 13) this is inconsistent with *Alcock*.

The decision in *Page* v *Smith* [1994] 4 All ER 522, CA, whilst not a psychiatric injury case, dealt with the illness myalgic encephalomyelitis (ME) as a nervous shock case. The court concluded that the ordinary fortitude test applies to participants in accidents as well as mere bystanders. There is further consideration of this case in chapter 8.

Summary

At present, then, we can say that the limits of event proximity are as stated in *McLoughlin* v *O'Brian*, with only the most unusual broadcast event meeting the criteria concerned, and the limits of relationship proximity are fluid, subject to evidence. It is interesting to consider the question of evidence and its relation to the decision in *Alcock* v *Chief Constable of the South Yorkshire Police*. It was accepted by the defence that if the plaintiffs established those required degrees of proximity then they would succeed. The courts were asked, therefore, to consider the proximity questions without hearing from the plaintiffs themselves. The sole witness was a psychiatrist highly experienced in treating Falklands War veterans, but no personal testimony was given to the court of any notion of how those spectators felt when they saw the television pictures. It may well be that it would have made no difference, but personal testimony must be of considerable importance when judges are considering whether an experience is sufficiently shocking. Further, no evidence was given about the degree of closeness of the relationships concerned. The decision indicates that there could have been evidence which would have compelled their lordships to acknowledge that a relationship between two brothers may be as close as that which may exist between a parent and child. There is no doubt therefore that much scope has been left to the imaginative and diligent litigator to establish claims of wider proximity.

It is also encouraging to consider the statement of Brennan J in the High Court of Australia in *Sutherland Shire Council* v *Heyman* (1985) 157 CLR 424 at p. 481:

> It is preferable, in my view, that the law should develop novel categories of negligence incrementally and by analogy with established categories, rather than by a massive extension of a prima facie duty of care restrained only by indefinable 'considerations which ought to negative, or to reduce or limit the scope of the duty or the class of person to whom it is owed'.

This was quoted with approval by Lord Bridge in *Caparo Industries plc* v *Dickman* [1990] 2 AC 605 at p. 618 and gives encouragement to the view that the categories of those who can claim for psychiatric injury will extend, albeit slowly or 'incrementally'.

It is tempting to overestimate the impact of the litigation ensuing upon the tragedy that took place at the Hillsborough stadium. That case was primarily about what we will call 'event proximity' under very exceptional circumstances. The very great majority of claims will not ever touch upon that issue and therefore it is vital not to exaggerate the effect of that case.

Even when proximity is a worrying and doubtful issue there is no doubting the importance of the individual case and its presentation. The practitioner will have the obstacle course of foreseeability and proximity to negotiate, but, given that policy, however described,[34] is to prevent the opening of those well-known floodgates, then the more individually compelling a case can be, the more likely will be the plaintiff to succeed.

---

[34] *Alcock* v *Chief Constable of the South Yorkshire Police* [1992] 1 AC 310 per Lord Oliver at p. 410.

TWO
The injury

In chapter 1, reference has been made to psychiatric injury resulting from a variety of distressing experiences. Damages are awarded in negligence only if a recognised psychiatric disorder has resulted, and it is proposed to look at such disorders which can occur as a result of such experiences.

Before considering specific disorders, it may be helpful to look at the way in which mental disorders are classified, and the way in which the terminology is used. It must be stressed that this is a brief and unsophisticated excursion through a very difficult area, with the intention only of setting the claim in its proper context. Difficult questions of psychiatric categorisation, techniques of diagnosis, suitability of treatment and so on are all the province of the medical experts whom the lawyer will instruct. It is hoped, however, that the following introduction will be of some help to the lawyer who is unfamiliar with psychiatric concepts.

CLASSIFICATION OF MENTAL DISORDERS

The work of physicians[1] in the eighteenth and nineteenth centuries led to the distinction between mental disorders which were caused by physical damage and those which were not so attributable. Those which have physical causes are 'organic', and those which have not are 'functional'. The functional group can be further divided into 'psychoses' and 'neuroses'. Generally it is true to say that psychoses are serious mental illnesses when the sufferer loses touch with reality whereas neuroses are less serious and less disruptive of 'normal' life. Schizophrenia is a psychotic illness, as is manic depression. However, depression is a widely used term which can be part of a number of illnesses, such as neurotic depression, or part of a personality disorder or an

[1] E.g., William Battie, *A Treatise on Madness* (London, 1758).

adjustment disorder. Because so-called psychotic conditions have little in common, save for their severity and loss of touch with reality many psychiatrists feel it is not useful to refer to them collectively.[2] Indeed, the latest edition of the international classification of mental disorders produced by the World Health Organisation (ICD 10), unlike previous editions, does not use the traditional division of neuroses and psychoses at all. However, it is outside the scope of this book to look at the merits or otherwise of the distinction.

Generally speaking most psychiatrists would agree that, in addition to psychoses and neuroses there are adjustment disorders, which can have similar symptoms to some neuroses but are dealt with separately because they have a different aetiology, i.e., cause. Finally, there are personality disorders, various forms of sexual dysfunction and substance abuse, and illnesses which are specific to children which are categorised separately.

Mental disorders have, of course, been classified over a very long period of time, and in a number of ways in the medical literature, but in the diagnostic context there are two main glossaries or guides to mental disorders: the *Diagnostic and Statistical Manual of Mental Disorders* published by the American Psychiatric Association, the current edition being the 4th, 1994, known as DSM IV; and *The ICD 10 Classification of Mental and Behavioural Disorders: Clinical Descriptions and Diagnostic Guidelines* which is part of the 10th revision of the international classification of diseases and related health problems, published by the World Health Organization, Geneva, 1992, known as ICD 10. There is some controversy in the field of psychiatry as to the usefulness in practice of such categorisations which inevitably fall short of proving a satisfactory classification system for all sufferers. However, both DSM IV and ICD 10 have a number of residual categories for psychiatric disorders which do not fit precisely into the more specific categories.

Basic classification

Psychiatric textbooks adopt different systems of classification but tend to follow the system below. This is based upon that contained in the *Concise Oxford Textbook of Psychiatry*, by Gelder, Gath and Mayou, 2nd edition, 1988.

Personality disorder
Mental impairment
Organic psychoses (underlying physical cause detected)
Functional psychoses (schizophrenia; affective psychoses; no underlying physical cause detected, although may be present)

[2] See M. Gelder, D. Gath and R. Mayou, *Concise Oxford Textbook of Psychiatry* (Oxford University Press, 1993) p. 46.

Neuroses
Adjustment disorder
Other disorders (includes alcohol and drug dependence, sexual deviance/
dysfunction etc., and disorders specific to childhood)

This is a very basic list and the formal classification systems are much more complicated, particularly DSM III R, which on the face of it, bears little resemblance to the above. That is not surprising as the formal classification systems are designed to assist the psychiatrist in diagnosis and treatment, and not as a broad description of mental illness.

Referring back to our broad classification system, there follows a brief description of the disorders concerned.

Personality disorder
This term is used to describe those who exhibit abnormal behaviour which is not attributable to either a mental illness or an intellectual impairment, and is said to have arisen through an 'uneven' development of their personality from childhood. Various 'types' of personality have been defined including the hysterical, obsessional, paranoid and depressive. Broadly speaking, a personality disorder does not necessarily have any causal connection with trauma or stress, although some may say that it can be environmentally induced by, say, the experiences of childhood. For example, studies have shown that clinical descriptions of borderline personality disorder have great similarities with descriptions of chronic post-traumatic stress disorder (PTSD), and particularly so when the victim has been subjected to repeated trauma over a long period of time, in cases of, say, repeated sexual abuse.[3] It is also acknowledged that in a small proportion of sufferers from post-traumatic stress disorder, an 'enduring personality change' can occur (see page 48). Furthermore, it is important to note that someone with a pre-existing personality disorder who is subjected to trauma or stress can seriously react to that incident and be, what may be thought to be, disproportionately affected by it. In other words they can be said to have an 'eggshell personality'. See *Brice* v *Brown* [1984] 1 All ER 997 (see page 120).

Mental impairment
This is essentially characterised as learning disability and refers to cases where intellectual impairment has been present since childhood (as opposed to dementia, where the onset is in adult life). It has no specific relevance to traumatically induced psychiatric disorder.

[3] See J. L. Herman and B. A. van der Kolk, 'Traumatic antecedents of borderline personality disorder' in A. van der Kolk (ed.), *Psychological Trauma* (American Psychiatric Press, 1987).

Organic psychoses

Organic psychoses are those psychoses (not neuroses) caused by physical disease or damage to the brain or nervous system, and therefore they can be caused by *physical* trauma and form part of a personal injury claim in the usual way.

Functional psychoses

Schizophrenia and some severe depressive illnesses are psychotic illnesses, but, as indicated above, psychotic illnesses are very difficult to define. They have severe symptoms, and are said to be characterised by lack of insight by the patient, but this is an imprecise attribute, given that there can be some insight in, for example, schizophrenic patients, and some lack of insight in some so-called neurotic patients. Sometimes trauma can be associated with a psychotic illness, but, as Scrignar says,[4] at best the link is tenuous. A person suffering from a psychotic illness can, of course, be adversely affected by trauma, and if that is the case, then the medical expert involved will have to address the effect, the treatment and the prognosis, whilst taking into account the psychotic illness. This may be an extremely difficult task. As Scrignar says: 'During legal proceedings, mental health professionals may feel that they are trying to untie the Gordian knot as they attempt to explain to the court the relationship of trauma, schizophrenia and PTSD'.[5]

Neuroses

This is a very wide category of mental disorder, and divides into many different subcategories, such as anxiety disorder, phobic disorder, obsessional neurosis. One or more of these conditions can be caused by distressing experiences. ICD 10 states that:

> the term 'neurotic' is still retained for occasional use and occurs, for instance, in the heading of a major group (or block) of disorders F40–48, 'Neurotic, stress-related and somatoform disorders'.[6]

It goes on to state at the introduction to F40, that: 'mixtures of symptoms are common (coexistent depression and anxiety being by far the most frequent), particularly in the less severe varieties of these disorders often seen in primary care'.

Neuroses can vary from minor emotional disruptions, i.e., everyday emotional reactions in a slightly exaggerated form, to quite serious disorders, which will be discussed further at page 45.

In DSM IV, PTSD is classified as an anxiety disorder.

---

[4] C. B. Scrignar, *Post-traumatic Stress Disorder*, 2nd ed. (New Orleans LA: Bruno Press, 1988) p. 120.
[5] Scrignar op. cit. (note 4), p. 121.
[6] Somatoform disorders are those which exhibit physical symptoms with no detectable physical cause.

Adjustment disorder

This is separately categorised for our purposes here because of its *specific* aetiology. ICD 10 states that these are:

> states of subjective distress and emotional disturbance, usually interfering with social functioning and performance, and arising in the period of adaption to a significant life change or to the consequences of a stressful life event.

It can include a grief reaction (see page 47). DSM IV states that: 'The essential feature of this disorder is a maladaptive reaction to an identifiable psychosocial stressor, or stressors'.

In ICD 10, PTSD is classified under the category of reaction to severe stress and adjustment disorders.

Other disorders

Included here is alcohol and drug dependence which can be the eventual outcome of alcohol and drug use following a distressing experience.

AETIOLOGY

Aetiology is concerned with all causes of mental disorder. Psychiatric disorders can be genetically determined or they can occur as a result of a naturally occurring disease, or they can be brought about by an external stimulus. The latter type of disorder can be said to be environmentally induced, and the main concern of this book is with certain external causes of mental disorder. In reality many mental disorders are caused by a complex interaction of external causes, genetic or similar predisposition, and physical illness. Psychiatrists classify causes as follows, although again a warning is appropriate that this is a general description only, and, inevitably, oversimplified.

Predisposing factors

Firstly there are the factors in the individual's physical make-up, determined by genetic, biological and similar considerations. Secondly, there are the factors of the individual's personality. We have seen that one type of mental disorder is a personality disorder, but an individual does not have to be suffering from a personality disorder to have a predisposing personality factor. Most people can be classified in a very rough and ready way as having a particular type of personality. This can affect the way in which they will react to external factors such as stress.

Precipitating factors

These include the external factors with which we are concerned in this book, such as trauma, and they also include physical factors such as cerebral tumours or the effect of drugs. A physical factor can have physical effects but also psychological effects due to the stress placed upon the individual concerned. This should be noted in particular in relation to head injury cases.

Perpetuating factors

These are factors which prolong the duration of the disorder concerned, and essentially will be secondary factors, such as the loss of a job which will prolong the original disorder. Stress can be a precipitating factor or a perpetuating factor.

Factual causation is essential for any action in damages to succeed. Jaspers[7] has formulated three criteria for deciding whether a psychological state is a reaction to events. First, the precipitating factors (often called stressors) should be sufficiently severe and closely related to the onset of the psychological state; secondly, there must be some clear connection between the stressor and the stress reaction; and thirdly, the reaction should disappear when the stressor is removed, unless of course there are perpetuating factors maintaining it. Although this sounds fairly obvious, it is important to bear it in mind, because there will often be socio-economic consequences of psychiatric injury (loss of job, inability to keep up friendships etc.), which will interact with the resultant disorder and affect diagnosis, prognosis and recovery.

HISTORY OF THE ILLNESS

Before going on to consider in more detail the relevant disorders which have been mentioned above, there follows a brief account of the history of traumatically induced psychiatric illness, which has been described by a variety of names depending upon the circumstances in which it has been inflicted.

The early history gives two notable instances in which psychological problems follow trauma; the first being the somewhat predictable circumstance of war, and the second in the less obvious situation of railway accidents.

To deal with the latter first, one of the most influential of the early doctors writing on the topic was John Eric Erichsen, Professor of Surgery at

---

[7] K. Jaspers, *General Psychopathology*, transl. J. Hoenig and M. W. Hamilton (Manchester: Manchester University Press, 1963) p. 392.

University College Hospital, London, who, in 1875, wrote *On Concussion of the Spine: Nervous Shock and Other Obscure Injuries of the Nervous System in Their Clinical and Medico-legal Aspects.* Although this deals with a variety of injuries to the spine resulting from falls and accidents of many different types, he comments that the most frequent cause, and certainly the cause of the most severe injuries is a railway collision. It is important to stress that he was referring to 'injuries' which normally have no obvious physical cause. His central thesis was that in trauma 'concussion of the spine' occurred causing molecular changes in its structure and inflammation of tissue. Although there was little in the way of pathological evidence available for most of the injuries, he did refer to the case of a man who died three and a half years after being involved in a railway accident in which, apparently, he suffered no external sign of injury. The post-mortem revealed signs of chronic inflammation of the brain, and the spinal cord.

The condition of spinal concussion or 'railway spine' as it came to be known was not always accepted by doctors and was attacked by Herbert Page who was surgeon to the London and North-West Railway. He attempted to discredit Erichsen and denied the existence of the condition of 'spinal concussion'. Instead, he introduced the concepts of 'nervous shock' and 'functional disorders', particularly by citing cases where manifestations of shock are greater in cases which caused the victim greater fright.[8]

Page seemed to identify fear as the prime cause of the disorder, and concluded that fear would probably be statistically greater, the more alarming the accident. In those days railways were, of course, the fastest way of travelling. Speeds which, at the end of the 20th century, would seem almost quaintly slow, could, no doubt, produce great alarm. If this is considered in conjunction with the size and powerful appearance of railway locomotives, then it is understandable that they could induce considerable fear into those who may have been involved in even the most minor incident. Charles Dickens was involved in a railway accident which left him with a great fear of rail travel.[9]

The other early experiences concerned war, the American Civil War being perhaps the first example of the recording of manifestations of psychiatric injury. Neurasthenia (physical and mental exhaustion) and other symptoms such as pains in the chest, breathlessness and weakness were recorded (da Costa's syndrome, known more usually today as neurocirculatory asthenia). The First World War produced, of course, countless cases of 'shell-shock' (although the rather crude assumption that it was literally due to the effect of exploding shells as opposed to the exposure to the multifarious horrors of war has long since been discredited), and by the end of the war there were

---

[8] See M. R. Trimble, *Post-Traumatic Neurosis* (Chichester: Wiley, 1981) for a good account of the history of diagnosis of traumatically induced disorders.
[9] L. T. C. Rolt, *Red for Danger* (London: Bodley Head, 1955).

over 20 army hospitals in the UK dealing specifically with shell-shock.[10]
Again, the Second World War produced psychiatric casualties, but not of the
same magnitude as in the First. Sophisticated diagnosis has developed since
then. Despite this, it was still the case that a great number of Vietnam war
veterans remained undiagnosed for many years.[11]

In more recent history, both the Falklands and Gulf wars have produced
victims of psychiatric illness directly attributable to their war experiences.

There are also a number of major civilian disasters, which have produced
large-scale victims of stress, such as the Australian bushfires, the American
Buffalo Creek flood, and events such as the capsize of the *Herald of Free
Enterprise* ferry near Zeebrugge in 1987. These have resulted in various
studies of the effects of major stress, disaster management and other areas.[12]

POST-TRAUMATIC STRESS DISORDER

The most commonly known psychiatric illness following trauma or stress is
post-traumatic stress disorder (PTSD), although it must be emphasised that
it is by no means the only disorder which can manifest itself, and
practitioners acting for plaintiffs should be alert to any suggestion by the
defence that because PTSD is not present then any psychiatric disorder
which is present is not related to the event concerned.

DSM IV

It was not until 1980, when the 3rd edition of the American Psychiatric
Association's Diagnostic and Statistical Manual (DSM III) was published
that PTSD was finally accorded a diagnostic heading. As already indicated
the current Manual is DSM IV, and PTSD is disorder number 309.81.
PTSD is classified as an anxiety disorder. DSM III R, 309.81, states:

> The essential feature of Posttraumatic Stress Disorder is the development
> of characteristic symptoms following exposure to an extreme traumatic
> stressor involving direct personal experience of an event that involves
> actual or threatened death or serious injury, or other threat to one's
> physical integrity; or witnessing an event that involves death, injury, or a
> threat to the physical integrity of another person; or learning about
> unexpected or violent death, serious harm, or threat of death or injury
> experienced by a family member or other close associate (Criterion A1).

[10] M. Stone, 'Shellshock and the psychologists' in W. F. Bynum, R. Porter and M. Shepherd
(eds), *The Anatomy of Madness*, vol 2 (London: Tavistock, 1985).
[11] M. J. Friedman, 'Post-Vietnam syndrome: recognition and management' *Psychosomatics*, vol.
22 (1981).
[12] See B. Raphael, *When Disaster Strikes* (London: Unwin Hyman, 1990).

The person's response to the event must involve intense fear, helplessness, or horror (or in children, the response must involve disorganised or agitated behaviour) (Criterion A2). The characteristic symptoms resulting from the exposure to the extreme trauma include persistent re-experiencing of the traumatic event (Criterion B), persistent avoidance of stimuli associated with the trauma and numbing of general responsiveness (Criterion C), and persistent symptoms of increased arousal (Criterion D). The full symptom picture must be present for more than one month (Criterion E), and the disturbance must cause clinically significant distress or impairment in social, occupational, or other important areas of functioning (Criterion F).

Traumatic events that are experienced directly include, but are not limited to, military combat, violent personal assault (sexual assault, physical attack, robbery, mugging), being kidnapped, being taken hostage, terrorist attack, torture, incarceration as a prisoner of war or in a concentration camp, natural or manmade disasters, severe automobile accidents, or being diagnosed with a life-threatening illness. For children, sexually traumatic events may include developmentally inappropriate sexual experiences without threatened or actual violence or injury. Witnessed events include, but are not limited to, observing the serious injury or unnatural death of another person due to violent assault, accident, war, or disaster or unexpectedly witnessing a dead body or body parts. Events experienced by others that are learned about include, but are not limited to, violent personal assault, serious accident, or serious injury experienced by a family member or a close friend; learning about the sudden, unexpected death of a family member or a close friend; or learning that one's child has a life-threatening disease. The disorder may be especially severe or long lasting when the stressor is of human design (e.g., torture, rape). The likelihood of developing this disorder may increase as the intensity of and physical proximity to the stressor increase.

The traumatic event can be re-experienced in various ways. Commonly the person has recurrent and intrusive recollections of the event (Criterion B1) or recurrent distressing dreams during which the event is replayed (Crierion B2). In rare instances, the person experiences dissociative states that last from a few seconds to several hours or even days, during which components of the event are relived and the person behaves as though experiencing the event at that moment (Criterion B3). Intense psychological distress (Criterion B4) or physiological reactivity (Criterion B5) often occurs when the person is exposed to triggering events that resemble or symbolise an aspect of the traumatic event (e.g., anniversaries of the traumatic event; cold, snowy weather or uniformed guards for survivors of death camps in cold climates; hot, humid weather for combat veterans of the South Pacific; entering any elevator for a woman who was raped in an elevator).

Stimuli associated with the trauma are persistently avoided. the person commonly makes deliberate efforts to avoid thoughts, feelings, or conversations about the traumatic event (Criterion C1) and to avoid activities, situations, or people who arouse recollections of it (Criterion C2). This avoidance of reminders may include amnesia for an important aspect of the traumatic event (Criterion C3). Diminished responsiveness to the external world, referred to as 'psychic numbing' or 'emotional anesthesia', usually begins soon after the traumatic event. The individual may complain of having markedly diminished interest or participation in previously enjoyed activities (Criterion C4), of feeling detached or estranged from other people (Criterion C5), or of having markedly reduced ability to feel emotions (especially those associated with intimacy, tenderness, and sexuality) (Criterion C6). The individual may have a sense of a foreshortened future (e.g., not expecting to have a career, marriage, children, or a normal life span) (Criterion C7).

The individual has persistent symptoms of anxiety or increased arousal that were not present before the trauma. These symptoms may include difficulty falling or staying asleep that may be due to recurrent nightmares during which the traumatic event is relived (Criterion D1), hypervigilance (Criterion D4), and exaggerated startle response (Criterion D5). Some individuals report irritability or outbursts of anger (Criterion D2) or difficulty concentrating or completing tasks (Criterion D3).

The diagnostic criteria are reproduced in appendix 1

ICD 10

The World Health Organisation classification in ICD 10 at category F43 lists disorders which are reactions to severe distress, and adjustment disorders. Post-traumatic stress disorder is defined as follows:

... a delayed and/or protracted response to a stressful event or situation (either short or long-lasting) of an exceptionally threatening or catastrophic nature, which is likely to cause pervasive distress in almost anyone (e.g. natural or man-made disaster, combat, serious accident, witnessing the violent death of others, or being the victim of torture, terrorism, rape, or other crime). Predisposing factors such as personality traits (e.g. compulsive, asthenic[13]) or previous history of neurotic illness may lower the threshold for the development of the syndrome or aggravate its course, but they are neither necessary nor sufficient to explain its occurrence.

[13] A personality disorder characterised by low energy.

Typical symptoms include episodes of repeated reliving of the trauma in intrusive memories ('flashbacks') or dreams, occurring against the persisting background of a sense of 'numbness' and emotional blunting, detachment from other people, unresponsiveness to surroundings, anhedonia, and avoidance of activities and situations reminiscent of the trauma. Commonly there is fear and avoidance of cues that remind the sufferer of the original trauma. Rarely, there may be dramatic, acute bursts of fear, panic or aggression, triggered by stimuli arousing a sudden recollection and/or re-enactment of the trauma or of the original reaction to it.

There is usually a state of autonomic hyperarousal with hypervigilance, an enhanced startle reaction, and insomnia. Anxiety and depression are commonly associated with the above symptoms and signs, and suicidal ideation is not infrequent. Excessive use of alcohol or drugs may be a complicating factor.

The onset follows the trauma with a latency period which may range from a few weeks to months (but rarely exceeds six months). The course is fluctuating but recovery can be expected in the majority of cases. In a small proportion of patients the condition may show a chronic course over many years and a transition to an enduring personality change.

It is interesting to note that in the earlier edition of DSM (DSM III R) the definition of PTSD was such that the sufferer had to have experienced an event that is outside the range of usual experience (i.e., outside the range of such common experiences as simple bereavement, chronic illness, business losses, and marital conflict), but that his requirement is no longer necessary under the DSM IV classification. This recognises the diversity of ways in which human beings can experience and be affected by stress, and is therefore to be welcomed.

Acute stress reaction
Both ICD 10 and DSM IV also describe acute reactions to stress which are what the lay person would regard as 'shock'. Such phenomena are short-term reactions only, but it is worth bearing in mind that they are specific psychiatric disorders, and *in consequence should be compensatable*. In DSM IV, 'acute stress disorder' is classified at 308.3. In ICD 10 the diagnostic guidelines for 'acute stress reaction' include daze, disorientation, agitation, sweating and breathlessness, usually lasting only two or three days. In cases such as *Nicholls* v *Rushton* (1992) *The Times*, 19 June 1992, where the plaintiff had suffered a nervous reaction which was described as 'falling short' of a recognised psychiatric injury, it may be that the plaintiff could be properly diagnosed as suffering from one of these short-term

disorders and could recover damages. The diagnostic criteria are reproduced in Appendix 1.

'The three Es'

Scrignar, in his book *Post-traumatic Stress Disorder* (see note 4), uses the definition of PTSD in DSM III R (the previous edition) and describes the specific sort of 'trauma' which is necessary as a stressor to precipitate PTSD by reference to 'the traumatic principle'. This, he says (pp. 13–14), is:

> any environmental stimulus which poses a realistic threat to life or limb, impacting on one, or more likely a combination of the five sensory pathways to the brain, if perceived as a serious threat to one's life or physical integrity, whether it produces physical injury or not, can be regarded as a trauma and precipitate a PTSD in a vulnerable individual. The central factor in the development of PTSD is not necessarily the type or duration of the environmental trauma, but whether the trauma poses a realistic threat to life or limb, and a person is consciously aware and has a full appreciation of the potential for serious injury or death to self or others. Also vital and a natural consequence is an intense activation of one's autonomic nervous system following exposure to the traumatic event.

The activation of the autonomic nervous system produces extremely intense, and frequent or persisting, anxiety; 'pathologic' anxiety. Scrignar says that anxiety is pathologic when the autonomic nervous system discharges: (a) so intensively that it renders an individual incapable of speech, movement or thought; (b) unpredictably and frequently in an attack-like manner, and (c) so regularly that chronic anxiety is the result. He describes five levels of anxiety, level 1 being normal, level 2 being mild symptoms of edginess, tension, feelings of nerves up to symptoms at panic level (level 5) of acute and intense feelings of impending doom, going crazy, going out of control, dying, or other thoughts of a cataclysmic nature.

Scrignar then goes on to identify the three sources of pathologic anxiety, what he calls the three Es. The first is the environment, i.e., the stressor which precipitates the PTSD. In the definition at DSM IV, 309.81, states that the stressor must also pose a threat to one's physical integrity, or a threat or serious harm to one's children, spouse, close relatives, or friends; or witnessing the destruction of one's home or community; or seeing another person who has recently been seriously injured or killed. The use of the word 'serious' in the definition is also difficult; who decides what is serious? Presumably it must be the plaintiff, i.e., the test must be subjective. The ICD 10 classification is no more helpful on this point, stating PTSD to be a response to a stressful event or situation 'of an exceptionally threatening or catastrophic nature, which is likely to cause pervasive distress in almost anyone', and also refers to the example of an accident as a 'serious' accident. It is at this point that it is worth stating again, that just because the criteria of PTSD are not satisfied, does not mean that the plaintiff's claim will fail. One or more other psychiatric disorders can be present. See the reference to Adjustment Disorder in the PTSD diagnosis criteria in DSM IV in Appendix 1 on page 174. It is also worth stating that *if* what is a relatively minor, say road accident, or perhaps a 'near-miss', *appears* to the victim to be extremely threatening, then this 'extremely threatening event' (or howsoever it is described) can be markedly distressing to almost anyone, so if the other symptoms of PTSD are there, then it appears that the definition can be satisfied in such a case.

Scrignar's second 'E' refers to encephalic events, also called cognitions, and concern thoughts, visual images, flashbacks, assumptions, beliefs, perception of external events and dreams. These encephalic events are always necessary for a diagnosis of PTSD to be made, and are what distinguish it from other anxiety disorders. The definition refers to them as recurrent and intrusive recollections of the event, recurrent and distressing dreams of the event and sudden feelings that the event was recurring. Scrignar calls them the videotapes of the mind, and they can be played back every day for months or years, keeping the trauma fresh in the mind. Such 'playbacks' can be triggered by physical sensations: Dr Morgan O'Connell, psychiatrist of the Royal Naval Hospital, Haslar has described to us the case of one young man on the *Herald of Free Enterprise* whom he treated. Every time he stood at the bar in a pub or similar he experienced these distressing flashbacks. It was discovered that he had been in the bar on the ferry at the time of the capsize; bottles of spirits were spilt, leaving an intense smell of alcohol, by which he was surrounded for some time after the capsize. The smell of spirits would bring back the images of the capsize with a vivid intensity.

Finally, Scrignar's third 'E' stands for endogenous events, which are physical sensations. These can be particularly difficult to differentiate from physical sensations produced by organic causes, particularly if the plaintiff was already ill before the event, or suffered actual physical injury at the event. If it is eventually established that the cause of the sensations is non-organic, then until the plaintiff accepts this, the PTSD will not be treatable.

These physical sensations remind the plaintiff of the event, which set off the encephalic events, i.e., the intrusive thoughts, dreams etc., which produce symptoms of anxiety (activation of the autonomic nervous system), which results in tension and unpleasant physical sensation, which reminds the plaintiff of the event, and so on. In other words, it has what Scrignar calls a 'spiral effect'.

These then, are the characteristics of PTSD. Survivor guilt, which was included as a characteristic in DSM III has since disappeared from the revised edition, but it is still thought to be an important factor.[14]

It is, perhaps, pertinent at this stage to enquire how frequently the specific criteria of PTSD will occur. Professor William Yule, and others at the Institute of Psychiatry, London University carried out assessments of 45 adult survivors from the *Herald of Free Enterprise* disaster, and all but three reached the DSM III (the edition of the manual at that particular time) criteria for PTSD. Many of them also satisfied diagnostic criteria for depression, anxiety and a pathological grief reaction. In his paper on the subject,[15] Professor Yule acknowledges that it cannot be concluded that 90 per cent of survivors suffered from PTSD, as the extent of the referral basis was not known, but he does conclude that comment is needed upon what was probably a high incidence, and goes on to cite Rachman,[16] who argued that extreme difficulties in emotional processing are associated with traumatic events in which the stimulus is intense, sudden (the *Herald* capsized in 45 seconds), dangerous (half the passengers were killed), prepared (i.e., prepared fears of drowning), uncontrolled and unpredictable. An event such as the capsize of the *Herald* should, therefore, produce a high level of psychiatric disorder. Professor John Gunn and Professor P. J. Taylor, also of the Institute of Psychiatry, state that the crucial factor about the likelihood of development of a psychiatric disorder seems to be prolongation of uncertainty about the final extent of damage to be inflicted.[17] Again, in relation to the *Herald* case, many of the victims were in the water for a very long time, with no way of knowing whether they would ever be rescued.

An extremely important factor for the practitioner is the way in which the sufferer's avoidance response can mask PTSD altogether. A study of 246 people exposed to an industrial disaster showed that those who were resistant to a first interview had suffered a higher degree of exposure to stress, and were more likely to have suffered from PTSD at the seven-month period than those who had agreed to a first interview. It was found that the resistance to interview was part of an avoidance response, and showed that without follow-up exercises the level of PTSD would have been underestimated.[18] A plaintiff who steadfastly denies psychiatric injury, therefore, may not only still be a victim, but may be even more seriously affected than more vocal contemporaries.

[14] See W. Yule, 'The psychological sequelae of disasters and resulting compensation', *Practical Reviews in Psychiatry*, ser. 2, No. 9 (1990), p. 6.
[15] Op. cit. (note 14).
[16] S. Rachman, 'Emotional processing', *Behav Res Ther*, vol. 18 (1980), p. 51.
[17] J. Gunn and P. J. Taylor (eds), *Forensic Psychiatry, Clinical, Legal and Ethical Issues* (London: Butterworth-Heinemann, 1993), p. 897.
[18] L. Weisath, 'Importance of high response rates in traumatic stress research', *Acta Psychiatr Scand*, vol. 80 (1989), p. 131.

ICD 10 states that symptoms should not generally be diagnosed as PTSD unless there is evidence that they arose within six months of the traumatic event, but that a 'probable' diagnosis may be made if more than six months elapsed provided the clinical manifestations are typical and no alternative identification of the disorder is plausible. Similarly DSM IV refers to delayed onset of PTSD, which delay can be a matter of years. Scrignar prefers the explanation that PTSD was there the whole time, but had not been diagnosed. There is some research to support this view, for example, a retrospective case review of 150 Israeli soldiers indicated that delay in seeking treatment explained most cases of apparently delayed-onset PTSD.[19] Suffice to say that the six-month period should be viewed with some caution. It is important to stress that we are here dealing with the diagnostic criteria for PTSD; other disorders have different patterns of development. For example, in ICD 10, at F62, enduring personality changes are dealt with, and it is stated that 'such enduring personality change is most often seen following devastating traumatic experience'.

The same degree of caution is necessary when it is considered that ICD 10 states that PTSD rarely lasts more than six months, although DSM IV is unspecific as to duration. There have been a number of follow-up studies carried out. For example, 14 years after the Buffalo Creek disaster of 1972, a follow-up study was done of 39 per cent of the living survivors.[20] Three quarters of the population had improved; less than 10 per cent had worsened. Of course, whether those who were still suffering were still suffering from PTSD rather than from, say, an enduring personality change, is debatable. It should be remembered that PTSD was not a recognised disorder in 1972, and diagnoses are made retrospectively on the basis of recorded clinical pictures. Follow-up studies, which are fairly infrequent in any event, can at present, therefore, give only an approximation of the duration of PTSD.

For a good review of the current position on PTSD see O'Brien, 'The Validity of the Diagnosis of Post Traumatic Stress Disorder' December 1994 JPIL p. 257.

OTHER DISORDERS

Neuroses

This is an enormous category of mental disorder. Neuroses can range from a very mild form of illness to an illness which severely disrupts the life of the

---

[19] Soloman et al. 'Delayed onset PTSD among Israeli veterans of the 1982 Lebanon war', *Psychiatry*, vol. 52 (1989), p. 428.
[20] Green et al. 'Buffalo Creek survivors in the second decade; stability of stress symptoms', *Am J. Orthopsychiatry*, vol. 60 (1990), p. 43.

sufferer. These include anxiety states, phobic states, some types of depression, obsessive compulsive disorder, somatoform disorders, and dissociative disorders. This discussion of other disorders is not intended to be in any way exhaustive, but contains general descriptions for the lay person of some of the disorders which can be environmentally induced and which may be induced particularly by trauma.

It has been acknowledged that environmental factors can play an important part in the development of neurotic disorders. A non-traumatic example is shown by studies that have indicated that workers on assembly lines report more neurotic symptoms than do comparable workers who have more control over their rate of work.[21] The ability of trauma to cause such symptoms is much less controversial.

The most common forms of neurotic illness after stress are anxiety states, phobic states and neurotic depression.

Anxiety states

ICD 10 gives no overall definition so it is useful to look at ICD 9 which said that they are:

> Various combinations of physical and mental manifestations of anxiety, not attributable to real danger and occurring either in attacks or as a persisting state. The anxiety is usually diffuse and may extend to panic. Other neurotic features such as obsessional or hysterical symptoms may be present but do not dominate the clinical picture.

Attacks of anxiety are often accompanied by a variety of bodily (somatic) symptoms, such as palpitations, excessive sweating, breathlessness, faintness, a sinking feeling in the stomach, nausea and shakiness. If anxiety attacks are very severe, then the sufferer can go into a panic. The sufferer may also have a persistent fear of some unfocused, unspecified disaster occurring.

If the anxiety has a particular focus then it is classified as a phobic anxiety. The phobia can be specifically linked to a stressful event, such as fear of travelling in motor vehicles or a fear of water.

Depression

The use of this term can create considerable confusion. ICD 10 has a whole block of disorders (F30–F39) which are called 'mood (affective) disorders'

---

[21] D. E. Broadbent: 'Chronic effects from the physical nature of work' in 'Working Life' (ed. B. Gardell and G. Johansson) London: Wiley 1981.

and which include depressive disorders. These can be of a varying degree of severity, but ICD 10 says:

> the individual usually suffers from depressed mood, loss of interest and enjoyment, and reduced energy leading to increased fatiguability and diminished activity. Marked tiredness after only slight effort is common. Other common symptoms are:
>
> (a) reduced concentration and attention;
> (b) reduced self-esteem and self-confidence;
> (c) ideas of guilt and unworthiness; . . .
> (d) bleak and pessimistic views of the future;
> (e) ideas of acts of self-harm or suicide;
> (f) disturbed sleep;
> (g) diminished appetite.

Depression can be caused by distressing experiences, and in ICD 10 various types of depressive reaction are included as reactions to stress and adjustment reactions. They can, of course, accompany other psychiatric disorders also caused by stress or trauma.

Somatoform disorders

These are characterised by the presence of physical symptoms for which there is no demonstrable organic cause. Both DSM IV and ICD 10 indicate that they can be associated with distressing experiences, but they are particularly difficult to treat because the patient will be unwilling to acknowledge that the physical symptoms are, in fact, psychological in origin.

A related matter is that psychiatric injury can have specific physical consequences, for example, it is thought that stress can have an adverse affect on the immune system.[22]

Dissociative disorders

These result in a partial or complete loss of the normal integration between memories of the past, awareness of identity and immediate sensations, and control of bodily movements, often associated closely in time with traumatic events.

Pathological grief

This phenomenon considerably occupied those involved in the *Herald of Free Enterprise* arbitration (see page 129). DSM IV refers to 'normal

---

[22] Calabrese et al. (1987) cited in Gunn and Taylor, op. cit. (note 17), page 933.

bereavement', and says that 'a full depressive syndrome' is a normal reaction to the death of a loved one. That would include such things as poor appetite, weight loss, insomnia and feelings of depression. Guilt, if present, is chiefly about things done or not done by the survivor at the time of death; thoughts of death are usually limited to the person's thinking that he or she would be better off dead or that he or she should have died with the deceased person. The person generally regards the feeling of depressed mood as 'normal' although help with loss of appetite or insomnia may be sought. The duration of 'normal bereavement' is variable, particularly between different cultural groups. Pathological grief is grief beyond this 'normal' reaction. DSM IV says that morbid preoccupation with worthlessness, prolonged and marked functional impairment and marked psychomotor retardation suggest that the bereavement is complicated by the development of a major depression. In ICD 10 grief reaction is described as an adjustment disorder, and can include depressive and anxiety reactions, which can be prolonged.

It was acknowledged by the arbitrators that an assessment of the difference between normal and pathological grief could only be done in a 'rough and ready fashion'. Because damages are not awarded for 'normal' grief, courts have the somewhat absurd task of trying to reduce damages by whatever part of the plaintiff's psychological state can be attributed to 'normal' grief only.[23]

Enduring personality changes

It is acknowledged that enduring personality changes can take place after extremely distressing experiences. ICD 10 at F62 defines such a change by reference to the extremity of the stress, i.e., it must be so extreme that it is unnecessary to consider personal vulnerability to explain its profound effect on the personality. Examples given of the sorts of extreme experiences are torture, disasters and hostage situations. Symptoms include a hostile or mistrustful attitude towards the world, social withdrawal, feelings of emptiness or hopelessness, a chronic feeling of being threatened and estrangement. It also states that long-term change in personality following short-term exposure to a life-threatening experience such as a car accident should *not* be included since recent research shows that such a development depends upon a pre-existing psychological vulnerability. An example of this can be seen in *Brice* v *Brown* [1984] 1 All ER 997 at p. 120.

Overlap of disorders

Many victims will develop more than one psychiatric disorder. This should present no particular problem for the practitioner, but it will probably have

---

[23] See *Hinz* v *Berry* [1970] 2 QB 40 discussed at page 119.

created diagnostic and treatment problems, and make prognosis more difficult. This was one of the features of the *Herald of Free Enterprise* arbitrators, see page 129.

Accident neurosis

In chapter 5 allegations of malingering will be considered. There is another concept, well-known to litigators, often described as 'accident', 'compensation' or 'litigation' neurosis. It means that some or all of the plaintiff's symptoms relate to anxiety about the personal injury claim and will resolve after settlement. An interesting follow-up study[24] was carried out on some 35 plaintiffs who had exhibited perplexing physical symptoms which could not be shown to have organic causes. The follow-up was to see whether they recovered markedly once their damages claims had been settled. The practitioner will recognise this allegation: it was said that they were suffering from accident or compensation neurosis. The result of the study showed that few of the claimants had recovered and such recovery as did take place was unrelated to the time of compensation. Interestingly, what did emerge from the study was that it appeared that an important factor inhibiting the recovery process was over-protectiveness on the part of relatives. It appears that no useful conclusions can be drawn about this phenomenon.

PREDISPOSITION

It is not surprising that there are types of personality which are more vulnerable to psychiatric injury. Scrignar says that predisposition to PTSD is correlated with preexisting autonomic hyperactivity or anxiousness. The anxiety can be part of a specific anxiety disorder, or it can be brought about by biological factors such as extreme fatigue or chronic sickness, or through substance abuse. He goes on to say:

> It must be concluded that no carefully controlled study has ever been conducted which definitively demonstrates that certain personality characteristics predispose a person to PTSD. Individuals with a higher than normal pre-morbid anxiety level apparently are more likely to perceive danger and develop PTSD. Whether a patient appears for psychiatric treatment depends more upon their personal coping skills and social support system.[25]

It is important to note Scrignar's conclusion that two patients with identical pre-morbid personalities, subjected to the same distressing experience, may

[24] Tarsh and Royston, 'A follow-up study of accident neurosis', *Br J Psychiatr*, vol. 146 (1985) p. 18.
[25] See page 86 Scrignar.

deal differently with the stress, and that the way in which they do so can affect whether they develop PTSD. He does not define 'personal coping skills', but social support can be readily identified. A victim without a supportive family or friends will be more vulnerable, as will a victim who ostensibly has a great deal of support, but is a naturally reticent character and does not utilise that support to the full. Sadly, one of the characteristic reactions to stress is a wish to move away from the disaster site,[26] which can mean that a victim moves away from familiar surroundings, family and friends and unwittingly exacerbates the situation. Sometimes support can be overused, in the sense that the victim acquires 'learned helplessness' and loses the capacity to appreciate his or her potential for influencing events and the subsequent course of his or her life, and so clings to the support group.[27]

Research is inconclusive as to the predisposing effect of age, gender and cultural background. A curious factor is the effect of previous traumatic experiences. It may be thought that they would in some way 'prepare' the victim and leave him less vulnerable. Research, however, points towards the reverse being true. Research on the firefighters in the Australian bushfires showed that those who had suffered previous traumatic experiences suffered more than those without such histories.[28] The 'pint pot' syndrome may be relevant: the human psyche can only take so much battering; once the pot is full then further assault will result in overflow and breakdown. On the other hand those who have had little or no experience of distressing but 'normal' life events, e.g., bereavement, job changes, moving home etc. may also be vulnerable.[29] Research is also inconclusive as to whether previous trauma can prevent the victim avoiding subsequent incidences of trauma/stress — 'learned helplessness'.[30]

DIAGNOSIS

Understandably, many psychiatrists and psychologists are impatient with a requirement of a strict diagnosis. The human psyche is enormously complex; it will not always be possible to say that a number of complicated symptoms set upon what is always a unique personality will result in a clear diagnosis happily conforming to the pictures painted by the systems of classification. In fairness to those systems, the difficulties of diagnosis and overlap of disorders are acknowledged, and there are many 'unspecified' categories where the more specific diagnostic criteria are not satisfied. The

[26] Masserman cited in Gunn and Taylor, op. cit. (note 17), p. 890.
[27] See M. E. P. Seligman, *Helplessness: on Depression, Development and Death* (New York: Freeman, 1992).
[28] McFarlane quoted in Gunn and Taylor, op. cit. (note 17), p. 893.
[29] See Gunn and Taylor, op. cit. (note 17), p. 894.
[30] Seligman coined the term, quoted by Gunn and Taylor, op. cit. (note 17), p. 894.

crucial point from the practitioner's point of view is that a 'positive' psychiatric illness is diagnosed, even if there are understandable difficulties in precise classification. Professor Gunn and Professor Taylor state:

> The term 'positive psychiatric illness' can embrace the whole range of morbid emotional responses as well as the ordinary form of neurotic and psychotic disorders. The doctor thus must attempt to determine the existence of any psychiatric disorder and its relation to the incident. The court is more concerned with the existence of disorder in itself, its attribution, and its consequences than with the niceties of diagnosis and classification. Diagnostic terms should be used simply and conventionally, but it is unnecessary to follow slavishly definitions from textbooks and glossaries such as the DSM III or ICD.[31]

An important point to note is that the reaction of the victim will not remain constant. Many studies have shown that the victim proceeds through a cycle of reactions. Gunn and Taylor review the literature, citing, first, the 'dazed' state, where victims seem unaware of their surroundings, then the euphoric state which is characterised by restlessness, altruism and perhaps relief at survival. The next stage is when reality impinges as the horror of what happened is recalled in detail. At this stage survival guilt and a sense of helplessness emerge.

Generally, it is thought that diagnosis can be difficult due to the fact that awareness of stress-related disorders is still fairly limited and patients may present a long time after the event. Their recollections of the event may be coloured by subsequent experiences; they may be obsessed with physical symptoms which are not organic or, upon the physical evidence, should not be causing the degree of pain or disablement complained of. There are constantly developing techniques to help in diagnosis. A number of self-assessment questionnaires are used by psychiatrists and psychologists, but which ones are used, and the degree of importance placed on each one will vary. Sometimes these are completed by the patient before seeing the expert, but sometimes the expert will want to interview the patient first, form an assessment and then ask for completion of the questionnaire(s) to confirm, or otherwise, the initial diagnosis. It is wise to note the preferences of the particular expert before exposing the potential patient to any of this type of documentation, and many of these questionnaires are subject to copyright restrictions (see page 98).

In considering the sort of information that may be elicited from the patient in order to diagnose and also assess the type of treatment necessary, and also prognosis, it is worth noting the list of headings in chapter 10 of Scrignar's

---

[31] Gunn and Taylor, op. cit. (note 17), pp. 102–3.

book on forensic evaluation: chronologic history; symptom inventory checklist; medical history; psychiatric history; medication; social history; antisocial behaviour; history of previous litigation; family history; personal history; and mental status examination (an assessment by the expert on the basis of the patient's mannerisms, speech patterns, thought processes and mood). It must be stressed that experts take different approaches, but the foregoing gives some indication of the sorts of information which will be sought.

TREATMENT

There are many ways in which victims of trauma can be helped. These include early screening for symptoms (gained through proper and immediate procedures implemented in the case of disasters), voluntary support groups and self-help, as well as the more conventional professional intervention. Whilst those who are victims along with others do not necessarily recover quicker than solitary victims, there is some advantage in knowing that others have suffered similar experiences so that relating to a peer group it is probably helpful.[32] Sometimes relatively simple strategies have been used with significant success in helping the victims of disaster. After the Australian bushfires of 1983, a leaflet entitled *Coping with a Major Personal Crisis* was devised which listed the sorts of experiences and symptoms which a victim might expect to undergo, describing them as normal, and giving simple advice. This leaflet was used after the Welton air crash, when an aircraft collided with private houses in Lincolnshire, without loss of life, and the reaction to this was investigated.[33] The leaflet was pushed through the door in every village, and 91 per cent of those who had received it had made some effort to read it, and 27 per cent had kept it. People appreciated the fact that someone was concerned, and also the attempt to normalise their experiences. Some local-authority social services departments publish literature advising people of the likely feelings they may experience following traumatic experiences (see appendix 3). The publication of a victims' newsletter also had beneficial effects following the Bradford fire and the *Herald of Free Enterprise* capsize. The newsletters would include requests for information, for contacts, poems and letters about loved ones who had died. Less than 2 per cent of victims rejected the newsletter whereas personal visits were refused by a large number. Victim support schemes can also be vitally important, although research shows that only about 1 per cent of those who report crime to the police are ever referred for help. In March

[32] Gunn and Taylor, op. cit. (note 17), p. 939.
[33] Lalonde et al. 'Community responses to a near disaster', presented at 1st European Conference on Post-traumatic Stress Studies, Lincoln 1988, cited in P. E. Hodgkinson, 'Technological disaster — survival and bereavement', *Soc Sci Med*, vol. 29 (1989), p. 351.

1986 there were, however, some 185,000 referrals.[34] Often this sort of help is enough; the mixture of practical advice, someone to talk to, and the reassurance that someone cares can resolve anxieties. Whoever supplies this service to victims, it is often described as counselling and can include informal counselling by social workers or more formal counselling by specially trained counsellors, such as bereavement counsellors, and can include one to one counselling and/or group therapy.

The importance of being able to talk about the event cannot be overestimated. This can be just as important for professionals as 'civilian' victims. Specific debriefing sessions can be held for rescue workers who are subjected to stress over an extended period of time following a large-scale disaster. The debriefing sessions organised following the San Francisco earthquake in 1989 were twofold: initial 'defusing' a few hours after the rescue work began, and a day or so later a formal three to five-hour session with a mental health professional.[35] Counsellors and others involved in the process may also require help.

The fact that the event affects possibly just one person does not, of course, diminish that person's needs to discuss the event, if necessary with an appropriate mental health adviser. Again, fairly simple techniques can be effective, such as training in progressive muscle relaxation.

An interesting study was carried out following the *Herald of Free Enterprise* disaster to ascertain whether the viewing of human remains by the bereaved was helpful or harmful.[36] The conclusion was that those who view may be more distressed in the short term, but less distressed in the long term. It was also concluded that no one should be encouraged to view, as there will always be individuals who will be badly affected by it, but that those who wish to do so should not be prevented. It is strongly advocated that suitably qualified 'helpers' should be available at the time the decision is taken. It should, however, be noted that the actual sight of the body can be one of the triggering events of psychiatric injury.[37] Needless to say, there should be no suggestion that the decision to view the body is a *novus actus* breaking the chain of causation, the decision to view a body being part of the normal consequences of a death.

Drug treatment

This will depend very much upon whether the victim is suffering from PTSD, or depression or some other psychiatric disorder. As far as PTSD is

[34] Gunn and Taylor, op. cit. (note 17), at p. 936 citing the work of Hough and Mayhew.
[35] See Armstrong et al. 'Debriefing Red Cross disaster personnel: the multiple stressor debriefing model', *Journal of Traumatic Stress*. vol. 4, No. 4 (October 1991).
[36] Hodgkinson et al., 'Viewing human remains following disaster: helpful or harmful?' (1993) 33 Med Sci Law 197.
[37] See *Hevican v Ruane* [1991] 3 All ER 65, QBD (decision reversed on appeal) — see page 163.

concerned, it seems to be acknowledged that drug treatment alone cannot resolve the problem.[38] Scrignar is neutral about the use of drugs in treating PTSD, stating that further research is necessary before conclusions can be drawn. However, he does consider the use of tranquillisers, antidepressants and sedatives. If depression is diagnosed as well as PTSD it is likely that antidepressants will also be given. The risk of diagnosing depression alone and masking as yet undiagnosed PTSD has been cautioned against in research.[39] There is also the danger of the prescription of drugs to those who may already be overusing alcohol and other substances to control their symptoms.

Psychological treatment

There are a large number of different theories and types of treatment which concentrate on altering behaviour and/or cognitive behaviour. Gunn and Taylor cite an example of behavioural treatment for morbid grief where patients who were taken through a period of guided mourning were compared with a control group who were encouraged to avoid thought of the deceased and given distraction techniques. Those who had been encouraged to write about their deceased loved ones and look at photographs of them improved significantly more than the control group.[40] The technique can be modified depending upon the trauma and resulting psychological state. For example, Dr Morgan O'Connell at the Royal Naval Hospital in Haslar encourages patients to produce collages based upon various memorabilia.

There are a number of different strategies used to treat patients psychologically. These include stress inoculation training, thought-stopping techniques, and other forms of what Scrignar calls encephalic reconditioning or cognitive restructuring, i.e., ways of changing those distressing 'videotapes of the mind', and desensitisation, which is a way of gradually re-exposing the victim to the scene of the trauma, or the phobic or anxiety-producing stimulus, such as water, car travel etc. Attribution theory is another way in which victims are encouraged to cope with a traumatic experience. According to this, the nature of the way in which an individual explains an event affects the way in which he will respond to it. Affirming that the explanation for the event is not the fault of the victim will help that victim to come to terms with it, to allay feelings of guilt and shame. Joseph et al.[41] concluded that there may be considerable scope for identifying vulnerable

[38] M. J. Friedman: 'Towards radical Pharmacotherapy for PTSD' Am. J. Psy. 1988 Vol. 145 p. 281.
[39] See Hodgkinson, 'Technological disaster — survival and bereavement', Soc Sci Med, vol. 29, No. 3 1989, pp. 351–356.
[40] Gunn & Taylor, op. cit. (note 17), p. 938 citing the research of Mawson et al. (1981).
[41] 'Attributions and symptoms after a maritime disaster', Br J Psychiatr (1991), vol. 159 p. 542.

individuals and for improving distress by altering people's perceptions of the causes of significant events that took place during the disaster. Scrignar also refers to the usefulness of family conferences, sleep training, and assertiveness training.

PROGNOSIS

There have been several follow-up studies undertaken in respect of victims of large-scale disasters,[42] but not enough, and not over a long enough period of time for any conclusions to be drawn from which useful generalisations can be made. Experts will make their prognoses on the basis of the severity of the symptoms, the degree of support the patient has, the way in which the patient has progressed, or not as the case may be, during the period from initial consultation to final report or trial, and so on. Often it will not be possible to say that the patient is cured; many of the techniques referred to above will be available to the patient throughout life to deal with anxieties, intrusive thoughts or images etc. which *may* return from time to time. Knowing that these techniques have worked in the past can be of considerable comfort to the sufferer. Some experts will use the questionnaire system to see how the patient is progressing.

CHILDREN

Are there any special problems relating to children who are exposed to trauma? It was once thought that children did not suffer from PTSD. Conclusions have been drawn, however, that children as young as eight can suffer the symptoms of PTSD.[43] The effects can go on for a number of years. Inevitably, the interaction with their parents can produce some confusing results, particularly if the parents have also been involved in the traumatic episode. Research has shown very different levels of distress reported by children when they were seen separately from their parents, after the *Herald* disaster, when children knew that their parents were trying to cope with their own distress.[44] Some differences, however, have been noted between adult and children's symptoms of PTSD; for example, it is more difficult to detect 'psychic numbing' in children. As Yule and Williams say: 'If anything, their pressing need to avoid situations that remind them of the accident drives them out of the house where it will be discussed and into a frenzy of social

---

[42] See, e.g., Gleser, Greg and Winget, *Prolonged Psychosocial Effects of Disaster: A Study of Buffalo Creek* (New York: 1981, Academic Press, 1981).

[43] W. Yule, 'The effects of disasters on children', *Association for Child Psychology and Psychiatry Newsletter*, vol. 11, No. 6 (November 1989).

[44] Yule and Williams, 'Post-traumatic stress reactions in children', *Journal of Traumatic Stress*, vol. 3, No. 2 (1990).

activities.' Clearly, this can mask psychological distress: it may well be thought that a child is unaffected if he appears to be full of energy and 'enjoying himself'. Yule and Williams also note with surprise the failure of teachers to note the problems the children were experiencing, but go on to say that this experience is similar to that in Australia following the bushfires, when McFarlane was thwarted in his attempts to study the children who saw the fires because schools would not co-operate saying it was best to let past things remain in the past. Another interesting point made by Yule and Williams is the value of group work with parents and children, considering that each may be trying to protect the other from their own distress.

Professor Yule worked with children who suffered in the *Jupiter* disaster (the ship carrying school children which sank near Athens in 1988) and gave valuable evidence in the case of *Gardner* v *Epirotiki SS Company & Others* [1995] PMILL January 1995, Vol. 10, No. 10. The reference to PTSD and children in the DSM IV diagnostic criteria should also be noted (see page 173).

THE FUTURE

Research produced as long ago as 1929[45] concluded that stress produces physical changes to the nervous system. Subsequent research has continued to confirm that a number of complex neurochemical changes take place within the nervous system following conditions of acute stress,[46] and in 1984, Bessel van der Kolk et al., produced a biological hypothesis that animals that have been exposed to 'inescapable shock' undergo changes in the chemical composition of their nervous systems, the extrapolation of which to humans suggests that opioid peptides play a vital role in the state of stress and its subsequent treatment and management.[47] This has fascinating and important implications for lawyers. One of the central problems in relation to establishing a successful claim for any form of psychiatric injury has always been that it is not 'physical' damage. If the future holds the possibility of producing evidence of actual physical damage to a plaintiff's neurochemical composition, then the question of proximity will disappear. There will remain, of course, the question of causation, but it would remove

---

[45] W. B. Cannon, *Bodily Changes in Pain, Hunger, Fear and Rage: An Account of Recent Researches into the Function of Emotional Excitement* 2nd ed. (New York, Appleton-Century-Crofts, 1929).
[46] H. Anisman, 'Neurochemical changes elicited by stress: behavioral correlates' in H. Anisman and G. Bigname (eds), *Psychopharmacology of Aversively Motivated Behavior* (New York: Plenum, 1978); D. Krieger, 'Brain peptides: what where and why', *Science*, vol. 222 (1983), p. 975.
[47] B. A. van der Kolk et al., 'Post-traumatic stress disorder as a biologically based disorder: implications of the animal model of inescapable shock' in B. A. van der Kolk (ed.), *Post-Traumatic Stress Disorder: Psychological and Biological Sequelae* (Washington DC: American Psychiatric Press, 1984).

one of the most difficult obstacles to a claim, and put psychiatric injury on a par with ordinary physical damage. This is all well into the future, but it could result in one of the most exciting developments in medical evidence.

More immediately, since the recognition over the past 10 years of so of the extent of traumatically induced disorders, a considerable amount of work has been carried out, and it is hoped that more follow-up studies will be carried out. Increased information about the effect of trauma of all kinds upon psychological development should bring a greater understanding and awareness.

THREE

Events that can cause psychiatric injury

SUDDEN TRAUMA

By sudden trauma, we mean a single event which is such as to make a sudden and immediately experienced impact upon one or more of a participant's senses. Establishing that the event fulfilled this criterion is crucial if the plaintiff has suffered psychiatric injury through fear for others or fear for him or herself. It should usually be a matter of common sense whether the event satisfies this criterion. A crime of violence is a sudden trauma, but we consider criminal injuries separately at the end of this chapter. Damage to property is usually sudden trauma and that is dealt with in chapter 4.

INJURIES CAUSED BY INTENTIONAL ACTS

Deceit

The case of *Wilkinson* v *Downton* [1897] 2 QB 57 established liability for psychiatric injury caused by a deliberate, as opposed to negligent, act of the defendant. In this case, the defendant, as a practical joke, informed the plaintiff that her husband had suffered an accident and was lying in a public house with both legs broken. She suffered injury as a result of this shock. Liability was established on the basis that this was a *wilful* act calculated to cause harm to the plaintiff. A claim in negligence for such damage would not have been allowable given the state of the law at that time. There is some force in the argument that *Wilkinson* v *Downton* liability is now of academic interest only, given the development of liability in negligence for psychiatric injury. However, it must be noted that the advantage of it is that, unlike a claim in negligence, it is not necessary to show that the injury was caused by some sudden impact or trauma upon the senses. In *Wilkinson* v *Downton*, of course, liability was established on the basis of a statement only.

It can also be said that the limitations placed upon liability in negligence by the concept of remoteness of damage are not appropriate in the case of intentional acts. If a certain result is intended, can it ever be said to be too remote? However, practical difficulties may arise inasmuch as although the *act* may be intentional, its *consequences* may not have been. Would recklessness as to the consequences suffice? It is also a moot point whether, in relation to an intended act, there is a requirement that the plaintiff has suffered a recognised psychiatric illness. If it can be established that the result was intended then it could be argued that non-medical mental distress would suffice. The following discussion covers a number of intentional torts where psychiatric injury could foreseeably be the consequence.

Harassment
The case of *Khorasandjian* v *Bush* [1993] QB 727 established, by a majority Court of Appeal decision, that there is a tort of harassment. That case was concerned with injunctive relief only, but there is no reason why damages could not be awarded and damages for psychiatric injury as well if the harasssment was the cause. It is submitted that damages for non-medical mental distress could also be recovered. Although *McCall* v *Abelesz* [1976] QB 585, CA, denied a remedy in tort in respect of landlord harassment, this was on the basis that an action would lie for breach of covenant for quiet enjoyment.

A developing area is that of sexual and racial harassment in the work place. Such claims are properly brought as sex/race discrimination claims, which include compensation for injured feelings. It is important to note that there is no longer a financial ceiling on discrimination compensation.

Intimidation
Coercion is an essential element of intimidation, and it is therefore, by its very nature, intentional. An example of the sort of situation where psychiatric injury or general distress could well result is illustrated by *Godwin* v *Uzioqwe* (1992) *The Times*, 18 June which concerned a 16-year-old girl who had been brought from Nigeria to work as a domestic servant and who had been treated as a drudge for two and a half years, with no proper food, clothing or social life. Damages of £20,000 were awarded for deprivation of these life essentials.

Discrimination and dismissal
Sex and race discrimination are other areas where psychiatric damage would be foreseeable. Actions in respect of unlawful discrimination, pursuant to the Sex Discrimination Act 1975 or the Race Relations Act 1976, other than in the field of employment, are brought in the county court just as any other

claim in tort, and the same heads of damage apply, although the statutes, for the avoidance of doubt, state that damages for injury to feelings can be brought.[1] Discrimination in the employment field is remediable through the industrial tribunal system, but the damages payable are equivalent to those that may be awarded in the county court and there is no financial ceiling.[2]

Although there is no similar head of damage in unfair dismissal law, compensation for the manner of dismissal can be recovered if it affects the employee's future prospects.[3] If the manner of dismissal causes a medical condition, e.g., psychiatric injury, rendering the dismissed employee either unfit to work, or unfit to work in his or her usual occupation, then the appropriate compensation can be awarded.

'CREEPING TRAUMA'

Although the majority of psychiatric injury cases do involve incidents of sudden trauma, which make an immediate impact upon the senses (e.g., natural disasters, man-made disasters, vehicles out of control, fire, flooding, explosion, violent crimes etc.), there are other examples of situations where psychiatric injury is incurred through more insidious means and where damages have been recovered. Although in *Alcock* v *Chief Constable of the South Yorkshire Police* [1992] 1 AC 310 the House of Lords stressed that the event-proximity requirement, i.e., that there had to be a sudden impact upon the plaintiff's mind, had to be adhered to (despite Lord Oliver's recognition (at p. 416) that 'It would be inaccurate and hurtful to suggest that grief is made any the less real or deprivation more tolerable by a gradual realisation'), it will be instructive to look at examples of some situations which can be described as 'creeping trauma'.

Professional negligence

Actions for professional negligence in all fields can arise in both contract and tort. In most non-medical cases there is a contract between professional and client. There is implied into most contracts the expectation that the professional will carry out professional activities with reasonable skill and care unless there are express terms to the contrary.[4] This implied term is now embodied in s. 13 of the Supply of Goods and Services Act 1982. The professional's tortious liablity arises by reason of the 'duty of care' principle, and any breach of the duty of care giving rise to foreseeable injury will

---

[1] Sex Discrimination Act 1975, s. 66; Race Relations Act 1976, s. 57.
[2] Sex Discrimination Act, s. 65; Race Relations Act 1976, s. 56.
[3] *Brittains Arborfield Ltd* v *Van Uden* [1977] ICR 211.
[4] The exceptions are contracts for finished articles, where it is more appropriate to say the implied term is that the article concerned will be fit for its purpose.

impose tortious liability upon the professional who owed the duty. It is generally thought that a doctor treating an NHS patient has no contractual relationship with that patient,[5] and any action brought by the patient will be brought in tort on the basis of breach of duty of care.

The question whether the professional who has a contractual relationship is also concurrently liable in tort has been considered by the courts on many occasions and has given rise to conflicting decisions. On the one hand, opinion has been that, whatever the contractual provisions, it seems inconsistent to deny that there is also a duty of care, and on the other hand, that if the parties have entered into a detailed contract in the full knowledge of its implications, the law should not insist on adding something to this. It is no coincidence, therefore, that the cases which seek to deny concurrent liability are those concerned with purely commercial contracts.[6] In any event, it must be understood that any contractual term which purports to exclude liability for death or personal injury is void.[7]

Medical negligence

The main area of professional negligence where personal injury of a psychiatric nature has arisen is medical negligence. The reason for this is clear: if anything goes wrong, i.e., if there is a breach of duty of care or a breach of a contractual term, then it will usually be discovered through physical injury, and, of course, once this has been shown, then any associated (i.e., factually caused) psychiatric injury will form part of the claim too.

A medical negligence claim can arise in a contractual situation, when the patient is paying privately, or in tort, if the patient is in receipt of NHS treatment. It is, of course, well established that a duty of care exists. The standard of care is still the standard proposed in *Bolam* v *Friern Hospital Management Committee* [1957] 1 WLR 582, in which McNair J directed the jury as follows (at p. 587):

> . . . [a doctor] is not guilty of negligence if he has acted in accordance with a practice accepted as proper by a responsible body of medical men skilled in that particular art.

In other words, the standard is the standard of a conventional medical practitioner and the fact that there are doctors who would have treated the patient differently does not matter. The standard concerned is objective, and takes no account of the particular doctor's level of skill or experience.[8]

[5] See *Pfizer Corporation* v *Ministry of Health* [1965] AC 512.
[6] See *Tai Hing Cotton Mill Ltd* v *Liu Chong Hing Bank Ltd* [1986] AC 80, PC.
[7] Unfair Contract Terms Act 1977, s. 3.
[8] See *Wilsher* v *Essex AHA* [1986] 3 All ER 801, CA.

Broadly speaking, the problem of causation is more difficult in medical negligence cases than in ordinary personal injury actions, the reason being that, usually, there will already be some injury or disease present. For example, in *Robinson* v *Post Office* [1974] 1 WLR 1176, the plaintiff sued the Post Office after suffering an injury received in the course of his employment, and also sued the doctor who administered an anti-tetanus injection without carrying out the appropriate test for an allergic reaction. Mr Robinson suffered from such a reaction, but it was found that even if the test had been administered properly, it would not have resulted in Mr Robinson's reaction being known in time.[9]

Frequently, the situation will be complex, and it will be impossible to say whether a particular cause is operating or not. In such cases the courts should normally take the view that the plaintiff succeeds if, on the balance of probabilities, the negligent act materially contributed to the injury or disease.[10]

However, the situation can become complicated when causation is considered before the damage suffered is identified, as in the case of *Hotson* v *East Berkshire Health Authority* [1987] AC 750. Due to the defendant's negligent treatment, the child plaintiff had suffered an injury which the trial judge found to be 75 per cent likely to occur anyway. On this likelihood, the judge awarded the child 25 per cent of his damages. The House of Lords rejected this approach, and said that the 75 per cent likelihood finding meant that on the balance of probabilities the judge had found that the negligence had *not* caused the injury. This meant that the plaintiff recovered nothing. What the plaintiff had suffered, however, was what is known as 'the loss of a chance', i.e., the chance in this case of receiving treatment which *may* have benefited him. Clearly the defendant's negligence caused *that* particular loss, and the decision in *Hotson* has been criticised on this basis.[11]

Causation is likely to be less of a problem with psychiatric injury, which is not usually a likely consequence of medical treatment. However, the difficulty could arise in cases where the treatment was itself for a psychiatric condition, or in sensitive operations such as sterilisations, where there could be some psychiatric consequences. It is important to remember here that if there are possible consequences which are likely to be unpleasant whether physically or otherwise, the doctors concerned are under a duty to inform the patient of these consequences, and failure to do so will give rise to a cause of action in negligence. Of particular relevance here is the fact that the obtaining of the patient's consent alone may not be enough. This is illustrated by *Wells* v *Surrey Area Health Authority* (1978) *The Times* 29 July 1978. Mrs Wells was due to give birth to her third child by Caesarian section,

---

[9] See also *Rance* v *Mid-Downs Health Authority* [1991] 1 QB 587.
[10] See *McGhee* v *National Coal Board* [1973] 1 WLR 1 and *Wilsher* v *Essex Area Health Authority* [1988] AC 1074.
[11] See, for example, M. A. Jones, *Textbook on Torts*, 4th ed. (London: Blackstone Press, 1993), p. 145.

and it was the hospital's practice to offer a sterilisation operation at the same time if the woman already had two or three children. Mrs Wells consented to the sterilisation operation whilst she was in labour, but later regretted it. She sued alleging assault on the basis that she had not been in a position to give valid consent. This was rejected by the court, but she succeeded in negligence as it was held that counselling is an important preliminary to sterilisation and the hospital had been negligent in failing to give her proper advice about it.

If psychiatric injury is suffered as a result of negligent treatment resulting in physical injury, then the requirement that the outcome must be sufficiently shocking or distressing to the person of average emotional constitution ('customary phlegm') still has to be satisfied. However, it should also be considered that even if the mishap was minor, it could result in phobic anxiety about medical treatment, particularly if an operative procedure has gone wrong whilst the patient was unconscious. Further-more, there appears to be no reason why a third party in a sufficiently proximate relationship should not recover damages for psychiatric injury caused by discovering a loved one in a condition of pain and suffering after some medical mishap. This would be particularly so if the medical treatment was to counteract some relatively minor ailment, i.e., the parties had no reason to expect anything other than the most minor discomfort. However, there is still the requirement of 'shock' see, for example *Sion* v *Hampstead Health Authority* [1994] 5 Med LR 170, considered on page 65.

In *Ackers* v *Wigan Health Authority* [1986] CLY 1048 the plaintiff had a Caesarian section operation to deliver her first child. She was not adequately anaesthetised, and was aware during the whole of the operation, but unable to indicate this due to the effect of the muscle relaxant administered before the operation. The operation lasted one and a quarter hours and she was in great pain and fear. As a result of this, she suffered a severe reactive depression, suffering from mood changes, irritability, insomnia, and a phobia about hospitals and anaesthetics. She was terrified when she learnt that her second child would be born by a Caesarian section, and she became frightened of further pregnancy, which adversely affected her sexual relationship with her husband. She also felt unable to face necessary surgery for other ailments which resulted in additional pain and discomfort. Although the prognosis was fairly optimistic, it did involve a course of therapy which would mean reliving her experiences which would be very unpleasant. She was awarded £12,000 in respect of general damages, wholly for psychiatric injury and £1,700 for the cost of future psychiatric treatment.

In *Biles* v *Barking Health Authority* [1988] CLY 1103 the plaintiff was diagnosed as suffering from PTSD as a result of a sterilisation operation carried out when she was 19. The operation turned out to have been unnecessary, and she underwent many operative procedures in an attempt to conceive. She had a tender scar across her lower abdomen. Her sexual function was impaired, although the prognosis in respect of this was good. At the time of trial she had been suffering from PTSD for seven years, her symptoms being depression and anxiety.

An interesting case is *Kralj* v *McGrath* [1986] 1 All ER 54. The plaintiff was admitted to hospital for the birth of her twins. One of the babies was lying in a transverse position in the womb, and the obstetrician put his arm inside the plaintiff in an attempt to turn the child around by manipulation of its head. These efforts were not successful and the baby was later delivered by Caesarian section. The child was born with severe disabilities as a result of the obstetrician's attempt to turn it and died some eight weeks later. The plaintiff and her husband already had one child and intended to have three. The claim for damages included a claim for aggravated damages due to the obstetrician's conduct and a claim for grief arising out of the loss of the child and a claim for financial loss of having another child to replace the dead child.

The claim for aggravated damages did not succeed; see page 116 for further discussion. It was also held that she was not entitled to damages for grief, but she had seen the child in its disabled condition and was entitled to damages for nervous shock caused by this and by hearing what had happened to it (this may be contrasted with the refusal of the courts to award damages when shock had been caused by hearing from a third party of the death or injury to a loved one, whereas here Mrs Kralj recovered because of *what had been done to her*). Furthermore, it was held that she was entitled to have those damages increased if, because of her grief at the loss of the child it would be more difficult for her to recover from her own injuries. She also recovered the financial loss which would result from a future pregnancy.

A case of some interest is *G* v *North Tees Health Authority* [1989] FCR 53. The plaintiffs were mother and child. The child had suffered from a skin complaint and in the course of the treatment the mother reported that the child was suffering from a vaginal discharge. A swab was taken, but, due to the negligence of the hospital it was mixed up with another one and it was reported that the swab from the child contained semen. The child was subjected to a very painful internal examination and was interviewed by social workers and police. Some four days later the mistake was discovered. The mother was already suffering from a phobic anxiety condition and this was exacerbated. The prognosis was good. The child suffered from nightmares and enuresis. She became preoccupied with sexual assaults and her genital organs, and developed a fear of both doctors and the police. The prognosis was similarly good, although it was thought that future gynaeco-logical procedures might make her anxious. The mother and child were awarded general damages of £5,000 each. A claim for aggravated damages was refused.

It should be noted here that not all medical malpractice actions are actions in negligence. A patient who has not been informed of the broad nature of the physical examination or surgical procedure which is carried out by a doctor cannot be said to have consented and the subsequent examination or surgery will constitute a battery, which is defined as a non-consensual touching.[12] Damages for psychiatric injury are recoverable in battery, and the issue of exemplary damages in such cases is discussed at page 117.

Another instructive case is *Waller v Canterbury and Thanet Health Authority* [1993] CLY 1453. Although only a county court decision, this is a somewhat unusual case involving the suicide of a 20-year-old man whose parents discovered his body hanging by a rope. The parents had warned the hospital of his suicidal tendencies and had been assured he would be kept within the hospital ward. In breach of this, he got out into a disused building where his parents found him. They both suffered depressive illnesses as a consequence and recovered damages.

Subject to the requirements of causation, psychiatric injury suffered by a patient who has been the subject of medical negligence is an uncontroversial head of claim. However, in *Taylor v Somerset Health Authority* [1993] PIQR P262, the psychiatrically injured party was the widow of the victim of medical negligence. After months of failure to diagnose and treat his heart disease, the plaintiff's husband suffered an unexpected and immediately fatal heart attack at work. He was taken to hospital and found to be dead. Shortly afterwards the plaintiff arrived at the hospital where she was told that her husband was dead. She was shocked and distressed. A few minutes later she identified her husband's body in the hospital mortuary which caused her further distress. As a result of these experiences she suffered a psychiatric illness. As a 'secondary' victim of the negligence Mrs Taylor had to satisfy the 'event proximity' test and failed. Firstly, because the judge held that there was no external, traumatic event, and secondly, because even if the fatal heart attack were found to be such an event, the communication of the bad news by the doctor was expressly excluded as a legitimate means of causation in *Alcock v Chief Constable of South Yorkshire Police* [1992] 1 AC 310, and the subsequent identification of the body did not form part of the immediate aftermath of the event. It went to the fact of the death as distinct from the circumstances in which the death came about.

In the case of *Sion v Hampstead Health Authority* [1994] 5 Med LR 170, the plaintiff had suffered a psychiatric illness as a result of the experience of sitting at his son's bedside for 14 days watching him deteriorate and fall into a coma. The son was a road accident victim but the plaintiff's claim was in respect of negligent medical treatment. The Court of Appeal rejected his claim because there was no evidence of 'shock', no sudden appreciation by sight or sound of a horrifying event, but a continuous process. In particular,

---

[12] See *Chatterton v Gerson* [1981] QB 432.

the court said, the son's death was not surprising but expected. A similar decision was made in *Taylorson* v *Shieldness Produce Ltd* [1994] PIQR 329. However, in *Tredget* v *Bexley Health Authority* [1994] 5 Med LR 178, damages were recovered by parents who were psychiatrically injured by the circumstances of the birth and subsequent death of their child caused by medical negligence. His Honour Judge White found that the illnesses were caused by the shock, the sudden and direct appreciation of sight or sound of a horrifying event.

As far as liability of a psychiatrist instructed by a local authority in an allegation of child abuse is concerned, in *M (A Minor) and Another* v *Newham London Borough Council and Others* [1994] 2 WLR 554, CA, (Sir Thomas Bingham MR dissenting) held that there was no duty of care owed to the child by the psychiatrist, only a duty to the local authority (see page 17).

It is interesting to note a recent settlement by the Ministry of Defence in respect of failure of the army to diagnose or treat PTSD suffered by a Falklands War veteran.[13]

Lawyers' negligence

The question of foreseeability of psychiatric damage is not a difficult one in the doctor–patient relationship. However, in other cases, if there is a breach of professional duty, whether it is a duty which has arisen through a contractual term or one imposed by the law of tort, then the connection between the breach and any subsequent psychiatric injury has to be established, factually of course, but also in the sense that legal causation must be proved. In other words the damage cannot be too remote. A claim in contract may succeed where one in tort would not, if the injury could be said to be within the contemplation of the parties to the contract, though the connection was too remote for liability in tort. The circumstances of the contract would have to be linked to the anticipated state of mind of the non-breaching party. In most professional contracts, of course, no such factors will be present. However, in the provision of legal services, there are a number of situations when the advice and action sought will be to alleviate or prevent a situation which is or is likely to cause psychiatric injury. It is essential, however, that the legal practitioner knows of the relevant factors or could reasonably be expected to know of them. In *Heywood* v *Wellers* [1976] QB 446, CA, the plaintiff had instructed solicitors to bring proceedings against a man to prevent him from molesting her. As a result of negligence on the part of the solicitors, the proceedings were ineffective. Damages were

[13] See Beggs, 'Successfully suing the MoD' NLJ, 11 March 1994, p. 369.

awarded in respect of anxiety, vexation and distress. Similarly, in *Dickinson v Jones Alexander & Co.* (1990) 6 PN 205, damages of £5,000 were awarded to the plaintiff for mental distress caused by the negligent failure of the defendant solicitors to remove her husband from the former matrimonial home and by negligent financial advice. At the time that the negligence took place, there was clear evidence that the plaintiff was suffering from the effects of the matrimonial situation which the defendants failed to alleviate, as they had a letter from her doctor saying she was 'suffering from an anxiety depression type of illness', and was being treated with tranquillisers, and that the doctor had no doubt that her condition had been brought on by her matrimonial situation. It appears that the £5,000 was awarded for 'non-medical' distress, but, had her condition been worse, then, upon the evidence available, she would probably have recovered for a specific psychiatric condition. The test, of course, is whether such damage would have been within the contemplation of the parties. In other words it will frequently be defeated as being damage which is too remote.

Damages were recovered in *Malyon* v *Lawrance, Messer & Co.* [1968] 2 Lloyd's Rep 539. In that case the plaintiff sued his former lawyers for failing to issue proceedings in a road traffic case within the limitation period. He claimed damages (*inter alia*) for business losses brought about by his inability to cope due to prolongation of an anxiety neurosis. It was held that it must have been obvious to the defendants from the information they held about the plaintiff and his claim, that his condition was worsening due to delay, and damages were recovered.[14] However, generally, it must be said that damages will be recovered only where the specific risk is known or should have been known.

In *McLeish* v *Amoo-Gottfried & Co.* (1993) *The Times*, 13 October 1993, damages were awarded to a plaintiff for mental distress caused by the negligence of a solicitor in the conduct of a criminal action, whereby he had been wrongly convicted of two charges of common assault on a police officer and a charge of possessing an offensive weapon. It was held that the very essence of the contract had been to ensure the plaintiff's peace of mind, and therefore it was foreseeable that he would suffer mental distress if the conduct of the case was negligent.

Al-Kandari v *J. R. Brown & Co.* [1988] QB 665 concerned a firm of solicitors who negligently allowed their client to recover his confiscated passport, thereby enabling him to kidnap his children. When taking the children, he used physical restraint upon his wife who suffered physical and psychiatric injury. The wife recovered damages from her husband's solicitors. French J held that a solicitor who had given an implied undertaking on behalf of a client, one object of which was to protect a third party, would owe

---

[14] See also *Wales* v *Wales* (1967) 111 SJ 946.

a duty of care towards that third party who ought to be within the solicitor's contemplation as someone who was likely to be so closely and directly affected by his acts that it was reasonably foreseeable that the third party was likely to be injured by the solicitor's acts.

Breach of confidence

Professional advisers and others receive information which is such that they are obliged to keep such information confidential. What if the adviser breaches that confidence, and such a breach causes psychiatric injury? As confirmed by *Attorney-General* v *Guardian Newspapers Ltd (No. 2)* [1990] 1 AC 109, information is confidential if it is imparted in circumstances where the recipient has notice, or has agreed, that the information is confidential and where it would be just that he should be precluded from disclosure. In *Furniss* v *Fitchett* [1958] NZLR 396, Mr and Mrs Furniss were both patients of Dr Fitchett, who was asked by Mr Furniss to supply to him a letter about his wife, confirming various matters that she had presented with, and concluding that she suffered from paranoia. Subsequently, and unbeknown to Dr Fitchett, Mr Furniss used the letter in divorce proceedings, and Mrs Furniss brought an action against the doctor, recovering (*inter alia*) damages for psychiatric injury. It was accepted that the letter was true, but it was held by the court that the duty of care owed to the patient was not limited to making sure the information was accurate. It also extended to the exercise of care in deciding whether to disclose the information at all. The duty to preserve confidences is not an absolute duty, and there will always be circumstances in which it will be possible to sustain the public interest defence.

Stress at work

There may be a number of workplace factors which will lead to some form of psychiatric disorder. These can range from lack of proper supervision or training to shortages of skilled staff and excessive working hours. Apparently in countries such as the United States, Japan and Australia, with no-fault worker's compensation schemes up to one in five claims are for stress-related problems.[15] There is a general duty on the part of an employer to take reasonable care for the safety of employees, and this can be summed up as the provision of competent, trained staff, adequate tools and materials and a safe system of work.[16] There may also be specific statutory requirements under the Health and Safety at Work Act 1974 and other legislation. In

[15] *The Guardian*, 26 October 1993.
[16] See *Wilsons & Clyde Coal Co. Ltd* v *English* [1938] AC 57.

addition, an employer is vicariously liable for the tortious acts of other employees. If psychiatric injury arises through an industrial accident then the normal rules will apply — proximity in space and time etc. However, here we will consider non-traumatically induced injury such as injury resulting from 'stress'.

An employee may suffer stress-induced psychiatric injury as a result of one or more of the employer's duties being breached by, e.g., being overworked, inadequately trained etc. An action for damages is sustainable if the employer is aware of the problem and has failed to take steps which could have been taken to reduce the stress. In *Johnstone* v *Bloomsbury Health Authority* [1992] QB 333, the Court of Appeal considered whether such a claim could be made in tort, if the contract provided, for example, for an excessive number of hours to be worked. The majority decision of the Court of Appeal was that the contractual relationship had to be looked at in the light of the implied terms of the contract, so the issue of tortious liability was not tackled head-on. It is a moot point, however, whether an employer can always avoid a duty of care by placing onerous express terms in the contract of employment. In *Walker* v *Northumberland County Council* [1995] 1 All ER 737, QB, the plaintiff was a social worker employed by the county council from 1970 until 1987. In 1986 he was off work, suffering from a nervous breakdown caused by stress at work. He was back after three months and it was agreed that he be provided with some assistance. In the event the help was very limited and after six months he suffered a second breakdown and had to give up work permanently. The court found that *both* breakdowns were caused by the defendant's breach of duty to provide a safe system of work. It is interesting that the issue of policy was discussed by the judge (Colman J), who said that this had no part to play in the context of the duty of care to an employee with whom a statutory body has a contract of employment. In *Gillespie* v *Commonwealth of Australia* (1991) 104 ACTR 1, it was held that a plaintiff who suffered an anxiety condition after being posted to a new embassy where conditions were very bad was owed a duty of care by his employer to prepare him adequately for this, but on the facts, it was found that the duty had been fulfilled.

Toxic trauma

This can be described as trauma which is caused environmentally but which is not perceived by one or more of the five sensory pathways to the brain (see page 42). Such trauma could be exposure to dangerous radiation levels or toxic substances of some kind. For any subsequent psychiatric illness to develop, it is essential for there to be cognitive awareness of the danger involved. Scrignar says:

As in other traumata which are perceived by one or a combination of the five senses, a variety of emotional responses can be expected. Some persons with good coping skills and a solid social support system would adapt quickly and experience no significant stress symptoms after four to six weeks. Others, who are 'worriers' and may have been suffering from a generalised anxiety disorder (GAD) prior to knowledge of exposure to invisible trauma, may have an exacerbation of the GAD or possibly develop a PTSD. Persons who develop a PTSD would have intrusive thoughts centring around exposure to the invisible trauma and its damaging effect upon their bodies, avoidance of all things believed to have been contaminated, and symptoms of increased arousal (anxiety). Encephalic events (cognitions) vivify the trauma, stripping away the cloak of invisibility. Official notification by governmental or medical officials of the hazards to health and the visible efforts and publicity attendant to populations in the danger area (warnings, evacuation, preventive measures, etc.) flesh out cognitions of dangerousness in the 'videotapes of the mind'. Accuracy of information and adequacy of preventive measures play an important role in a person's ultimate response to invisible trauma.[17]

There may be physical damage to the body's physiological structure caused by exposure to toxic substances which can have behavioural effects.

Tortious actions in respect of pollution in various forms are not uncommon. These can be in respect of negligence, nuisance, the rule in *Rylands* v *Fletcher* (1868) LR 3 HL 330 or breach of statutory duty. Some of these actions can, of course, include a claim for damages for personal injury, although causation is always a difficult issue.[18] The interesting question is whether the law would allow a claim for psychiatric damage. If there is associated physical injury then there will be no need for the 'sudden impact' rule to be complied with. However, what of those who develop psychiatric injury after exposure to toxic substances in respect of which there have been (as yet) no physical manifestations of poisoning.

If there is immediate physical harm but not to the plaintiff or those sufficiently proximate to him, the question of communication of bad news may be relevant.

Through exposure to the risk, even if there is no organic damage, awareness of the risk, and the possibility of illness developing, can produce psychiatric disorder. In respect of the latter, a number of particular claimants come to mind, such as those living within close proximity to places such as Sellafield, and other nuclear processing plants; those who have been

---

[17] C. B. Scrignar, *Post-traumatic Stress Disorders*, 2nd ed. (New Orleans LA: Bruno Press, 1988), pp. 64–65.
[18] C. Pugh and M. Day, *Toxic Torts* (London: Cameron May, 1992).

close to an industrial explosion such as the one which took place at Flixborough, near Scunthorpe in 1974. At Flixborough 29 people died and over 100 were injured. Many homes in the vicinity were destroyed. After a fire and an explosion at the Walmsly Chemical Plant in Barking, East London, a major evacuation was organised as it was feared that a toxic cloud from the fire could contain significant levels of cyanates. At Bhopal, India, in 1984, a cloud containing methyl isocyanate escaped rapidly into the atmosphere at a time when the victims were sleeping. Many physical disorders developed, such as pulmonary oedema and blindness. Then there was the incident at Three Mile Island, and, of course, Chernobyl. Many physical illnesses from such incidents take years to manifest themselves; it is little wonder that the cloud hanging over those who may eventually succomb to such illnesses can have serious psychological effects.

Is there any liability for psychiatric injury caused by a fear that physical illness will result from exposure to or proximity to contamination? Mullany and Handford cite a number of cases[19] where psychiatric injury has resulted from situations akin to the *Donoghue* v *Stevenson* [1932] AC 562 scenario, but where the resulting injury was purely psychiatric, e.g., the Australian case of *Vance* v *Cripps Bakery Pty Ltd* [1984] Aust Torts Rep 80–668, where the plaintiff recovered damages for a phobia caused by the realisation that he had eaten bread containing a dead mouse; the Canadian case of *Curll* v *Robin Hood Multifoods Ltd* (1974) 56 DLR (3d) 129, where the plaintiff was shocked by discovering a partly decomposed mouse in a bag of flour. In these cases there was no physical damage yet recovery was made for what, presumably, were justifiable fears.

There does not appear to be any difference between these sorts of cases and the case of a plaintiff who has suffered exposure to some form of environmental contamination but has not (as yet) been physically injured by it. There may never be any physical damage but if there is a significant risk of injury then why should the plaintiff not recover for suffering the fear of that injury? Plaintiffs in this situation are sometimes described as 'the worried well'. The plaintiff will recover, of course, if the contamination is part of a traumatic event or its immediate aftermath which the plaintiff has experienced directly, but otherwise, despite the liberal Commonwealth decisions above, English law is unlikely to allow recovery, at least in negligence.

If the plaintiff has an interest in land and his or her use of enjoyment of that land has been interfered with by the contamination, does this make a claim for psychiatric injury easier to sustain? It may do so, as the tort will turn on whether the defendant's use of the land was reasonable. In other words the defence that the defendant took all reasonable care is not available

[19] *Tort Liability for Psychiatric Damage* (London: Sweet & Maxwell, 1993), p. 213.

in the same way as it is in negligence. This distinction, however, may be more apparent than real. It was established in *Overseas Tankship (UK) Ltd* v *Miller Steamship Co. Pty Ltd, The Wagon Mound (No. 2)* [1967] 1 AC 617 that in nuisance 'although negligence may not be necessary, fault of some kind is almost always necessary and fault generally involves foreseeability'. In addition, if there is also physical damage then it is generally thought that liability must be fault-based, as opposed to amenity damage.[20] Furthermore, *Cambridge Water Co.* v *Eastern Counties Leather plc* [1994] 2 WLR 53 confirms that only plaintiffs who can show that the damage of that type or kind was foreseeable can succeed in an action for nuisance or, indeed, for damage sustained under the rule in *Rylands* v *Fletcher* (1868) LR 3 HL 330.

In California it is possible to claim damages for fear of illness. In *Potter* v *Firestone Tyre & Rubber Co.* (1994) *Lloyd's List*, 4 March 1994, the plaintiffs lived near the Crazy Horse landfill site in Salinas. They discovered that toxic chemicals had contaminated their domestic water wells, and that the defendant company had been dumping toxic waste in violation of landfill regulations and the company's own policy. The California Supreme Court held that to recover damages for negligent infliction of emotional distress arising out of exposure to carcinogens in the absence of physical injury, plaintiffs must establish, first, that they have been exposed to a toxic substance which threatens cancer and, secondly, that the fear stems from knowledge, corroborated by reliable medical or scientific opinion, that it is more likely than not that they will develop the cancer. However, the latter requirement was not necessary if the defendant's conduct amounted to oppression, fraud or malice.

Action for damages for psychiatric injury caused by this sort of 'invisible trauma' are untested in the UK. The first action is awaited with interest.

CRIMINAL INJURIES

It is appropriate to consider criminal injuries separately because in most cases the victim will not seek compensation through an ordinary civil action but will pursue a claim through the statutory criminal injuries scheme.

If a criminal act results in physical injury then any claim for psychiatric injury will normally be uncontroversial. Most people convicted of a criminal offence will not be worth suing in the ordinary civil courts so most cases are dealt with by way of applications to the Criminal Injuries Compensation Board. The original scheme came into force on 1 August 1964 and has since been modified. The present rules governing applications are contained within the 1994 Tariff Scheme which applies to all applications for

[20] *Read* v *J. Lyons & Co. Ltd* [1947] AC 156.

compensation received on or after 1 April 1994. This modification is currently the subject of challenge in the courts. Paragraphs 8.3 to 18 describe the circumstances in which compensation may be awarded. The claimant must have suffered physical or mental injury directly attributable to a crime of violence or a threat of violence. This includes arson and poisoning, and injury caused by animals if the animal is deliberately set upon the victim, or there has been a failure to control the animal amounting to recklessness. If the claimant is an employee of a railway company and sees another person injured or killed as a result of trespassing on the railway, there is also an entitlement. Similarly in cases of the discovery of a body on or beside the track, or if the claimant were 'involved in the immediate aftermath of the incident'. The scheme also covers claimants who are involved in the prevention of an offence or the apprehension or attempted apprehension of an offender. Shock due to loss of possessions is outside the scheme. It seems, therefore, that although, for example, arson is included in the scheme, if any injury suffered is attributable only to the shock of seeing home or other possessions destroyed, then no compensation is payable under the scheme.

There is no definition of crime of violence, and the guide to the scheme states, 'We judge every case on the basis of its circumstances' (para. 8.5). In addition, s. 109(1)(a)(ii) of the Criminal Justice Act 1988 states that a personal injury is a criminal injury when it is directly attributable to conduct constituting an offence which requires proof of intent to cause death or personal injury or recklessness as to whether death or personal injury is caused. It has been held that committing suicide is not a crime of violence — *Craig* v *CICB* (1992) *The Scotsman*, 23 December and *R* v *CICB Ex parte Webb* [1987] 1 QB 74.

It should be noted here that the *conduct* constitutes an offence, whatever actual damage is caused, and the key elements are intention or recklessness. In the case of *Brown*, 12 February 1993, CICB Appeal Board, Leicester, a woman who suffered head injuries and 'psychological problems' when a raw potato thrown at a fellow employee missed him and hit her instead was found to be a victim of a crime of violence as this was regarded as a case of transferred malice and it did not matter that the woman had not reported matters to the police. For that reason, compensation is not payable in respect of road traffic incidents except where the injury is due to a deliberate attempt to run the victim down. The scheme specifically includes arson and poisoning, and it includes sexual abuse such as rape, incest and buggery, and also indecent assault. A person engaged in law enforcement activity is covered by the scheme. It is interesting to note the specific inclusion of the offence of trespass on a railway in para. 8.8 so as to cover the cases of shock produced in railway workers who came upon cases of suicide or attempted suicide, and drivers of trains that have hit people attempting suicide. If the victim is subjected to fear either of physical injury[21] or incarceration, or fear for a loved one or whatever fear may be induced by the criminal act and this causes psychiatric injury, then the victim is entitled to compensation under the scheme if the injury is 'directly attributable'.

Personal injury is 'directly attributable' if the incident from which the injury arose would be considered by a reasonable person who knew all the facts to be a substantial cause of the injury, but not necessarily the only cause.[22] One who witnessed the violent killing or injuring of another and who suffered psychiatric injury as a result of that will satisfy the 'directly attributable' condition. In *R v CICB Ex parte Johnson* (1994) *The Times*, 11 August, the Queen's Bench Divisional Court held that the direct attributability test did not function according to the same criteria as the reasonable foreseeability test for nervous shock. The case concerned a woman who was psychiatrically injured after discovering the body of a friend who had died as a result of a violent crime. The court held that psychiatric injury (as opposed to mere shock) had to be proved as did causation, but *not* foreseeability.

Fagan v *Crimes Compensation Tribunal* (1982) 150 CLR 666 is an interesting Australian case on the interpretation of the Crminal Injuries Compensation Act 1972 of Victoria, which resulted in damages being awarded to a boy who was aged five when his mother was murdered, and who suffered 'nervous shock' as a result. He was at school at the time of the murder, and the case hinged on the interpretation of the statute concerned; whether the injury was 'by or as a result of the criminal act'. The High Court held that the tribunal considering the application had erred in applying the common law principle of remoteness rather than simply looking at the words of the Act. If the latter approach was taken then it had to be said that the child had suffered his psychological injury as a result of a criminal act. This has interesting implications if applied to our own scheme and the words 'directly attributable'. It is important to note that under the scheme not every mental injury is compensatable. Mental injury is defined as a 'disabling mental disorder where the psychological and/or physical symptoms and disability persist for more than six weeks from the incident'.

There is a lower limit on compensation, currently £1,000. Compensation used to be assessed on the same basis as general civil damages, but, unfortunately, under the new tariff scheme, as from 1 April 1994, major changes are proposed to the calculation of compensation (currently the subject of challenge in the courts). Since the scheme was introduced in 1964, compensation has been awarded by a body of lawyers on the same basis as in the ordinary civil courts. Under the new scheme, civil servants will now deal with the issue of quantum. The individual's particular

[21] Criminal Injuries Compensation Board Report (1983), p. 20: the case where compensation was awarded to a young girl who had been forced into prostitution through threats of violence.
[22] See *R v Criminal Injuries Compensation Board, ex parte Ince*[1973] 1 WLR 1334, CA.

circumstances will be ignored. There will be no provision for loss of earnings or other financial loss. Injuries are to be grouped into 25 bands with a single payment in each band. This is a retrograde step and will significantly reduce the compensation payable to the most severely damaged claimants. It is also contrary to the European Convention on the Compensation of Victims of Violent Crime.

As far as violence within the family is concerned, under para. 2.4 of the scheme (as in paragraph 8 of the old scheme) if the applicant and the person who injured the applicant were living together in the same household at the time of the incident, compensation cannot be paid unless the person who caused the injury has been prosecuted (unless there are good reasons why this could not happen) *and* the parties have stopped living together for good.

It is not necessary that the offender should have been convicted, but the Board may withhold or reduce compensation if an applicant has not taken, without delay, all reasonable steps to inform the police or other appropriate authority of the circumstances of the injury with a view to bringing the offender to justice. However, it is appreciated that in the case of young children, they may have been too young or too frightened to know what to do, and there is a discretion in such cases. In addition, the requirement that the parties have stopped living together for good may not be strictly applied, although compensation will not be paid if there is any likelihood that the perpetrator of the crime will benefit from it.

As far as time limits are concerned, claims should be made within one year of the incident (it used to be three years), except that the Board may in exceptional cases waive this requirement. Cases involving children are often treated as exceptional. It must be noted, however, that where the incident occurred before 1 October 1979 any late claim will be governed by the terms of an earlier scheme under which no compensation was payable if the victim and the offender were living together at the time as members of the same family.

The tariffs applicable are set out in appendix 2.

FOUR

The causal connection between trauma and injury

This chapter looks at the causal mechanism which exists between the originating event and the subsequent psychiatric injury. Although whatever the cause of action, factual causation will have to be proved, it is in the area of negligence that the causal connection raises special problems.

To establish liability in negligence, the causal mechanism must, of course, satisfy the test of factual causation, but the test of whether the factual causal link will be admitted in law depends upon the elements of foreseeability and remoteness and all that those entail. Put simply, the law says that the psychiatric injury must have been caused by some sort of 'shock' to the senses.

WHERE THERE IS ASSOCIATED PHYSICAL DAMAGE

Physical injury to the plaintiff

It is worth repeating that the majority of cases involving psychiatric injury will also involve actual physical injury to the plaintiff. In such cases, subject as ever to factual causation and proof of injury, there should be no difficulty in sustaining the psychiatric part of the claim. However, see *Harrison* v *State Government Insurance Office* [1985] Aust Torts Rep 80-723 discussed on page 87.

It is also worth pointing out the importance of considering the possibility of psychiatric illness following a head injury.

Physical injury to another person

Where damages are sought for psychiatric injury caused by witnessing injury to another it is common to regard the other person as the primary victim, and the plaintiff in the psychiatric injury case as the secondary victim. However, it must be stressed that the secondary victim in this context is someone to whom a duty of care is owed and *not*, for example, a person who suffers financially when his business partner is injured and unable to work, someone to whom no duty is owed and who cannot be compensated. The plaintiff in the psychiatric injury case has an action in his or her own right which is independent of the action of the so-called primary victim.

Physical damage to property

Whilst the majority of cases of traumatically induced psychiatric injury are caused by bodily injury to the plaintiff or someone sufficiently proximate to the plaintiff, or by fear of such injury, it is possible to recover damages in cases of property damage, see *Attia* v *British Gas plc* [1988] QB 304. In this case the defendants set fire to the plaintiff's house whilst installing central heating. There was no dispute that a duty of care was owed, the question was whether this type of damage, i.e., psychiatric injury, was foreseeable, and it was held that it was.

Another example of property damage is the Australian case of *Campbelltown City Council* v *Mackay* (1989) 15 NSWLR 501, where it was stated that in negligent property damage, damages could be awarded for vexation, worry and distress as well as for psychiatric injury.

The precise nature of the relationship between the plaintiff and the property (e.g., does the plaintiff have to have a proprietary interest?) has yet to be fully explored, but it may be that the courts would use some variant on the 'proximity theme' in order to decide whether to admit any claim.

An interesting question is whether property can include animals. In *Davies* v *Bennison* (1927) 22 Tas LR 52 damages were awarded for the shock of seeing a pet killed, but the action was in trespass. However, in *Campbell* v *Animal Quarantine Station 632* p. 2d 1066 (Hawaii 1981) the Supreme Court of Hawaii awarded damages for mental distress to the owners of a boxer dog which died in the back of an overheated van on its way to a veterinary hospital. There was no psychiatric injury.

WHERE THERE IS NO ASSOCIATED PHYSICAL DAMAGE

Rescuers

First let us look at the case of rescuers. There is a traumatic event of some kind, maybe a minor road accident, or maybe a large-scale industrial explosion or transportation disaster. It is well established that those who go to the scene, either as volunteer helpers or in their professional capacity as members of the emergency services, are vulnerable to both physical or psychiatric injury or indeed both. It is also well established that any injury they suffer is foreseeable. In *Haynes* v *Harwood* [1935] 1 KB 146, a police constable successfully claimed damages after he was injured when he stopped a runaway horse on a crowded street. It was confirmed in *Baker* v *T. E. Hopkins & Son Ltd* [1958] 1 WLR 993, CA, that a duty is owed to rescuers. Morris LJ quoted with approval the American case of *Wagner* v *International Railway Co.* (1921) 133 NE 437 in which Cardozo J said:

> Danger invites rescue. The cry of distress is the summons to relief. The law does not ignore these reactions of the mind in tracing conduct to its consequences. It recognises them as normal. It places their effects within the range of the natural and probable. The wrong that imperils life is a wrong to the imperilled victim; it is a wrong also to his rescuer.

As to any possibility of the defence of *volenti* being raised, it has been stated that:

> ... the doctrine of assumption of risk does not apply where the plaintiff has, under an exigency caused by the defendant's wrongful misconduct, consciously and deliberately faced a risk, even of death, to rescue another from imminent danger of personal injury or death, whether the person endangered is one to whom he owes a duty of protection, as a member of his family, or is a mere stranger to whom he owes no such special duty.[1]

Once it has been shown, therefore, that the defendant has been negligent towards the victims of an accident and that the requirements of foreseeability have been met in respect of those persons, then others who go to their aid will meet the criteria of both event and relationship proximity (see pages 81–87). These persons will almost certainly include members of the usual emergency rescue teams, but may also include lay people who happen to be in the vicinity. The unfortunate Mr Chadwick was one such rescuer, when a serious railway accident occurred some 200 yards from his home in Lewisham on 4 December 1957.[2] He went to the scene immediately and stayed there helping in the rescue activities for some 12 hours. As a result of his experiences that night he suffered what was described as an 'anxiety neurosis'. He was described as a man who before the accident had been of 'a happy disposition' who 'got on extremely well with people'. Indeed he was described as being cheerful and allaying fears of those railway passengers whom he comforted and helped that night. Mr Chadwick recovered damages against British Railways Board for the psychiatric injury he received as a result of helping in that rescue. It was held (*inter alia*) that injury

---

[1] A. L. Goodhart, 'Rescue and voluntary assumption of risk' (1935) CLJ 192 at p. 196.
[2] *Chadwick* v *British Railways Board* [1967] 1 WLR 912.

by shock was foreseeable in those circumstances; that the fact that someone would attempt to rescue the victims of the accident was foreseeable and that a duty was therefore owed to such persons; and that the fact that the risk run by the rescuer was not of the same kind as that run by the persons being rescued did not deprive the rescuer of his remedy; on the contrary, the very situation of a rescue involves unexpected things happening. Although a decision at first instance, *Chadwick v British Railways Board* [1967] 1 WLR 912 has been approved subsequently by the House of Lords in a number of cases, and in particular in *McLoughlin v O'Brian* [1983] 1 AC 410 and in *Alcock v Chief Constable of the South Yorkshire Police* [1992] 1 AC 310. Note also *Wigg v British Railways Board* (1986) *The Times*, 4 February 1986, in which a train driver recovered for the psychiatric injury suffered after searching for a passenger (a victim of the defendant's negligence) on the railway track and finding him dead. Tucker J said that although the plaintiff could be described as a rescuer, the presence of a train driver on the track was foreseeable anyway. This must be on the basis that although a mere bystander cannot recover, the train driver, being present in the course of his employment, satisfied the required relationship proximity.

What of the extent of the rescuer's involvement? Will it be enough if he runs to the scene of the accident, sees the horrifying scenes and hears the cries of pain coming from the victims, only then to run, say, to a telephone for help, and then participate no further? The defendant's argument will be that this person was not sufficiently proximate to the event, either in terms of physical closeness to the scene of suffering or in terms of being involved for any period of time. The defendant might argue that if such a person could recover it would invite any number of claims from bystanders who were involved in no significant way in the rescue operation, and that effectively it would be allowing a claim by a 'mere' bystander (see page 87). The fact of alerting others by a telephone call or other means is irrelevant. The plaintiff's lawyer may wish to argue otherwise and, on the basis of policy, say that such a person who through compassionate impulses became involved at all and as a result suffered psychiatric injury should not be denied compensation. The plaintiff's lawyer will cite *Owens v Liverpool Corporation* [1939] 1 KB 394, in which damages were recovered by mourners at a funeral, who were relatives of the deceased, for shock caused by the negligence of a tram driver in damaging the hearse upsetting the coffin. The defendant will look to the speech of Lord Oliver in *Alcock v Chief Constable of the South Yorkshire Police* [1992] 1 AC 310 who, referring to *Owens*, said: '... it is doubtful how far the case, which was disapproved by three members of this House in *Bourhill v Young* [1942] 2 All ER 396 ... can be relied upon'.

Suppose there is a large-scale accident and the rescuer is one of many who help, so that he does not experience a full picture of the suffering involved, but sits, say, on the periphery of the accident, comforting an injured person who is covered in blood, crushed, perhaps disfigured, and moaning in pain. Will this person recover for any subsequent psychiatric injury caused by this experience? The answer must be that in this case the requirements of proximity are met, as to argue otherwise would reach the absurd result that a rescuer must meet with a certain number of victims to qualify. However, in *McFarlane* v *E. E. Caledonia Ltd* [1994] 2 All ER 1, a worker on a support vessel in the Piper Alpha rescue operations who moved blankets and assisted two walking injured as they arrived on the support vessel was found not to be a rescuer.

What of psychiatric injuries to the rescuer who is a member of the emergency services? In the case of *Ogwo* v *Taylor* [1988] AC 431 the House of Lords decided that there is no principle which precluded a professional fireman from recovering damages from a person who had negligently started a fire and in which the fireman was injured. It was decided that his injuries were foreseeable, and therefore he should recover compensation, but confirmed that the rescuer should not take unnecessary risks. In *Piggott* v *London Underground* (1990) *Financial Times*, 19 December 1990 (news item), a total of £34,000 damages was awarded to four firemen who suffered psychiatric injury during the King's Cross fire in 1987, which was the first time that damages had been awarded *primarily* for psychiatric rather than physical injuries. The latter award was not universally approved, as the *Daily Telegraph* leader of 20 December 1990 stated:

> The concept of seeking damages for stress incurred in the course of professional duties ... seems to us unworthy and distasteful. Indeed, we would argue that men and women who find the stresses of dangerous but respected and rewarding jobs too much to bear should simply seek different employment.

The writer of that piece perhaps did not see that there is no essential difference between this claim and a claim by someone in a dangerous occupation for physical injury caused by the defendant's negligence. There is an implicit assumption in that piece that the firemen could in some way have avoided suffering this type of injury. Suffice to say that however dedicated the fireman or member of the other rescue crews may be, that is no bar to him pursuing his claim, if the facts are otherwise in his favour. Compensation for psychiatric injury suffered by rescuing a fireman was also made in *Hale* v *London Underground* (1992) *The Times*, 5 November 1992 and in February 1995, 14 police officers settled their claims following the Hillsborough disaster and this produced another outraged editorial, this time in *The Times*, 4 February 1995.

Non-rescuing witnesses

People who have suffered psychiatric injury from witnessing physical injury to others but who did not act as rescuers will usually have to establish the degree of proximity required for a claim in negligence in two ways: what can be called 'event proximity' and 'relationship proximity' respectively.

Event proximity

'Event proximity' means that the bystander must witness either the accident itself or its immediate aftermath, and that the experience of the accident or immediate aftermath must be by sight or hearing.

The whole concept of 'event proximity' was explored in much detail in the case of *McLoughlin* v *O'Brian* [1983] 1 AC 410. It is worth looking at the case in some detail. Mrs McLoughlin's husband and three children were all involved in a road accident. At the time Mrs McLoughlin was at home and, some two hours after its occurrence, was informed about the accident by a neighbour who took her to the hospital two miles away. When she arrived there she was informed that one child had been killed, and she was allowed to see her husband and the other children. She claimed that the shock of seeing them resulted in severe psychiatric illness. The court of first instance and the Court of Appeal had both found against her, holding that, since she had not been at or near to the scene of the accident, she was not entitled to recover damages for the resultant shock. The House of Lords allowed her appeal. It was accepted that proximity to the accident should be close both in time and space because the claim is essentially for shock-induced illness. However, their lordships decided that to insist upon the plaintiff seeing or hearing the event directly was impractical and unjust, and that someone who comes very soon upon the scene should not be excluded. The crucial part of Mrs McLoughlin's case was the state in which she found her husband and children. It appeared that they had yet to be given any attention at the hospital. Lord Wilberforce summarised what she experienced thus (at p. 417):

> She was taken down a corridor and through a window she saw Kathleen, crying, with her face cut and begrimed with dirt and oil. She could hear George shouting and screaming. She was taken to her husband who was sitting with his head in his hands. His shirt was hanging off him and he was covered in mud and oil. He saw the appellant and started sobbing. The appellant was then taken to see George. The whole of his left face and left side was covered. He appeared to recognise the appellant and then lapsed into unconsciousness. Finally, the appellant was taken to Kathleen who by now had been cleaned up. The child was too upset to speak and simply clung to her mother. There can be no doubt that these circumstances,

witnessed by the appellant, were distressing in the extreme and were capable of producing an effect going well beyond that of grief and sorrow.

It was this sort of scene which impressed their lordships as being sufficiently 'shocking' to be part of the 'immediate aftermath' of the accident.

It is essential to note from *McLoughlin* v *O'Brian* that the 'immediate aftermath' is not calculated in a strictly temporal sense. Whilst for most practical purposes the further away from the accident one is in time, the less likely the 'immediate aftermath' criteria are likely to be satisfied, it is not necessarily going to be so in every situation. Mrs McLoughlin was some two hours or more away from the time the collision took place when she experienced its effects. However, the appearance of her family was unchanged from that time. In the Australian case of *Jaensch* v *Coffey* (1984) 155 CLR 549, Deane J considered the meaning of 'aftermath' in some detail (at pp. 607–8):

> The facts constituting a road accident and its aftermath are not, however, necessarily confined to the immediate point of impact. They may extend to wherever sound may carry and to wherever flying debris may land. The aftermath of an accident encompasses ... the extraction and treatment of the injured. In a modern society, the aftermath also extends to the ambulance taking an injured person to hospital for treatment and to the hospital itself during the period of immediate post-accident treatment. ...
> In the present case ... the aftermath of the accident extended to the hospital to which the injured person was taken and persisted for so long as he remained in the state produced by the accident up to and including immediate post-accident treatment.

Consequently, if the plaintiff sees the primary victims either at the scene of the accident, or elsewhere, in a state of physical dishevelment or distress and pain, would this satisfy the criteria concerned, even if this is many hours later? On the basis of *Jaensch* v *Coffey*, there is no reason why a claim should not succeed, but the decision in *Alcock* v *Chief Constable of South Yorkshire Police* [1992] 1 AC 310 is not encouraging in this respect inasmuch as the 'eight hours or so' which had elapsed between the incident and the time that Mr Alcock identified his brother-in-law at the mortuary was said to have removed the identification outside of the 'immediate aftermath' (per Lord Ackner at p. 405). With respect, it is submitted that the identification of bodies *can* be regarded as part of the immediate aftermath on the *Jaensch* v *Coffey* test.

It could be argued that perception of the event through senses *other* than sight and sound, e.g., smell and touch, would be sufficient. One of the diagnostic criteria for PTSD in DSM IV concerns the exposure to internal or external cues that symbolise or resemble an aspect of the traumatic event and this is not sense specific. Whilst such an experience would no doubt occur under very unusual circumstances, on the authorities cited above (*McLoughlin* v *O'Brian*; *Jaensch* v *Coffey*), it would satisfy the criteria concerned. Scrignar[3] describes the experiences of a coroner's assistant attending at the scene of an air crash, where the stench of burning flesh was a strong factor in the experience of trauma.

Again, the witnessing may take place before any accident takes place, or, indeed, even if little or no injury is suffered as a result of it. *Dooley* v *Cammell Laird & Co. Ltd* [1951] 1 Lloyd's Rep 271 illustrates this. Mr Dooley, a crane driver, operating the defendant's crane, was loading a full canvass sling of material from a quay into a ship's hold when he saw the rope begin to break. He attempted to move the crane so that if the material fell it would fall into the sea, but before he could achieve this the rope broke and the load fell into the hold. As a result he suffered sciatica and 'nervous shock'. The claim for damages for both these injuries was accepted by Donovan J, who stated (at p. 277) that it was obvious that if one is loading material in this way, and if men are working on the deck or in the hold, then they may become injured or killed and that:

> if the driver of the crane concerned fears that the load may have fallen upon some of his fellow workmen, and that fear is not baseless or extravagant, then it is ... a consequence reasonably to have been foreseen that he may himself suffer a nervous shock.

For the particular application of relationship proximity to this case see page 84.

The court will, of course, need to be convinced that the incident was sufficiently distressing to the plaintiff. The test is whether the event itself is such that a person of normally phlegmatic disposition would be likely to be affected. This is not always easy to reconcile with the rule that one takes one's victim as one finds him. However, it is important to note that the rule is not about remoteness of damage, but is about foreseeability. Was it foreseeable that *this* person would suffer psychiatric injury so as to be owed a duty of care? Once that is established, then the tortfeasor must indeed take his victim as he finds him. This was considered at length in the case of *Bourhill* v *Young* [1943] AC 92. Lord Wright said (at pp. 109–10):

> Does the criterion of reasonable foresight extend beyond people of ordinary health or susceptibility, or does it take into account the peculiar susceptibilities or infirmities of those affected which the defendant neither knew of nor could reasonably be taken to have foreseen? ... A blind or

---

[3] C. B. Scrignar, *Post-Traumatic Stress Disorder*, 2nd ed. (New Orleans LA: Bruno Press, 1988), p. 60.

deaf man who crosses the traffic on a busy street cannot complain if he is run over by a careful driver who does not know of and could not be expected to observe and guard against the man's infirmity.

... whether there is duty owing to members of the public who come within the ambit of the act, must generally depend on a normal standard of susceptibility.

Of course, once it has been established that the situation would have been shocking to one who possesses normal susceptibility, then the fact that *this* particular plaintiff reacted in a way which could not have been foreseen, e.g., because of an eggshell personality, does not affect liability or damages any more than susceptibility to physical injury affects liability for negligently causing physical injury.

What sort of event will be sufficiently shocking to the person of 'customary phlegm'? It is important to remember that it does not necessarily have to be horrific in the sense of involving death or serious injury, or even involving standard 'horrors' such as copious amounts of blood. For example, the case of *Lucy* v *Mariehamns Rederi* [1971] 2 Lloyd's Rep 314, the plaintiff was struck by a large quantity of oil in the course of his employment. He suffered no physical injury, but developed an anxiety neurosis which was accepted as being a result of the accident and for which damages were awarded accordingly. One must assume that, for no physical injury whatsoever to have resulted, the blow struck must have been fairly insignificant, but it was sufficient to set up the claim as long as the plaintiff could show actual illness and the necessary causal link, which he was able to do. However, see the case of *Page* v *Smith* [1994] 4 All ER 522, considered on pages 14–16 and 167–168.

Relationship proximity
The successful plaintiff, however, will not have been successful just by satisfying the event proximity criteria. Normally, the successful plaintiff who has only witnessed a distressing event will have to show that as well as satisfying the requirements of proximity to the event, he or she also has what can be called 'relationship proximity'. The secondary victim (the plaintiff) should normally stand in a certain relationship to the primary victim. The relationship does not have to be in the common sense of the word, i.e., family relationship. That relationship may be one of rescuer to primary victim, as seen above. The plaintiff recovered damages in *Dooley* v *Cammell Laird & Co. Ltd* [1951] 1 Lloyd's Rep 271 because he was in a special relationship to those likely to be injured: the essential element in that case was that the plaintiff was put in the position of believing that *his* actions would have been the cause of any injury to his fellow workers. The Australian case of *Mount Isa Mines Ltd* v *Pusey* (1970) 125 CLR 383

similarly allowed recovery of damages by a plaintiff who, after an explosion, discovered the badly burned body of his workmate and subsequently developed a schizophrenic condition.[4]

A relationship of proximity can arise in a number of ways. Suppose you are cutting long grass at the front of your house with a scythe. There is no fence between you and the highway, but you are well away from the footpath. You are swinging the scythe to and fro in the normal way, when a small child of perhaps two or three who, due to the negligence of the local authority employee to whom the care of the child has been entrusted, suddenly rushes towards you at the precise moment that you are swinging the scythe in the direction of the oncoming child. You make every attempt to control the scythe, but cannot avoid the child suffering dreadful injuries. You suffer psychiatric injury. This, we would suggest, would establish the necessary relationship proximity, should you be inclined to take action against the local authority concerned.[5] This may sound somewhat fanciful, but the illustration shows that there are exceptions to the rule that the relationship has to be an intimate one, and these exceptions do not necessarily have to be the established ones such as rescuer and primary victim and the like. In *Alcock* v *Chief Constable of the South Yorkshire Police* [1992] 1 AC 310, Lord Oliver considered the problem of involuntary participants in a negligently caused event, concluding that the fact that the defendant's negligence has brought the plaintiff into the event is enough to establish a relationship of proximity and all that then has to be considered is foreseeability of the type of damage caused (at 408). This criteria would, of course, still have to be satisfied in the hypothetical case mentioned above. A somewhat different case, but one illustrative of the difficulties in the area of nervous shock is *Chester* v *Waverley Corporation* (1939) 62 CLR 1. In this case the High Court of Australia rejected the claim of a mother psychiatrically injured when, in her presence, the dead body of her child was recovered from a flooded trench which had not been fenced properly by the defendant authority. The injury was held not to be foreseeable.

Generally, however, the relationship is likely to be one of some intimacy. The only examples of successful claims so far in the UK are those of spouses or the parent–child relationship, although a parent–foster-child relationship has been involved, without specific comment.[6] Persons in similar 'quasi' relationships should not have difficulty establishing their claims if the emotional ties are more or less identical with those in the formally legalised relationship. Here therefore would be included cohabitees, children not formally adopted but treated as the natural children of the party concerned

[4] See also *Wigg* v *British Railways Board* (1986) *The Times*, 4 February 1986.
[5] See *Carmarthenshire County Council* v *Lewis* [1955] AC 549 where the House of Lords considered the liability of a local authority for escaped schoolchildren.
[6] *Hinz* v *Berry* [1970] 2 QB 40, CA.

(see *Long* v *PKS Inc.*, *Lloyd's List*, 16 April 1993, California, where a foster-mother recovered), siblings who can establish especially close ties, and stepparents and stepchildren. The inclusion of cohabitees is the most obvious, but can present problems. A court may, for example, be reluctant to consider a claim when the parties' relationship is of short duration and their period of cohabitation is short. However, there is no doubt that a relationship of identical or shorter length would not be queried if the parties were formally man and wife. The test will be the strength of the relationship. Similarly, a homosexual couple living together should be treated the same as heterosexual cohabitees. In the case of *Dunphy* v *Gregor* 642 A 2d 372 (N.J. 1994) the New Jersey Supreme Court held that an unmarried cohabitant could recover damages after witnessing her partner being hit by a car and being dragged 240 feet down the roadway.

Do the parties have to be living together at all? Again, a couple engaged to be married, particularly if their relationship is of some duration, can hardly be held to be in a different category to those who have recently chosen to live together. And why should there be a requirement that they be formally engaged at all?

Do the siblings have to be of a certain age to justify their claim? It would be a harsh judge indeed who denied the claim of a minor child who witnessed the distressing death of the sibling to whom he was devoted. And if that devotion survives into adulthood, why should the sibling be denied his claim simply because they are no longer children? There are many other close relationships: grandparents and grandchildren; aunts and uncles and their nieces and nephews; devoted platonic friendships and so on.

The judgment in *Alcock* v *Chief Constable of South Yorkshire Police* [1992] 1 AC 310 sent a clear message that categories would not be devised and boundaries would not be drawn. If the evidence is there of the intimacy of the relationship and the injury is proved and the legal requirements satisfied then no relationship is excluded.

The tortfeasor who causes or threatens self-injury

What if the appropriate event proximity and relationship proximity are established: does this mean that the plaintiff can recover damages for psychiatric injury caused by the negligence of the tortfeasor hurting or threatening his or her *own* safety? The dictum of Deane J in *Jaensch* v *Coffey* (1984) 155 CLR 549, at p. 604 that in order to succeed the injury must have been sustained 'as a result of the death, injury or peril of *someone other than the person whose carelessness* is alleged to have caused the injury' (emphasis added) specifically precludes such a claim, but in *Alcock* v *Chief Constable of South Yorkshire Police* [1992] 1 AC 310 this wholly anomalous position was considered by Lord Oliver as being 'curious and wholly unfair' (at p. 418). It has not been in issue in the English courts (not being dealt with in *Bourhill* v *Young* [1943] AC 92 where there was insufficient proximity to the incident in which the defendant had injured himself negligently) but in Australia, on the authority of *Jaensch* v *Coffey* it was said in *Harrison* v *State Government Insurance Office* [1985] Aust Torts Rep 80-723 that damages could not be recovered. In that case a wife suffered minor physical injuries in a road accident in which her husband was killed and which was due to his negligence. Her claim for psychiatric injury was eventually allowed simply because it was impossible to separate the psychiatric injury caused by the accident itself and that caused by the shock of her husband's death.

The 'mere' bystander

By the 'mere' bystander we mean someone who can establish 'event proximity' but has no special relationship with the primary victim.

Normally such a person has little hope of establishing a claim, but it is not entirely out of the question. Lord Ackner stated in *Alcock* v *Chief Constable of the South Yorkshire Police* [1992] 1 AC 310 at p. 403:

> . . . why does it [the duty] not eventually extend to bystanders? As regards the latter category, while it may be very difficult to envisage a case of a stranger, who is not actively and foreseeably involved in a disaster or its aftermath, other than in the role of rescuer, suffering shock-induced psychiatric injury by the mere observation of apprehended or actual injury of a third person in circumstances that could be considered reasonably foreseeable, I see no reason in principle why he should not, if in the circumstances, a reasonably strong-nerved person would have been so shocked. In the course of argument your lordships were given, by way of an example, that of a petrol tanker careering out of control into a school in session and bursting into flames. I would not be prepared to rule out a potential claim by a passer-by so shocked by the scene as to suffer psychiatric illness.

McFarlane v *E. E. Caledonia Ltd* [1994] 2 All ER 1 is not encouraging in this respect as the Court of Appeal held that witnessing the Piper Alpha oil rig explosions did not entitle the plaintiff to recover damages (see page 13).

FEAR AND IMAGINED HARM

Fear for injury to oneself

Although it is now uncontroversial law, it should be remembered that one of the earliest cases in England on 'nervous shock', *Dulieu* v *White & Sons* [1901] 2 KB 669, established the principle that damages could be recovered for the condition which had been produced by fear for *oneself* and indeed that case stated that *only* fear for *oneself* would do. (It is now established that fear for injury to *others* will also found a claim.) In consequence, the case of 'the accident I almost had and *thought I was going to have*' can result in a successful claim for damages for psychiatric injury. It will, of course, have to satisfy the foreseeability requirements. The incident itself will have to satisfy the 'person of customary phlegm' test, i.e., be distressing to a person of ordinary fortitude.[7] A word of caution is appropriate here, however: we have already pointed out that damages are not recoverable for 'shock' in the general sense; there must be an identifiable psychiatric illness.[8] The great majority of near-misses will not, it is hoped, result in any such illnesses. Those that do should have no difficulty as far as proximity is concerned, subject, as ever, to the additional requirements of factual causation and proof of injury. Normally, the fact that one fears for oneself is enough to establish a sufficiently close physical proximity. However, it must be reasonable to fear for oneself. The reasonableness of the fear will be demonstrated either by the fact that the plaintiff was within the physical area of the risk or by the fact that the nature of the event (sudden, dramatic etc.) was such as to make the plaintiff reasonably fear for his or her own safety. This was considered by the Court of Appeal in *McFarlane* v *E. E. Caledonia Ltd* [1994] 2 All ER 1 where it was found that the plaintiff could not reasonably have been in fear for his own safety when he was on a support vessel which was some 550 metres away from the Piper Alpha oil rig which exploded in the North Sea in 1988. Stuart-Smith LJ said (at p. 11):

> The [support vessel] was never in actual danger. . . . If indeed the plaintiff had felt himself to be in any danger, he could have taken refuge in or behind the helicopter hangar, which was where non-essential personnel were required to muster. The judge [at first instance] thought it was entirely understandable that the plaintiff and other non-essential personnel should wish to see what was happening on the Piper Alpha. I agree with this. What I do not agree with, is that someone who was in truth in fear of his life from spread of the fire and falling debris should not take shelter. Only someone who is rooted to the spot through fear would be unable to do so. The plaintiff never suggested that; he accepted that he had moved about quite freely and could have taken shelter had he wished.

The House of Lords in *Hicks* v *Chief Constable of the South Yorkshire Police* [1992] 2 All ER 65 identified fear 'of whatever degree' as a normal human emotion and not therefore compensatable unless, of course, it is causative of a recognised psychiatric illness.

[7] See *Bourhill* v *Young* [1943] AC 92, at p. 117.
[8] But there is a recognised psychiatric illness, albeit of short duration, known as acute stress disorder, or acute stress reaction, see page 41.

Imagined harm to oneself

The plaintiff must normally experience at least part of the event through his or her own unaided senses. So, for example, a claim for damages was disallowed when the plaintiff, who worked at a school, suffered psychiatric injury as a result of realising that she had narrowly escaped being attacked and possibly killed by a burglar who entered the school at a time when she would have been on duty had she not swapped her shift with another.[9]

Fear for injury to another — real and imagined

As in the case of the plaintiff's fear for injury to him or herself, fear of injury to another must be induced by the unaided senses of the plaintiff. In *Hambrook* v *Stokes Brothers* [1924] 1 KB 141 the plaintiff suffered psychiatric injury as a result of seeing a runaway lorry go downhill towards a position where she had just left her children. Shortly afterwards she was told by a bystander that one of her children had been hit. It was held by the court that recovery of damages was possible only on the basis that the injury was caused by the sight of the runaway lorry and not by the communication of bad news.

In *King* v *Phillips* [1953] 1 QB 429 although the incident (a taxi backing towards a place in the road where the plaintiff believed her child to be playing) was perceived by the plaintiff's unaided senses, she was held to be an unforeseeable plaintiff, being positioned some 70–80 yards away and looking out of the window of her home. This is a case which has attracted some criticism.[10]

In *Dooley* v *Cammell Laird & Co. Ltd* [1951] 1 Lloyd's Rep 271, the plaintiff was operating a crane when the cable broke, causing a load to fall into the hold of a ship. The plaintiff suffered psychiatric injury as a result of his fear for the harm that may have been caused to his fellow employees below (in fact, no one was injured). The defendant was held to be liable. See also *Mount Isa Mines Ltd* v *Pusey* (1970) 125 CLR 383.

To differentiate between real and imagined harm is illogical as Mulaney and Handford state:

> Shock victims who genuinely and honestly believe that they have killed or injured another are for all intents and purposes in the same position as if the imagined facts were true . . . and provided that mistaken belief proved to be genuine and honestly held and causative of psychiatric injury, these types of case should be treated the same as any other.[11]

[9] *Wilks* v *Haines* [1991] Aust Torts Rep 81-078.
[10] See, for example, A. L. Goodhart, 'Emotional shock and the unimaginative taxi driver' (1953) 69 LQR 347.
[11] N. Mullany and P. Handford, *Tort Liability for Psychiatric Damage* (London: Sweet & Maxwell, 1993), pp. 222–3.

One might go on to say that the belief should be reasonable in all the circumstances, as it would be illogical to insist that fear for oneself must have reasonable grounds but fears for another need not. For the avoidance of doubt, it must be stressed that the shock victim in this case must not be the negligent party, although there may be contributory negligence.

Acquiring information other than through the unaided senses of the plaintiff

Being told bad news
Generally there is no prospect of recovering damages if the psychiatric injury results from being told bad news.[12] However, there are a number of Commonwealth cases where damages have been recovered when the plaintiff has been involved in the same accident in which a loved one died and was informed of the death some time after the accident.[13] It may be that the difficulty in separating the shock of the accident from the shock produced by hearing of the death was at least partly responsible for these favourable decisions and partly the fact that the injury, or the immediate prospect of the injury, to the loved one, would have been witnessed by the plaintiff. However, there must be *some* perception with the unaided senses, in which case there is no bar to recovery just because the psychiatric injury may have been caused *partly* by hearing the news.

Nevertheless, in the Australian case of *Petrie* v *Dowling* [1992] 1 QdR 284, the plaintiff recovered for injuries caused by being at a hospital in the expectation that her daughter had suffered only minor injuries, and being told that she had, in fact, died. It is unlikely, given the tone of the House of Lords decisions in *McLoughlin* v *O'Brian* [1983] 1 AC 410 (see per Lord Wilberforce at p. 423) and *Alcock* v *Chief Constable of the South Yorkshire Police* [1992] 1 AC 310 that this decision reflects the present position in English law.

Television and radio broadcasts
The clear judicial disapproval in *Alcock* v *Chief Constable of the South Yorkshire Police* [1992] 1 AC 310 of allowing recovery when a plaintiff suffered injury after a simultaneous television broadcast (far less for a recorded transmission) means that it would be an exceptional case which succeeded in this respect. The example given of such an exceptional case by Nolan LJ in the Court of Appeal in *Alcock* was that of children travelling in a balloon which suddenly burst into flames, the impact of which on live television would be as great or greater than the actual sight of the accident. Lord Ackner in the House of Lords in *Alcock* suggested that there could be 'many other such

---

[12] See *Hambrook* v *Stokes Brothers* [1924] 1 KB 141.
[13] *Andrews* v *Williams* [1967] VR 831 and *Kohn* v *State Government Insurance Commission* (1976) 15 SASR 255 and *Schneider* v *Eisovitch* [1960] 2 QB 430.

situations', so recovery has not been ruled out completely in the case of live broadcasts. However, it is clear that the wholly subjective speculations by judges as to what may be more or less shocking than real life, points up the inadequacies of the present state of the law. Furthermore, it is inexplicable why a live broadcast of, say, the balloon, is likely to be more shocking than a recorded broadcast which is seen by a plaintiff with no previous knowledge of the incident.

Does the communicator acquire any liability for the communication of bad news?

In *Alcock* v *Chief Constable of South Yorkshire Police* [1992] 1 AC 310, their lordships referred to the broadcasting code of ethics, which the authorities could be expected to follow, and which code precluded them from showing the suffering of recognisable individuals. It was suggested that if this code was breached, this would be a *novus actus* breaking the chain of causation. Leaving aside the question whether it would make any difference whether the breach of the code was *intentional* or not (see page 58), is there likely to be any liability for a communication, negligent or otherwise? Presumably, a distinction can be drawn between false information and information which is true but which is communicated in a insensitive and thereby shocking manner? Where false information is given due to negligence there is little in the way of English case law to support a claim. In *D* v *National Society for the Prevention of Cruelty to Children* [1978] AC 171 Lord Denning MR distinguished between false information in the *Wilkinson* v *Downton* [1897] 2 QB 57 sense, i.e., when there is a deliberate deceit, and false information due to negligence. In the latter case it was said there would be no liability. The rule in *Hedley Byrne & Co. Ltd* v *Heller & Partners Ltd* [1964] AC 465 has no application here either, as one of the essential elements of the tort of negligent misstatement is that the recipient of the information relied upon it, as opposed to simply received it. Could it be argued (somewhat tortuously, it is admitted) that the recipient relied upon it being true and therefore suffered loss on this basis? It seems unlikely.

Problems also arise in the second type of case, where the information which is conveyed is true, but is given in an insensitive manner. It was said in *Mount Isa Mines Ltd* v *Pusey* (1970) 125 CLR 383 that there is no duty to break bad news gently. However, in *Petrie* v *Dowling* [1992] 1 QdR 284, a case examined by Mullany and Handford,[14] damages were recovered by a mother who was told in a blunt manner by a nurse that her daughter was dead. This appears to be an example of a Commonwealth case which is more generous than we are led to hope for in the English courts.

---

[14]N. Mullany and P. Handford, *Tort Liability for Psychiatric Damage* (London: Sweet & Maxwell, 1993), p. 189.

FIVE

Identifying the plaintiff as a sufferer

In this chapter we look at some of the practical difficulties that may arise in identifying psychiatric injury. This is of practical importance for lawyers because people who wish to pursue claims for physical injuries often do not realise the possibility that psychiatric injury may also be involved. In other circumstances, the client may claim to have suffered psychiatrically, and the lawyer may need to know how to proceed further. This chapter, therefore, aims to give some practical advice for circumstances such as these.

THE IMPORTANCE OF IDENTIFICATION

Lawyers acting for both plaintiffs and defendants should be aware of the difficulty of identifying psychiatric injury. Early identification will assist with the progress and settlement of the case. It may well be that the plaintiff is suffering from physical symptoms which are difficult to resolve; the specialists concerned may be unable to make a firm prognosis. In these circumstances, the defendant may be alleging an element of functional overlay (a much over-used term which has no clear meaning but is used to suggest that there is a 'psychological' element to the plaintiff's physical symptoms), or even malingering, which will, no doubt, be strongly denied. These sorts of problems, and there are many variations on the theme, can delay settlement and increase costs. If there is some psychiatric injury then the sooner it is identified the better, so that it may be treated, and, it is hoped, resolved, and so that its relationship to the physical disorders can be clarified, and, again, it is hoped, resolved. Research shows that plaintiffs are more interested in recovering their health than in receiving compensation (see The Law Commission Report No. 225: 'Personal Injury Compensation: How much is enough?'). The sooner the illness is identified the sooner the treatment can be done.

It is worth pausing here to consider the importance of tact on the part of the legal advisers involved. Most victims will not be aware that they are suffering from an identifiable illness. In the majority of cases they will have also suffered physical trauma, and may ascribe any difficulties they have to that. They may feel hostile towards the doctors treating the physical illness, believing them to be either incompetent or unsympathetic. Many will not wish to accept that they have a psychiatric disorder. This would be particularly so if the physical injury incurred was relatively minor; they may fear accusations of being weak and faint-hearted. There is no doubt that there is a fair amount of public opinion which would brand them so.[1] They may also fear the stigma and misery of being diagnosed as mentally ill and dread the treatment. The legal adviser should therefore approach the plaintiff with a fair degree of sensitivity and reassurance. It is important to stress that the phenomenon of psychiatric injury is well-known, and that many others have suffered similarly without accusations of weakness, and, importantly, without being told that they are 'mad'. It is worth relating the following story which may be of help even with the most stiff-upper-lipped person.

On 12 December 1931 Winston Churchill was in New York on a lecture tour, when he was struck by a taxi whilst trying to cross Fifth Avenue. He suffered two cracked ribs, scalp wounds, slight injury to the pleural cavity and some general bruising. In other words, his injuries were minor ones. Rest was prescribed, and he and his wife went to the Bahamas, arriving for New Year. Some eight days or so later he experienced a nervous reaction, experiencing lack of concentration, a feeling of inadequacy, insomnia, apathy. He later wrote in the *Daily Mail*: 'I certainly suffered every pang, both physical and mental, that a street accident or, I suppose, a shell wound can produce'.

It has been subsequently stated by a professor of clinical psychiatry[2] that 'it can be surmised from documented evidence that Churchill not only suffered from physical injuries as a result of the car accident, but developed PTSD as well'. He went on to say 'Unlike most commoners, Churchill was able to quit work (depart from his lecture tour) to rest and recuperate in the Bahamas with his wife, personal secretary, a nurse and the rest of his entourage'. In other words Churchill was in the very best position to recover and yet even then he did not make an immediate recovery. It is extremely unlikely that most victims of PTSD and other reactive disorders will have any of these material and social advantages.

---

[1] See *Daily Telegraph* leader, 20 December 1990, discussed on page 80.
[2] C. B. Scrignar, *Post-traumatic Stress Disorder* (New Orleans LA: Bruno Press, 1988), p. 83.

IDENTIFYING SYMPTOMS OF PSYCHIATRIC INJURY

In the case of a head injury, the plaintiff's lawyer should always be alert to psychiatric injury, but in all forms of injury, its possibility should be recognised. If the legal adviser is concerned that there may have been psychiatric injury amounting to an identifiable illness, what sort of signs might he or she look for?

It is vital to remember that a number of psychiatric injuries and conditions can be caused by trauma. Because of the detail of diagnostic criteria of PTSD, and because of the wide publicity received for PTSD in the wake of the *Herald of Free Enterprise* arbitrations and other recent disasters, it is tempting for the practitioner to think in terms of PTSD and little else. Certainly this condition has received, in recent years, the main focus of attention in psychiatric injury litigation. This is partly due to the prominence of PTSD in the traumatic effects caused to the victims in the spate of disasters in the late 1980s. It is also partly because PTSD is probably the most commonly diagnosed psychiatric injury in an accident situation. But as we have said earlier, PTSD is not the only psychiatric injury and an open mind as to the possibility of a variety of psychiatric illnesses is, therefore, vital.

The plaintiff may have been involved in a 'disaster', by which we mean a major incident as defined, for example, by the Cranfield Disaster Prepared-ness Centre as:

> Any situation resulting from natural or man-made catastrophe demand-ing total integration of the rescue, emergency services and life support systems available to those responsible for the affected areas together with the communication and transportation resources required to support relief operations.

In such a case, it is possible that, before the victims seek legal advice they will have had discussions with social workers and doctors experienced in dealing with the effects of trauma. When they see a legal adviser for the first time they may have already told their story several times, and been made aware of the possibility of some psychiatric disorder developing. It is certainly to be hoped that they would have had such an opportunity, as the appropriate degree of care at this stage is essential if the victims are to cope socially and psychologically with the after-effects.[3] If this is the case, then they will already have been alerted to the possibility of psychiatric illness and it should be relatively easy to ask what, if any, steps have been taken to deal with this. Earlier messages about symptoms manifesting themselves, and the

[3] There are a number of texts which deal generally with disasters and their consequences for survivors. A good account is provided by B. Raphael in *When Disaster Strikes* (London: Unwin Hyman, 1990).

availability of help can be reinforced. The adviser will go on to point out that psychiatric disorder is a legitimate head of damage, and should be carefully assessed in a similar way to the physical injury (if any) suffered.

Regrettably, even in the case, of a major disaster, the medical and social service resources may not have been as readily available as desired. A victim may therefore seek legal advice 'cold', and it will be left to the legal adviser to consider for the first time the possibility of traumatically induced psychiatric injury. A number of local authorities have produced leaflets and similar literature for distribution in the aftermath of disasters (see appendix 3).

Victims of incidents which fall short of being disasters will almost always seek legal advice totally unaware of possible psychiatric injury. It will be difficult to identify whether they are in fact suffering. It is relatively easy and acceptable for the adviser to tell someone who has been involved in a disaster that psychiatric injury is possible and to ask the appropriate questions to determine whether medical assessment is necessary. A victim of a relatively minor traffic accident will not immediately spring to mind as being a sufferer or potential sufferer. It would not be desirable to encourage practitioners or their clients to find illness where there is none, or to encourage pursuit of the psychiatrist's couch once the ambulance has gone out of sight. This is where the interviews with the client are so important for the plaintiff practitioner. A large part of contact time will be taken up with straightforward factual questions of what took place — 'How fast do you think you were travelling?' etc. — but it can be illuminating at the first interview simply to ask for a general description of what happened. It may be that the most distressing parts of the incident will either be described with emotion in some vividly remembered detail, or, just as significantly, there will be an avoidance of aspects of which the client simply cannot speak. These may be no more than warning signs for the adviser concerned (store them away and remember them at future interviews, and see if the reaction is still the same), or they may be so obviously distressful that, at that stage, the possibility of psychological after-effects is broached with the client. Even then, the practitioner should not be assuming psychiatric injury. Most accidents produce ordinary shock and distress; in most cases, nothing more serious will develop, and the client should not be made to dread becoming psychiatrically ill as a natural consequence of his or her misfortune. By contrast, it should be remembered that even if the initial interview indicates the most phlegmatic of clients, one of the characteristics of PTSD is 'psychic numbing', which can mean that there is a *failure* of emotional response, easily mistaken for unconcern. Achieving the correct balance is not easy. The fact that others were affected more seriously than the client may produce great feelings of guilt, which will cause a suppression of memories and anxieties on the basis that he is lucky and should gratefully get on with his life. There is also the phenomenon of 'delayed onset' of PTSD recognised in DSM IV and ICD 10 (see page 45), and defined as such if the onset of symptoms was at least six months after the trauma.

Plaintiff practitioners will be aware that frequently a client is accompanied by a spouse or other close relative or friend. If psychiatric illness is a possibility then it can be a great help for the legal adviser to elicit the views of someone close to the plaintiff who may be aware of personality changes since the incident, such as distressing dreams, increased irritability, or increased consumption of alcohol. Even if the plaintiff denies symptoms, by conscious or unconscious suppression, it is likely that the spouse or similar will not collude in this denial. For the same reason, it is usual for the expert psychiatrist or psychologist to want to see a close friend or relative of the victim.

Generally, the plaintiff's lawyers should simply be alert to the possibility of traumatically induced psychiatric disorder without being obsessive about it, and through the continuous lawyer-client relationship be sensitive to new indications of its existence, deterioration or (it is hoped) improvement.

POST-TRAUMATIC STRESS DISORDER

What of specific indicators? Having said that PTSD is only one of the psychiatric disorders which can result from trauma, it is an important one, on which a great deal of work has been carried out in recent years. As, has already been said, the main springboard for understanding the diagnostic criteria of PTSD is DSM IV and ICD 10. From this Scrignar[4] has compiled a table of the cardinal characteristics of PTSD:

(a) Nervousness.   The person is apprehensive, on edge, tense, jumpy, easily startled, and fearful.

(b) Preoccupation with the trauma.   The person talks a great deal about the accident, speculating that more serious injury or even death could have occurred.

(c) Pain or physical discomfort.   The person complains of pain or physical discomfort that appears disproportionate to the actual injury incurred.

(d) Sleeplessness.   The person complains of insomnia with resultant tiredness and fatigue.

(e) Flashbacks and nightmares.   The person relives the trauma during flashbacks or nightmares with similar emotional reactions as if the accident were happening again. Intrusive thoughts related to the trauma are common.

---

[4] See C. B. Scrignar, *Post-traumatic Stress Disorder*, 2nd ed. (New Orleans LA: Bruno Press, 1988), pp. 89–90.

(f)   Deterioration of performance.   The person experiences inability or difficulty in carrying out usual life activities such as work, family responsibilities, social and recreational activities, or any activity engaged in before the trauma.

(g)   Phobia.   The person experiences fearfulness and avoidance of the place where the accident occurred or extreme apprehension associated with some activity related to the trauma.

(h)   Personality change.   The person becomes withdrawn, moody, irritable, distracted, forgetful, and unlike his or her usual self.

(i)   Dudgeon.   The person gives expression to frequent unprovoked outbursts of anger with complaints about the carelessness of others and a retributive attitude. Quarrelsome behaviour may be evident.

(j)   Depression.   At some point following the trauma the person feels 'blue' or 'down in the dumps'. A loss of self-confidence, a pessimistic attitude, brooding about past events, or feeling sorry for self may be noted. Social withdrawal, lack of pleasure, and a look of sadness on the face of a person formerly cheerful and outgoing may be extant.

This account of the symptoms of PTSD may be more useful in understanding a client who has PTSD. It is also important to remember that in the *Herald of Free Enterprise* arbitration it was stressed that these are guidelines only. This should also be kept in mind when instructing experts.

These symptoms do, of course, have further effects, so that the plaintiff may have sought sleep and solace in alcohol which itself has caused physical illness.

All of these characteristics will affect the ability of the plaintiff to work. Loss of a job after the incident, if there is no other compelling reason, may therefore be an indicator. Again, all of these characteristics are likely to put a strain on relationships. Marital or other close relationship discord can therefore be an indicator if it comes after the incident with no previous signs that the relationship was breaking down. Quarrelsome behaviour which is untypical of the plaintiff's previous behaviour may result in incidents of violence with or without the involvement of the police or prosecution. This may also be an indicator. The inability to concentrate and sleeplessness and, indeed, many of the other characteristics, may mean that the plaintiff has abandoned previously enjoyed hobbies and social activities.

What is clear from this interaction of symptoms is that, without diagnosis, the condition will worsen because the plaintiff's social circumstances will be progressively deteriorating. Recovery will be delayed if there is no adequate social and emotional support, which is unlikely to be the case if the plaintiff's marriage has broken down and he or she has quarrelled with family and friends. Financial matters will become an additional burden if a job is lost. The lack of a job and enjoyable social activities will mean that the plaintiff's time will be used almost exclusively to consider his or her unhappiness; there will be no distraction and no respite. The plaintiff's lawyer must be alert to identify these signs which will have a potentially major effect on the medico-legal analysis of the client's claim. Further if there is no possibility of a successful claim for legal reasons, the lawyer should advise the client about the possibility of medical assistance in the form of counselling and other treatment.

It is not suggested that the practitioner has to possess some unrealistic level of intuition, merely that he or she should be aware of the phenomenon of psychiatric injury and notice if an indicator presents itself.

THE EFFECT OF PSYCHIATRIC INJURY ON PHYSICAL INJURIES

Psychiatric disorders can affect physical injuries in a number of ways. A plaintiff whose psychiatric disorder has not yet been recognised but who has some physical result of the incident can concentrate upon that as being the sole aspect of his or her unhappiness. Furthermore, the physical injury is itself a constant reminder of the trauma and, indeed, disproportionate pain or physical discomfort is a recognised characteristic of PTSD. A plaintiff will, for example, be far more troubled by a scar if seeing it always recalls the event which caused it, and the recollection of that event causes distress. The general 'knock-on' effect of psychiatric symptoms on social and financial circumstances can also mean that the plaintiff is not recovering quickly from the physical injuries. Of course, coping with the stress of financial deterioration (which can lead to social problems) is a common consequence of physical injury alone, and care needs to be taken not to confuse signs of such stress with psychiatric disorder; in that case what is needed is an interim payment, not the help of a psychiatrist.

USE OF QUESTIONNAIRES FOR ASSESSMENT

Those who treat psychiatric injury, whether psychiatrists or psychologists, use a number of questionnaires to assess their patients. The General Health Questionnaire (GHQ) was designed to be a self-administered screening test. It focuses on breaks in normal function, i.e., normal for that person, and therefore concentrates on two major areas: first the inability of the patient to continue his normal functions, and secondly, the appearance of new phenomena of a distressing nature. Examples of the questions are:[5]

---

[5] Extract from General Health Questionnaire 30 © David Goldberg 1978, reproduced by permission of the publisher, NFER-Nelson.

HAVE YOU RECENTLY:

been able to concentrate on whatever you're doing?	Better than usual	Same as usual	Less than usual	Much less than usual
felt capable of making decisions about things?	More so than usual	Same as usual	Less so than usual	Much less capable
been getting scared or panicky for no good reason?	Not at all	No more than usual	Rather more than usual	Much more than usual

The GHQ consists of 30 questions and it stresses the importance of all 30 questions being answered. It must be said, however, that the GHQ is a closed clinical document and may be purchased only by those with medical or psychology qualifications though it is possible that a psychologist who purchases it may give it to a lawyer for controlled use with the client. This may be particularly useful as a screening mechanism where the client may be reluctant to visit a psychiatrist or psychologist because of the 'stigma' associated with doing so. Indeed, particularly in the case of children, or very nervous clients, this may be appropriate as a sensitive method of checking whether the client needs full medical assessment. Even so, it does not necessarily follow that the initial assessment by the plaintiff in conjunction with the practitioner will be welcomed by the expert. Some psychologists, for example, prefer to interview the plaintiff *before* the GHQ or any other clinical questionnaire is completed as they believe more telling results can be obtained this way. It is, therefore, important to liaise with the experts and deal with each case on an individual basis.

Other surveys which are, again, subject to copyright and various restrictions are:

(a) **The Beck Depression Inventory.**   This was designed to measure the behavioural manifestations of depression and in particular to provide a quantitative assessment of intensity. It is said to discriminate effectively between varying degrees of depression; it is also able to reflect changes in the intensity of depression after an interval of time.

(b) **The Revised Impact of Event Scale.**   This questionnaire was specifically developed as a result of research into the characteristic experiences of individuals with post-traumatic stress disorder related to a specific trauma. The 15 items provide self-report data on the extent to which the person has experienced intrusive thoughts and exhibited avoidance behaviour in relation to a specific trauma during the previous seven days — i.e., it focuses on a person's current response level.

(c) **The Beck Anxiety Inventory.**   This is a 21-item self-report that measures the severity of anxiety in adults. It was constructed to measure symptoms of anxiety which are minimally shared with those of depression, such as those symptoms measured by the Beck Depression Inventory.

(d) **The Beck Hopelessness Inventory**. This measures the extent of negative expectancies about the immediate and long-range future. It is designed to measure the extent of negative attitudes held during the previous seven days.

(e) **The Structured Clinical Interview for PTSD (SCID)**. This is an interview checklist used to evaluate the presence or absence of PTSD, and has been held to be diagnostically reliable but poor in assessing severity of the disorder.

(f) **The Clinician Administered PTSD Scale (CAPS)**. This scale is designed to assess intrusive and distressing recollections of traumatic events and can also record sleep difficulties, irritability, outbursts of anger, poor concentration, hypervigilance and exaggerated startle response.[6]

GENUINENESS OF SYMPTOMS

'Malingerer' means someone who deliberately pretends to be suffering from an illness or disability usually, but not necessarily, for gain. Indeed, if a 'rational' motive is not present (another may be fear, e.g., military deserters) then the person concerned is almost certainly suffering from what is classified in DSM IV as a factitious disorder, which is deliberate feigning of symptoms, but is part of a personality disorder. Malingering is to be contrasted with functional disorders such as these. We are of the opinion that the problem of malingering can be dealt with satisfactorily by competent doctors and lawyers, and is no more prevalent in psychiatric disorder cases than it is in those of a physical nature.

There is no doubt that, at times, genuineness of symptoms has unduly preoccupied participants in litigation, because where disorders which have no organic manifestation are concerned, there is a common conception that they are easy to feign, and difficult to detect. However, because no medical expert wishes to be successfully duped, and certainly not in the public forum of a court room, any expert should take great care to apply stringent checks in any case where malingering is an issue. It is worth the plaintiff's lawyer reminding the defence of this in appropriate cases, and also of the remark of Richard Asher:

> The pride of a doctor who has caught a malingerer is alike to that of a fisherman who has landed an enormous fish and his stories (like those of the fisherman) many become somewhat exaggerated in the telling.[7]

[6] See Shepherd et al, 'Assessing general damages: a medical model', NLJ, 4 February 1994, p. 162.
[7] R. Asher, *Talking Sense — a Selection of his Papers*, ed. Sir Francis Avery Jones (London: Pitman Medical Publishing, 1972).

Great care should be taken to ensure that the consequences of the injury to the plaintiff, such as slow ability to return to normal life, are not written off as malingering. The Law Commission Report No. 225: 'Personal Injury Compensation: How much is enough?', stresses the fact that even so-called minor injuries can have profound effects on the lives of victims and their families, and that health and normal life were far more important than financial compensation pp. 204-214.

Indications of malingering include inconsistencies in the relating of history of the illness, and possibly in the accounts of the traumatic event itself (although given the possibility of post-traumatic amnesia and non-chronological recollection of the event, the latter should be treated with care). In addition the longer the case is studied, the more likely the conclusions drawn will be accurate. Scrignar says:

> the clinician must make a diagnosis based on history of a trauma, self-report of symptoms by patient, psychological tests, interviews with relatives or friends, review of records and mental status examination.[8]

DSM IV states at V65.2 that:

> Malingering should be strongly suspected if any combination of the following is noted:
> (1) medicolegal context of presentation, e.g. the person's being referred by his or her attorney to the physician for examination;
> (2) marked discrepancy between the person's claimed stress or disability and the objective findings;
> (3) lack of cooperation during the diagnostic evaluation and in complying with the prescribed treatment regimen;
> (4) the presence of antisocial personality disorder.

Item (1) should be disregarded for the purposes of this chapter, as we are specifically concerned with cases of referral by lawyers. Scrignar himself is cautious about (3) and (4).[9] Firstly, the genuinely ill can be contrary, although he does go on to say that in due course they can usually be persuaded to cooperate, whereas the malingerer, through fear of discovery, may continually try to thwart attempts to diagnose or treat. Secondly, he cautions: 'When evaluating patients, the clinician must be aware of the difference between antisocial personality disorder and intermittent antisocial behaviour; one must be suspicious of malingering in the former, while in the latter, the interpretation is not necessarily that of an unreliable scoundrel'.[10]

[8] Scrignar, op. cit. (note 4), p. 145.
[9] Scrignar, op. cit. (note 4), pp. 144–5.
[10] Scrignar, op. cit. (note 4), p. 145.

An interesting development in psychiatric diagnosis is that of 'script-driven imagery'. In this form of testing the subject meets with the psychiatrist who elicits specific information concerning events in the subject's past. From this information, a 30-second 'script' is written and recorded for each event. The scripts are then played back to the subject, who is told to imagine the event described in the script as vividly as possible. Whilst this is taking place, the subject's heart rate, sweat gland activity, muscle tension etc. are measured. A value is ascribed to each measurement, both before and during the time the subject imagines the event. These values are then subjected to statistical analysis. In an American case in September 1993[11] the plaintiff was a woman who had been involved in a head-on collision. She developed nightmares, a fear of driving and other PTSD symptoms. Testing, by using script-driven imagery yielded a 99 per cent probability of PTSD.

It is important to be aware of other areas where malingering is sometimes alleged, e.g., back injuries. Most practitioners, whether they are acting for the plaintiff or the defendant, would accept that such cases do not present all that often, and do not raise insuperable difficulties. In cases where malingering is suspected, then the usual steps are to interview the appropriate people with whom the plaintiff has contact, and look at any relevant social, work and, indeed, litigation history. There is a developing trend for the defence to use secret video recordings of the plaintiff, this is often found in a back injury case. Obviously, physical symptoms, or lack of them are easier to detect in cases of physical injury.

THE CHILD VICTIM

It may be thought that the child who suffers from one or more psychiatric disorders is in some ways easier to identify, as usually a parent will be the child's mouthpiece, and will have been watching carefully the physical (if any) effects of the event, which attention will have made the psychological effects easier to identify. Even when there has been no physical injury a parent may have been particularly attentive following the child's exposure to trauma. It may also appear more appropriate to the plaintiff's lawyer to enquire whether the event has affected the child in a non-physical sense, and, of course, the risk of a parent not being eager to cooperate is extremely unlikely.

On the other hand, studies have shown that parents and other carers tend to try and stifle the need of a child to talk about the distressing experience, and to reassure themselves that it has not adversely affected the child.

---

[11] See Pitman et al. 'Psychophysiologic testing for post-traumatic stress disorder', *Trial*, April 1994.

William Yule, Professor of Applied Child Psychology, University of London Institute of Psychiatry, has argued that studies have shown that traumatically induced emotional disturbances in children are flawed in their methodology, and also says:

> Another reason for the failure to recognize and report the severity of the effects of disasters on children is the understandable but misplaced reaction of adults who do not want to consider the horrors the children have faced. After some disasters, people in authority have prevented researchers interviewing children; schools have ignored the event or paid it cursory attention, arguing that children are getting over it and no good is done by bringing it all up again. The result is that children quickly learn not to unburden themselves to teachers who then take a long time to link the drop off in standards of work and impaired concentration with the intrusive thoughts the children are experiencing.[12]

There is less material on the effect of trauma on children and it was believed at one time that children did not suffer from, for example, PTSD. DSM IV has this to say about children:

> Diminished interest in significant activities and constriction of affect both may be difficult for children to report on themselves, and should be carefully evaluated by reports from parents, teachers and other observers. A symptom of post-traumatic stress disorder in children may be a marked change in orientation toward the future. This includes the sense of a foreshortened future, for example, a child may not expect to have a career or marriage. There may also be 'omen formation', that is, belief in an ability to prophesy future untoward events.
>
> Children may exhibit various physical symptoms, such as stomach-aches and headaches, in addition to the specific symptoms of increased arousal noted above.

One of the awards in the *Herald of Free Enterprise* arbitration concerned a 14-year-old boy whose mother and elder brother were killed; he, his father and sister survived. He was diagnosed as suffering from PTSD and a prolonged depressive adjustment disorder. It is also instructive to read the judgment in *Gardner* v *Epirotiki SS Company & Others* [1995] PMILL January 1995, Vol. 10, No. 10, which is a case arising out of the sinking of the boat *Jupiter* near Greece in 1988. The plaintiff was 14 at the time and suffered the most terrifying experience when the boat was rammed by

---

[12] 'The effects of disasters on children', *Association for Child Psychology and Psychiatry Newsletter*, vol. 11, No. 6 (November 1989).

another vessel. She spent some time in the sea as she watched the *Jupiter* disappear into the water. She developed PTSD, together with severe depression, a generalised anxiety state, and phobia, particularly for water. Giving judgment for the plaintiff, Mr Justice Wright described her symptoms thus:

> ... since the events of October 1988 and to the present time she has suffered and continues to suffer, now at about monthly intervals, and if she gets very tired, of vivid dreams of the actual event with additional horror, such as the windows of the lounge coming in followed by the water. These nightmares cause her to awake feeling distressed and unwell. She also has other vaguer dreams of being trapped and in danger. She can usually sleep through these but wakes in the morning unrefreshed and unwell. Both these kinds of dreams are significantly more disturbing to her than the childish nightmares she used to have prior to the incident.
>
> After the event she had a continuous headache for almost six months. This condition has significantly improved, but she still thinks that she gets rather more headaches than she should. On a number of occasions since October 1988 she has, whilst waking, experienced 'flash-backs', a sudden reaction or feeling as if the traumatic event were recurring, a phenomenon which is a particular feature of PTSD. She last had such an experience in the early part of 1992.
>
> Quite apart from that, she is persistently bedevilled by intrusive thoughts of the traumatic events. Throughout the three years that she was at school after the accident, she had great difficulty sleeping. If she composed herself to sleep she found the thoughts, and the sensation of the noises, mental pictures and smells associated with the event bearing in on her so as to make her feel ill. She found that the only way to get to sleep would be to watch television until she went off or simply to read herself to sleep. Nothing less would suffice to distract her mind from the intrusive thoughts of the accident. Even now, while she is at University, she has difficulty getting off to sleep, and usually has to read for about an hour into the small hours before she can succeed. . . .
>
> In order to keep the intrusive thoughts and feelings at bay, she has developed a technique which she describes as 'an internal monologue'. Sometimes she repeats what people are saying to her, and when she is not in conversation she sings songs to herself or keeps up a conversation with herself in order to keep her mind occupied. This technique requires a conscious effort on her part, and I entirely accept her when she says that she finds it exhausting. These intrusive thoughts, and the necessity to resort to this defensive technique and the impact upon her concentration have all, I am satisfied, had a catastrophic effect upon her educational attainments, and I shall have to return to this topic later.

I am satisfied that, as she describes, she suffers from a high degree of anxiety, which, as it so often is, is associated with a marked degree of irritability which her mother confirmed. She is hyper-anxious about losing articles, which she associates with the fact that she lost all her property in the accident, and she behaves irrationally if she mislays even an unimportant article. When it is found, she feels sensations of guilt. She suffers from a degree of claustrophobia and finds crowded places, particularly on public transport, difficult. Wherever she goes she finds herself looking for escape routes.

Her appetite has been diminished, and she has developed a well marked phobia for water. Even so mundane an operation as filling a bath induces intrusive thoughts in her, and she normally takes showers instead. While she is able to swim she can only do so if she concentrates on swimming lengths; she cannot enjoy being at the pool with her friends, as the sound of splashing and shouting upsets her.

Her summary of herself is that from a relatively placid outgoing stable character with no real anxieties, she has turned into an introverted neurotic worrier. She takes deliberate steps to avoid any 'triggering' experiences, and finds herself unable to watch scenes on the television or at the cinema involving water or indeed any catastrophes.

The plaintiff was awarded (inter alia) the sum of £17,500 general damages and the sum of £12,500 for future loss of earnings given the detrimental effect of the incident on her education.

Although the medical expert may make all the appropriate enquiries of schools and any other agencies involved, the lawyers involved should also be aware of these other sources of information on the child's behaviour, and be prepared to make enquiries. It is important not to rush a child's case because it is especially difficult to make an accurate prognosis for a child.

SIX

Assessing damages

Damages for psychiatric injury are, of course, subject to the general law of damages, and the main principle of damages is to be compensatory, but note what is said below about punitive damages. The usual rule that damages should compensate only for actual loss applies to damages for psychiatric injury. It is proposed to look at some of the main considerations on the award of damages in a psychiatric injury case.

Until recently there was not a great deal of authority on assessment and quantum of damages in this area. The *Herald of Free Enterprise* arbitrations which are included in full at the end of this chapter reviewed the issues involved in assessing damages in a psychiatric injury case.

THE ONCE-AND-FOR-ALL RULE

Where damages result from the same cause of action, they are assessed once and for all, so that any loss which will or may occur in the future must be assessed. If there is only a probability that there will be future deterioration or loss then that will be valued according to the percentage risk of the deterioration or loss which may occur.

PROVISIONAL DAMAGES

In most cases of psychiatric injury the once and for all rule will apply. For example in the *Herald of Free Enterprise* arbitrations, it was decided by the arbitrators that the risk of future problems and the vulnerability of a plaintiff to future injury should be taken into account when assessing damages.

However, there are some cases where it is not appropriate to assess the damages for this future risk, which may be of some serious and debilitating development, and for which the essentially modest sum of damages which would be assessed at trial would be entirely inadequate. The Administration of Justice Act 1982 made provision for this sort of situation by inserting s. 32A into the Supreme Court Act 1981 which gives the court a power to assess damages in two stages if:

> there is proved or admitted to be a chance that at some definite or indefinite time in the future the injured person will, as a result of the act or omission which gave rise to the cause of action, develop some serious disease or suffer some serious deterioration in his physical or mental condition.

For the county court the power to award provisional damages is in the County Courts Act 1984, s. 51. In order for the court to make an award of provisional damages a claim for provisional damages must have been pleaded. It is also important to note that the adjective 'serious' qualifies the disease or deterioration and *not* the risk; in fact the word 'chance' suggests that the plaintiff does not have to show that he or she is likely to suffer such deterioration on a balance of probabilities.

It may be appropriate to consider provisional damages in a psychiatric injury case if the plaintiff has been involved in a particularly horrifying incident and appears to have suffered no psychiatric ill-effects but there is psychiatric evidence to suggest that a serious breakdown could occur later in life. For a high-earning and ambitious plaintiff, the consequences of this could be devastating, and provisional damages should be considered. What has to be established is a 'clear and severable risk rather than a continuing deterioration'.[1] There is evidence that mental breakdowns can occur many years after a traumatic event,[2] which would make it appropriate to award provisional damages.

The procedure is that when damages are assessed in the first place, the risk is ignored, but the judgment will state the precise nature of the disease or deterioration for which damages are reserved and should usually fix a time limit for a further claim.

EFFECT OF ILLNESS OR ACCIDENT SUPERVENING BEFORE ASSESSMENT OF DAMAGES (*NOVUS ACTUS* OR *NOVA CAUSA*)

The law in this area is complex. One of the leading cases is *Baker* v *Willoughby* [1970] AC 467, which concerned a later, unconnected accident. The plaintiff had sustained a fractured leg as a result of the defendant's

---

[1] See *Cowan* v *Kitson Insulations Ltd* [1992] PIQR Q19.
[2] See C. B. Scrignar, *Post-traumatic Stress Disorder*, 2nd ed. (New Orleans LA: Bruno Press, 1988) pages 96–99.

negligence. This had left him with some permanent disability, pain and risk of osteoarthritis. Before the trial his leg was shot by armed robbers and had to be amputated. The House of Lords held that since his earning capacity and enjoyment of life had been reduced by the first accident, he was entitled to damages for this *as a continuing condition* notwithstanding the fact that the supervening attack had made his condition a lot worse. However, as the pain could not continue, nor was there now any future risk of osteoarthritis, damages under that head were not recoverable.

In *Jobling* v *Associated Dairies Ltd* [1982] AC 794 a different approach was taken by the House of Lords, without actually disapproving *Baker* v *Willoughby*. *Jobling* v *Associated Dairies Ltd* concerned a supervening *illness* and damages were reduced on the basis that the illness would have supervened regardless of the original accident. The difference between illness and accident is not entirely clear; it may be that illness is thought to be something already written into a person's physical development *before* the original accident took place, whereas a subsequent tortious event is pure chance. On this basis, however, it would be necessary to distinguish between different *types* of illness, and treat, say, a permanent disability brought on by a chance infection as the same as one brought about by a tortious act. On the other hand if the distinction is made to avoid a victim of two torts missing out on compensation from both tortfeasors then this would not make sense either.

The case of *Pigney* v *Pointer's Transport Services Ltd* [1957] 1 WLR 1121 is illustrative of this point in relation to psychiatric injury. The facts were that Mr Pigney sustained head injuries in July 1955 due to the negligence of the defendants. He commenced proceedings, but in January 1957 before the hearing of the action, he committed suicide. His widow continued the action, and also brought one of her own under the Fatal Accidents Acts. The question for the courts was whether the suicide, which it was accepted had been committed in a fit of depression brought about by a condition of acute anxiety neurosis induced by the accident and the injury incurred therein, was a *novus actus interveniens* which broke the chain of causation between Mr Pigney's injury and his death. It had been established that Mr Pigney was not insane as judged by the standard laid down in the M'Naughten rules, and it was held that if he had been then that would have made the chain of causation complete. Pilcher J found that the suicide did not break the chain of causation, and that, furthermore, the widow's action was not barred by public policy considerations (suicide was then an offence) because any damages would accrue to her and not to her late husband's estate.

DAMAGES WHERE THERE IS A PRE-EXISTING CONDITION

A pre-existing condition may cause an apportionment of damages, a discount for the contingency of the condition developing in any event, or an increase in damages.

An apportionment will be appropriate in cases where it can be shown on the evidence that the plaintiff was already *suffering* from the effects of a psychiatric disorder and the defendant will only be liable for the additional disorder. In practice, of course, it may be difficult, if not impossible, for the medical evidence to make it clear how the damages should be apportioned.

If the plaintiff was not actually suffering from any psychiatric disorder at the time of the accident, but had a predisposition towards such illness, then the court *may* discount the damages to take account of the condition developing in any event (see the CICB case of Beattie considered on page 125). This has to be contrasted with the situation where the plaintiff has the psychological equivalent of the eggshell skull: the eggshell personality. In such a case the plaintiff may appear to be disproportionately ill, but full damages will be payable however serious the condition may be (see *Brice* v *Brown* [1984] 1 All ER 997 discussed on page 120).

Again, in practice, the difference between these two situations can be difficult to see. An analogy can be drawn with some orthopaedic cases. Ageing causes degenerative changes in the spine, and most people remain unaware of these for most of their lives. However, an injury can sometimes result in osteoarthritis, for example, which may never have otherwise happened. The defendant in such a case may point to X-rays which show the pre-existing changes and state that the illness would have manifested itself sooner or later. The plaintiff will say that the illness would never have occurred but for the injury. In a psychiatric injury case, the point at issue will not be x-rays but the plaintiff's medical history.

The plaintiff should beware of any suggestion that his or her psychiatric disorder could have been triggered by some other event. Whilst the courts do, of course, regularly make discounts in damages to allow for special factors (e.g., the plaintiff may not work up until normal retirement age), no discount will be made in either general or special damages if the triggering event would *itself* give rise to a claim in damages or some other form of compensation, for example, a future negligent traumatic event.

CERTAINTY OF LOSS

The difficulties outlined above are similar to those faced when the loss sustained is simply uncertain. It is well established that mere difficulty in assessment and lack of precision and certainty are not reasons for denying an award of damages.[3] Courts often make awards for the loss of a chance, e.g., loss of a job opportunity or career, but see the case of *Hotson* v *East Berkshire Health Authority* [1987] AC 750 (at page 62).

Damages can be awarded for risk of relapse. Psychiatric injury can leave a plaintiff very vulnerable to a relapse which may be triggered by a relatively ordinary event. The degree of vulnerability will depend entirely upon the medical evidence. Consider this in relation to an award of provisional damages described above (page 107) and the *Herald of Free Enterprise* findings (see page 132).

DAMAGES CLAIMED MUST NOT BE TOO REMOTE

Remoteness was considered in chapter 1, and is a concept primarily concerned with liability. However, it is worth noting that even if some of the consequential damage is compensatable, the same will not necessarily apply to all loss and expense which flows from the injury. As we have seen in chapter 1, foreseeability is not the sole test. Damage will not be too remote either if it was a direct consequence of the accident or if it was an indirect but foreseeable consequence.[4] If the damage has left the plaintiff vulnerable to risks then if he suffers further damage as a result of the realisation of those risks, then unless that was wholly due to the negligence or intentional act of himself or a third party, the plaintiff will recover for the additional damage.

The case of *Robinson* v *Post Office* [1974] 2 All ER 737, CA, illustrates this point. The plaintiff suffered a cut shin due to the negligence of the defendant. He was given an anti-tetanus injection to which he was allergic, as a result of which he developed encephalitis and brain damage. It was held by the Court of Appeal that, although it was not foreseeable that he would suffer such a reaction to the injection, the chain of causation was not broken, as it was the original injury which was being treated, and in addition, the defendant must take the plaintiff as he finds him, with his allergy. There was some argument that the doctor was negligent because he had not carried out the test properly to ascertain whether the plaintiff was allergic, but the court decided that there was no negligence, and in any event the weakness would not have been revealed within the stipulated period of time.

However, in *McKew* v *Holland & Hannen & Cubitts (Scotland) Ltd* [1969] 3 All ER 1621, (a Scottish case) the pursuer suffered an injury which left him with a weak knee liable to give way. As a result, when he attempted to go down a steep flight of stone steps without the help of a stick, he fell and broke both legs. It was held that he could not recover damages for the injury he received when he fell, as he had behaved unreasonably and this had broken the chain of causation.

[3] See *Chaplin* v *Hicks* [1911] 2 KB 786, CA.
[4] See *Hughes* v *Lord Advocate* [1963] AC 837 and *Morrison Steamship Co. Ltd* v *Greystoke Castle* [1947] AC 265.

Remoteness of damage in the specific context of psychiatric injury, needs to be further examined in a number of cases.

Meah v *McCreamer* [1985] 1 All ER 367

The plaintiff was a passenger in a car driven negligently by the defendant. As a result of the injury suffered, which included severe brain damage, he developed a psychiatric injury in the form of a serious personality change. He became aggressive, violent and dangerous and attacked a number of women. As a consequence of these attacks he was sentenced to life imprisonment and classified as a category A prisoner. He claimed damages (*inter alia*) for the psychiatric injury and his incarceration for life as a category A prisoner. He was awarded general damages of £45,750. Although the evidence indicated that before the accident, Mr Meah had been convicted of a number of offences and had a poor employment record, there was no evidence of his being violent towards women; indeed he had had several successful relationships. The medical evidence was that his personality was altered by the head injury in the direction of a coarsening and an exaggeration of pre-existing traits, and a loss of emotional control. He had an 'eggshell personality'. Woolf J concluded that but for the accident he would not have committed the acts of violence, although some discount was made for the finding that he would probably have spent time in prison. The full damages were £60,000, discounted by 25 per cent because of the plaintiff's contributory negligence in travelling as a passenger with a driver whom he knew to be drunk.

Meah v *McCreamer (No. 2)* [1986] 1 All ER 943

Two of Mr Meah's victims, Mrs W and Miss D, one of whom had been raped by him in terrifying circumstances, and the other of whom had been seriously assaulted sexually were awarded damages of £10,250 and £6,750 respectively against him[5] they brought an action against the driver and the driver's insurers to recover the amounts awarded to the two victims. The action failed. Adopting what Woolf J referred to as a 'robust' approach, the damages awarded to Mrs W and Miss D were too remote to be recoverable. They were not in respect of the plaintiff's own injuries or *direct* financial loss, and if the plaintiff were to recover it would expose the defendants and other defendants in similar cases to an indefinite liability for an indefinite duration. It was also held that it would be contrary to public policy for the plaintiff to be indemnified for the consequences of his crimes.

Malcolm v *Broadhurst* [1970] 3 All ER 508

This is an interesting case on the question of remoteness of damage generally, but it does involve consideration of the 'eggshell personality' rule.

---

[5] See *W* v *Meah* [1986] 1 All ER 935.

The case concerned a husband and wife who were injured in a road accident. The husband suffered head injuries which caused his intellectual deterioration and a serious diminution of learning power, and changed his personality and behaviour so that he became irritable in the home, bad tempered and, on occasions, violent towards his wife. The prognosis was poor. The wife recovered from her physical injuries after some three to four months, but she did suffer from a pre-existing nervous condition which was exacerbated by the accident. This had improved after a year, but for some seven months she was incapacitated from work solely because of the effect on her vulnerable personality of the husband's changed behaviour. In addition to her full-time job, before the accident, the wife had worked part-time for her husband, but was no longer able to do this, as, due to the effect of the accident, he no longer worked himself. She returned to work after seven months, but the medical view was that her husband's behaviour would be likely to cause her to develop nervous symptoms from time to time. However, the wife was unable to obtain part-time work in addition to her full-time job.

The difficult question of remoteness of damage that the court had to decide was whether she was entitled to loss of wages in respect of both her full-time and part-time job, and her nervous disability from which she suffered due to the effect on her of her husband's changed behaviour.

It was held that the exacerbation of her nervous condition was a foreseeable consequence of injuring her on the principle of the 'eggshell personality', and that it was reasonably foreseeable that if the husband was severely injured when the wife was temperamentally unstable, her instability might be adversely affected by the injury done to the husband. She was, therefore, entitled to damages to compensate her for loss of wages from full-time work for that period of seven months, and to a sum (assessed at £150) for her nervous disability over those months and the slight risk of future nervous trouble.

However, Geoffrey Lane J also held that she was not entitled to compensation for the part-time wages lost. This loss was not foreseeable. His lordship said (at p. 512):

> If the wife herself had not been injured there is no doubt that she would not have been entitled to recover under this head. The defendant could not reasonably have foreseen that by injuring the husband he would be depriving the wife of her only means of part-time employment. Does the fact that she herself has a cause of action against the defendant arising out of the same accident give her the right to recover?

Since both the cause of action and the recoverability of damages depend on foreseeability, the answer logically should be the same in each case. Logic, however, is not always an infallible guide in problems of remoteness of damage. The 'eggshell skull' principle itself, for example, is hard to reconcile logically with the foreseeability test. Geoffrey Lane J went on to say:

> It seems to me that the only way in which the defendant could be made liable under this head would be by saying that he must take his victims as he finds them not only in relation to their physical infirmities but also in relation to their infirmities of employment. That would be an extension, and in my judgment an unwarrantable extension, of the present law.

This may be contrasted with *Pigney* v *Pointer's Transport Services Ltd.* [1957] 1 WLR 1121 (see above page 108).

Cowan v *National Coal Board* 1958 SLT (Notes) 19, Scotland, Court of Session, Outer House

This was an action brought by the widow of a workman who suffered an injury to his left eye, become mentally ill as a result of the injury and committed suicide some three months after the accident. Damages were claimed in respect of the suicide, but recovery was denied. Lord Cameron said (at p. 21):

> ... if it were held to be established that the deceased had received a comparatively moderate injury through the negligence of the defenders and had thereafter become depressed and worried because of fear for his future working capacity or physical health and then had committed suicide under the influence of such depression and worry no doubt it might be inferred that the suicide was consequent upon that injury. ... In the present case not only is there no proof of injury to the skull or brain but there is no physical connection between the initial injury (assuming it to have been caused by the defenders' negligence) and the assumed suicide.

The correctness of this decision can be doubted, but what may have been being considered was a straightforward anxiety about the future in material terms, rather than the more subtle and less rational feelings of anxiety and depression which can result from a traumatic incident.

McLaren v *Bradstreet* (1969) 119 NLJ 484

The three plaintiffs were passengers in the defendant's car, which met with an accident. The defendant died as a result, but the plaintiffs suffered minimal physical injuries. They were all young siblings and lived with their parents. Their mother was neurotic and was obsessed with the accident, constantly talking about it. The plaintiffs suffered from dizziness, shyness, occasional blackouts and other symptoms. Two of the plaintiffs said they were unable to work for two years following the accident, and the third for seven years. The defendant's medical evidence was that the mother's personality was such that the plaintiffs' symptoms would have cleared up within a few months if she had not influenced them to exaggerate and perpetuate them. She was held to have instigated a form of family hysteria. This evidence was accepted by the court, and the Court of Appeal held that while it was true that a tortfeasor had to take his victim as he found him, he did not have to take his family. The hysteria here was not foreseeable and the chain of causation was broken.

GENERAL DAMAGES

General damages consist of damages for pain, suffering and loss of amenities of life. It is interesting that in negligence there are no recoverable damages for 'ordinary' mental distress or shock if there have been no physical injuries.[6] If there have been physical injuries, then, although it is not described as such, in a sense there are always damages for mental distress, as this is part of pain and suffering. According to McGregor,[7] 'pain' is the immediately felt effect on the nerves and brain, while 'suffering' is distress not directly connected with any bodily condition, and would include fright at the time of the injury, and 'fright reaction' (*Thompson* v *Royal Mail Lines Ltd* [1957] 1 Lloyd's Rep 99), fear of future incapacity — in relation to health, sanity or the ability to make a living — and humiliation, sadness and embarrassment caused by disfigurement. If there is a physical injury, therefore, any non-medical distress which is suffered in excess of that which is to be expected, e.g., a bad case of fright which did not go so far as to develop into a recognisable psychiatric illness, would be claimed under this heading. Damages for pain and suffering are, of course, entirely dependant upon the type of injury sustained. It should always be considered, however, whether the bad case of fright could be said to be an acute stress reaction.

The other aspect of general damages is 'loss of amenities of life'. These include injuries to the senses,[8] sexual dysfunction,[9] loss of marriage prospects, loss of enjoyment of family life,[10] loss of enjoyment of work[11] and loss of a holiday.[12]

---

[6] See *Nicholls* v *Rushton* (1992) *The Times*, 19 June 1992, but note 'acute stress reaction' discussed on see page 41.
[7] *McGregor on Damages*, 15th ed. (London: Sweet & Maxwell, 1988), p. 956.
[8] See *Cook* v *J. L. Kier & Co. Ltd* [1970] 1 WLR 774.
[9] See *Cook* v *J. L. Kier & Co. Ltd* [1970] 1 WLR 774.
[10] See *Hoffman* v *Sofaer* [1982] 1 WLR 1350.
[11] See *Morris* v *Johnson Matthey & Co. Ltd* (1967) 112 SJ 32, CA, where a substantial sum was awarded for the loss of the joy which a craftsman found in his craft.
[12] See *Marson* v *Hall* [1983] CLY 1046.

In an award for psychiatric injury, loss of amenity can have great significance. Disorders such as depression and post-traumatic stress disorder can affect all aspects of the sufferer's life. For example, clinical depression can mean that the plaintiff suffers from insomnia in varying degrees, loss of libido, sometimes to the extent of impotence, loss of interest in work and leisure activities, and impaired concentration. There may be an effect on enjoyment of work or any hobby which requires a degree of concentration. In addition, of course, the plaintiff may suffer from depressive feelings such as hopelessness, exhaustion, low self-esteem etc which can permeate everything he or she does. Similarly, affective and neurotic disorders can be just as debilitating. An anxiety neurosis, for example, means that there is unreasonable fear without any particular focus. These attacks are often accompanied by a variety of symptoms: palpitations, excessive sweating, breathlessness, faintness, nausea etc. A phobic anxiety can also seriously curtail the plaintiff's activities, particularly if it concerns something of a commonplace nature, such as travelling in a vehicle, or being left alone. Again, the symptoms in the later stages of PTSD — phobic anxiety, inordinate attention to physical discomfort and normal physiological processes so that the plaintiff may become obsessive about bodily sensations etc. — will all interfere with enjoyment of the normal activities of life. Loss of amenities of life will, in these sorts of cases, be substantial. As Birkett J stated in *Griffiths v R. & H. Green & Silley Weir Ltd* (1948) 81 Ll L Rep 378:

> . . . I can conceive of very few things so painful as to be continually unwell; to lose the savour and zest for life. . . . I think I must award a fairly substantial sum.

SPECIAL DAMAGES FOR PECUNIARY LOSS

Obviously, all the usual special damages apply in exactly the same way as in the case of physical injury. When considering, however, loss of earning capacity or handicap in the labour market or loss of a career, it should be remembered that psychiatric injury can have serious consequences for a plaintiff's employability.[13] Plaintiff lawyers will be aware that, whilst there is always a duty to mitigate loss, allegations by the defence that the plaintiff is not making enough efforts to resume working should receive a robust response, subject, of course, to the evidence, both medical and non-medical, supporting the plaintiff whose injuries are such that work is as yet impossible. It should also be remembered that damages can be awarded for

---

[13] See *R v Liverpool City Council* [1989] CLY 1255 and *Steventon v Cotmor Tool and Presswork Co* [1990] CLY 1587, both cases considered below at page 125.

loss of housekeeping capacity, whether or not the plaintiff intends to employ anyone.[14]

If the plaintiff's marriage breaks down as a result of his or her injuries, and, undoubtedly, psychiatric injuries can put a great strain upon a marriage, then the plaintiff can recover damages to cover certain aspects of the consequent financial loss. In *Jones* v *Jones* [1985] QB 704, CA, the injured husband recovered damages for part of the amount of the lump sum he had been ordered to pay to the wife in divorce proceedings. The whole of the lump sum was not recovered as it was held that the wife would have shared in the general damages that the husband was awarded. The damages did not cover the maintenance order on the grounds that the husband might have a reduced tax liability because of this, and also the wife might remarry.

Medical expenses must be 'reasonable', but there is no obligation on the plaintiff to make use of NHS or other 'free' treatment even if this is available.[15] The cost of convalescence, again, subject to it being reasonable, is also recoverable.

OTHER DAMAGES

Aggravated and exemplary damages

Aggravated damages were defined in *Rookes* v *Barnard* [1964] AC 1129, HL, as compensation for injuring the plaintiff's feelings. In other words they depended upon the motives or manner of committing the wrong of the defendant. They would, therefore, be appropriate usually only in cases of assault, or some other form of deliberate infliction of injury. The suitability of an award of aggravated damages was considered in *Kralj* v *McGrath* [1986] 1 All ER 54. It was stated that it would be inappropriate to introduce the concept of aggravated damages into claims for breach of contract and negligence. In that case it was found that a doctor had treated his patient in a horrific and wholly unacceptable way, but it was held that if aggravated damages were allowed into this sort of case, it would be difficult to keep them out of many negligence cases. Woolf J said (at p. 61):

> If the principle is right, a higher award of damages would be appropriate in a case of reckless driving which caused injury than would be appropriate in cases where careless driving caused identical injuries. Such a result seems to me to be wholly inconsistent with the general approach to damages in this area, which is to compensate the plaintiff for the loss that she has actually suffered.

[14] See *Daly* v *General Steam Navigation Co. Ltd* [1981] 1 WLR 120.
[15] Law Reform (Personal Injuries) Act 1948, s. 2(4).

However, we would suggest that there is scope for the award of exemplary damages for non-consensual sterilisations which, in appropriate cases could reflect the severity of any resulting psychiatric injury. There are a number of cases where women have been sterilised without seeking their consent, usually when undergoing a Caesarian operation and when the surgeon, aware that the woman had a number of children, decided that it would be in her 'best interests' to sterilise her.[16] Such operations, apart from evidencing an extraordinary arrogance on the part of the surgeons concerned, are batteries and not just negligence, and it is suggested that plaintiffs should be awarded aggravated damages in appropriate cases.

Exemplary damages were not distinguished from aggravated damages until the case of *Rookes* v *Barnard*, and they have little or no part to play in personal injury cases. They are punitive in nature and are usually considered as punishment for oppressive or arbitrary action by government servants or persons making a profit out of their wrong, which may exceed the compensation payable to the plaintiff. However, should that action have resulted in psychiatric injury, then it would not be inappropriate to award them, subject to the restrictions placed upon awarding them by *Rookes* v *Barnard, Cassell & Co. Ltd* v *Broome* [1972] AC 1027, and *AB* v *South West Water Services Ltd* [1993] 2 WLR 506, which confirmed the unsatisfactory criterion that exemplary damages can be awarded only if the type of tort is one in respect of which an award was made prior to 1964, which does not include negligence.[17]

The Law Commission's Consultation Paper No. 132 stated that it is difficult to maintain the present position on any basis of principle, and provisionally concluded (at para. 6.8) that exemplary damages should be put on a principled basis:

> . . . we consider that there is intrinsic value in protecting personality rights and in empowering citizens to enforce those rights . . . it will be necessry to decide whether legislation should make provision for such awards according to a generally drawn statutory test, a test which confined the availability to specific wrongs, a detailed legislative scheme, or a combination of these.

MITIGATION OF LOSS

The plaintiff is under a duty to mitigate his or her loss. What if a psychiatrically injured plaintiff refuses the necessary medical treatment

---

[16] See, for example, *Hamilton* v *Birmingham Regional Hospital Board* (1969) BMJ 456, *Devi* v *West Midlands Regional Health Authority*, 9 December 1981, CA, see Nelson-Jones and Burton *Medical Negligence Case Law*, (London: Fourmat Publishing 1990).
[17] See Alan Reed, 'The end of the line for exemplary damages?' (1993) 143 NLJ 929.

which may reduce loss? An *unreasonable* refusal (and the burden of proof will be on the plaintiff to show that it was reasonable to refuse) will mean a reduction in damages to a level which it is deemed would have been appropriate if the treatment had gone ahead and the anticipated degree of recovery had been made.[18] The test of reasonableness is objective: would a reasonable man have refused? It also does not matter whether it is the plaintiff's own medical adviser or the defendant's adviser who recommends the treatment, although the plaintiff would certainly want to seek his own doctor's advice before proceeding. However, it must be remembered that with injuries of a psychiatric nature, the refusal of treatment can be part of the condition or can be reasonable simply because the plaintiff does not wish to relive the trauma. An important finding of the *Herald of Free Enterprise* arbitrations (see page 132) was that it may be reasonable for the survivors to refuse medical treatment.

'Compensation neurosis'

The precise meaning of this term (sometimes called 'litigation or accident neurosis' is elusive. Sometimes medical reports state that a plaintiff's condition is likely to improve, perhaps to the point of complete recovery, once the case is settled. This is often a euphemistic way of saying the plaintiff is malingering. However, it can be a reference to the inevitable stress of the litigation process, and consequences such as financial hardship, which can inhibit the plaintiff's recovery, or even exacerbate the plaintiff's condition. This is particularly likely to be the case in a claim following psychiatric injury. Dr James Thompson at the Middlesex Hospital has researched into post-disaster victims and the effect of the subsequent legal and administrative procedures and found that these procedures exacerbated their injuries.[19] This is no fault of the victim and should not be used as an argument to reduce damages. A report containing such an opinion should not be agreed by the plaintiff's lawyers unless there is also agreement about precisely what is meant by it. Two cases which deal with this issue are have already been considered: *Lucy* v *Mariehamns Rederi* [1971] 2 Lloyd's Rep 314, see page 120 and *Malyon* v *Lawrance, Messer & Co.* [1968] 2 Lloyd's Rep 539, see page 67.

Exacerbation of physical injuries

A plaintiff's physical injuries may be exacerbated by the psychiatric injury that he or she has suffered. Thus, it is important to identify the psychiatric

---

[18] See *Morgan* v *T. Wallis Ltd* [1974] 1 Lloyd's Rep 165.
[19] Radio 4 transmission 'Shockwaves' 28 April 1991.

injury as soon as symptoms become apparent. Damages can be awarded to cover both exacerbation and prolongation of physical injuries. See *Kralj* v *McGrath* [1986] 1 All ER 54.

LEVEL OF DAMAGES — THE MAIN CASES

It is well established that judges are free to inform themselves of appropriate levels of damages from any reasonable source.[20] In other words there is no doctrine of precedent on matters of quantum. Naturally, as in any other area of personal injury law, the authorities on quantum set the guidelines for practitioners and the courts. Many would be surprised at the extent of the authorities on cases involving psychiatric injury. Here we review the landmark cases on quantum that have marked the progression towards the point where the Judicial Studies Board *Guidelines for Assessment of General Damages in Personal Injury Cases*, 2nd ed. (Blackstone Press, 1994), now record the following:

(a)	severe psychiatric damage:	£22,500 to	£45,000
(b)	moderately severe damage:	8,500 to	20,000
(c)	moderate damage:	2,500 to	7,500
(d)	minor damage:	500 to	1,500

Hinz v *Berry* [1970] 2 QB 40, CA

This was the first really significant case on quantum. The plaintiff was picking flowers at the side of the road with one of her children when she saw a car run into the stationary van where her husband and the other seven children (some were the foster children of the couple) were preparing a picnic. Her husband was killed and the children were injured. It was said that she had a robust character, and that but for witnessing the accident she would have stood up well to the bereavement. However, at the trial some five years after the event she was still suffering from morbid depression. The trial judge awarded her £4,000 damages in respect of the depression. The defendant appealed. The Court of Appeal upheld this award, saying that although it was high, it was not wholly erroneous. The duration of the illness was said to make it a very exceptional case. Pearson LJ said:

It should not be for the whole of the mental anguish which she has endured during the last five or six years. It should be only for that additional element which has been contributed by the shock of witnessing the accident, and which would not have occurred if she had not suffered that shock.

In 1994 this award of £4,000 would have been worth £32,200.

[20] See, for example, *Waldon* v *War Office* [1956] 1 WLR 51.

Lucy v *Mariehamns Rederi* [1971] 2 Lloyd's Rep 314

Here, the issue to be decided concerned an anxiety neurosis suffered by the plaintiff and how far this was due to the plaintiff's own intentional actions. The plaintiff was struck by a large quantity of oil in the course of his employment, and, although not physically injured, developed an anxiety neurosis as a result. Despite having suffered no apparent physical injury, the plaintiff complained of it having hurt his eyes. He was sent to an eye specialist who concluded that there was nothing wrong with his eyes. He also found it difficult to sleep; difficult to lie comfortably in bed at night; he felt lethargic, with no interest in household jobs or social activities. There seemed little dispute between the parties that the symptoms, *at some point*, had been genuine, and were still continuing at the trial of the matter, over three years after the accident. The defendant contended that to begin with it had been a genuine anxiety neurosis, but that the plaintiff had recovered from it some six months after the accident. Due to an intentional assumption or exaggeration of symptoms at that time he caused his illness to continue, and this exaggeration had subsequently become part of his make-up and he was incapable of voluntarily reversing it.

The plaintiff had been examined by his psychiatrist some six months after the accident, and had appeared to have recovered, being optimistic about going back to work. Much was made of this at the trial, together with the fact that the plaintiff when first giving evidence had been tearful and trembling, but that this condition improved as the evidence continued, and particularly under cross-examination. Geoffrey Lane J, however, accepted the plaintiff's expert witness's conclusion that his condition deteriorated because when he got back to work he found he could no longer drive a crane, but was relegated to a less responsible job. Geoffrey Lane J also concluded that the plaintiff's condition was due entirely to the result of the accident. This was in part based upon some hesitation on the part of the defendant's medical expert, and in part upon the evidence of both the plaintiff and his wife. The genuineness of the wife's evidence was particularly important: 'I cannot believe that a man like Mr Lucy would, under any circumstances, deliberately inflict that sort of torture on his family' (at p. 317).

Geoffrey Lane J also concluded from the report of the defendant's expert witness that the matter which really caused the anxiety neurosis to continue so long was the very litigation itself, and that within six months he would be fully restored to health.

The damages awarded for pain and suffering were £1,100, some three and a half years after the accident, with a prognosis of complete recovery within six months. The 1994 equivalent of this was £8,162.

Brice v *Brown* [1984] 1 All ER 997

This is an important case both on remoteness and on quantum. The plaintiff was a middle-aged woman who had suffered from a hysterical personality disorder since childhood. The effect of that disorder upon her life, however, was relatively minor, inasmuch as symptoms were relatively moderate and infrequent, and generally the plaintiff and her family of husband and three children led a happy life. In 1980 she and her daughter were passengers in a taxi which was involved in a collision with an oncoming bus. The plaintiff suffered minor injuries only, but her daughter had a very badly cut head, although she recovered quickly from this. Shortly afterwards, the plaintiff became moody, unable to sleep and neglected her household jobs. This gradually became worse; she attempted suicide on a number of occasions and her behaviour became increasingly bizarre, to such an extent that she was admitted to hospital under the Mental Health Act on three occasions.

The plaintiff sought damages for her condition and for the cost of future care. There was no dispute that her illness was genuine, although there was some dispute between the experts as to its precise nature, the defendant contending that it was endogenous depression, unconnected with the accident. On the medical evidence, Stuart-Smith J did not accept this and found that the accident had aggravated and made patent the underlying personality disorder.

It was submitted by the defendant that even if this was the condition, as she had an underlying personality disorder, she did not have a normal standard of susceptibility, and a hypothetical reasonable man could not foresee that the psychiatric results would eventuate. However, it was held that the circumstances of the accident were such that 'nervous shock' might result to a mother of a normally robust constitution, and the fact that the consequences were so much worse than a normal person would suffer was immaterial.

General damages were awarded of £22,500. In 1994 the equivalent would have been £37,350, and is substantial. In view of that we quote extensively from the description of the plaintiff's illness as given by Stuart-Smith J:

The accident . . . occurred on 2 February 1980. . . .

On 8 February 1980 she consulted a partner of the general practitioner's practice and was prescribed an analgesic, presumably for the chest pain of which she was complaining. . . .

On 1 April 1980 she again consulted a partner in the general practitioner's practice who recorded a reactive depression to a road traffic accident. . . .

The family went for a holiday in Italy shortly after this time but it was not a success. On 28 April she again consulted her general practitioner and different drugs were prescribed. She went again on 2 May. It is quite clear that by this time her condition had reached a somewhat worrying state. She describes seeing or dreaming about evil spirits. She thought she was dying, and she believed she had got cancer. She was prescribed

Mogadon for sleeping and anti-depressants. By this time her husband described her condition as very bad. She appears to have thought that both her husband and Julie [a daughter] were trying to poison her. On 29 May she attempted suicide by drinking a bottle of wine after she had taken a large quantity of tablets. There is no reason to suppose that that was anything other than a genuine attempt to take her life. She was admitted to hospital.

... the hospital notes indicate violent changes of mood and bizarre behaviour on the part of the plaintiff. The hospital seems to have diagnosed a depressive illness, seemingly brought about by the accident. Towards the end of her stay there she was allowed home at weekends. On 22 June another serious attempt at suicide was made. She was returned to hospital. There appears to have been a further attempt on 30 June. Early in July she was found in a compromising position with a male patient. It seems that she had sexual relations with him. This got back to the plaintiff's husband, who was extremely angry both with her and with the hospital. She appears to have made another, probably this time half-hearted, attempt at suicide, and on 10 July to the evident relief of the hospital she discharged herself. I think they were thankful to get rid of a troublesome patient.

Over the next few months she continued to behave in a most bizarre way. She wandered off for sometimes weeks at a time and sometimes days. She probably behaved like a prostitute in London and elsewhere. She slept rough in the woods and did not take any proper food. The hospital were reluctant to take her back. She was rejected at home for her unsocial behaviour and because her husband, understandably I think, thought that she was some sort of moral danger to the girls. On 14 September she was again admitted to the Queen Elizabeth II hospital pursuant to s. 136 of the Mental Health Act 1959, having been found in a destitute state. She remained there until 29 October. The picture again presented by the notes is one of changing moods but on the whole, isolated, sullen, uncooperative, secretive and not taking drugs. The plaintiff's husband described her as being unrepentant, aggressive and like a nasty spoilt child. . . .

On her discharge from the Queen Elizabeth II hospital on the second occasion the plaintiff lived at home. Her husband described her as awful. He said: 'The intensity of crying and screaming got worse; I could not bear it'. On 10 November he came home to find the house in darkness. The plaintiff was in the hall. She had pulled out the main cable where the electricity comes into the junction box in an attempt to kill herself. He found her shaking and she would not let him near her. She was admitted to Hillend hospital following that, under s. 29 of the Mental Health Act 1959. Again her history was taken from the patient and she appears to have related her symptoms to the accident. Her behaviour in hospital as recorded in the hospital notes continued to be bizarre. She was convinced that she was suffering from venereal disease. She certainly had some infection in the genital region but it does not appear to have been venereal disease. The hospital appears to have diagnosed recurrent depression in a neurotic personality following the road traffic accident. She was allowed home over Christmas 1980 ... she was discharged from Hillend hospital early in January 1981, and since that time she has lived at home. ...

Since January 1981 her condition has to some extent stabilised though her behaviour remains highly abnormal. Her present state is described by her husband. She spends most of her time in one room. She covers the window with a blanket, and even in the extremely hot weather which we have been experiencing recently she does not open the window and she stays in there, the room being like an oven. In the winter time she is in there nearly all the time. In the summer she will go out for walks in the fields. She goes uninvited into the neighbours' gardens and is often most inappropriately dressed, wearing either a bra and knickers or in hot weather one or two hot jerseys. She is unable to cook or wash her own clothes. She can now take a bath and does bath herself, but until comparatively recently she had to be bathed, and her husband described it in a graphic phrase, 'like bathing a cat'. She has peculiar habits in relation to her toilet. She apparently was reluctant to use the WC and would urinate on the floor ... she now for the most part uses the bucket. ... She lives largely on biscuits. ... She pleads with people in a pathetic way to cut off her head and kill her. She wrings her hands and appears to be miserable a great deal of the time. She seems to want to play with children and continues to do bizarre and inappropriate things like untying the laces of her son-in-law's shoes; but there is no doubt that there has been some improvement. She is no longer vicious or aggressive. She is slightly less reluctant to mix with the family, and she seems to be making some response at last to overtures of affection. But there is no doubt that at the moment she is severely deranged. She needs supervision. She cannot be left alone for long. ... She has to be cooked for, tidied after, shopped for and have her clothes washed.

This graphic description should leave no doubt that Mrs Brice's damages of £22,500 were not in any way excessive. It is also a fascinating, if harrowing, account of the way in which a relatively minor road accident could reduce a normal life to one so far removed from anything that could be described as satisfactory. It is interesting to contrast Mrs Brice's condition with that of Mr Meah (see page 111). Mrs. Brice may have fallen short of committing any crime as a result of her condition, but it would not have been surprising if she had fallen foul of the criminal law, for example, by destroying property or damaging life by fire. Presumably had she been sued in respect of this damage and had attempted to recover her losses she would have been treated in exactly the same way as Mr Meah.

The following are summaries of a number of other cases on quantum. Where appropriate we have multiplied the damages to give the 1994 figure. In some cases the figure for general damages includes a sum for physical injury which has not been dealt with separately at trial or in the report, but where this is the case, we have indicated this.

Bartlett v *Arnold Cook Ltd,* 7 July 1981, Kemp C4-024

This is an interesting case inasmuch as it considered the issues raised by so-called functional overlay. The plaintiff had suffered back strain due to an accident at work. The trial took place two years or so after the accident, and the trial judge found that his continuing symptoms were partly due to functional overlay and partly to 'conscious exaggeration'. The Court of Appeal reversed the trial judge's findings and held that the plaintiff had suffered a marked degree of psychiatric damage as a result of the accident and that due weight had not been given to the medical evidence. General damages were awarded of £6,500, consisting of £3,500 for pain and suffering and loss of amenity and £3,000 for loss of earning capacity. (1994 figure: £13,325.)

S, 21 October 1986, CICB, London

A woman, aged 31 at date of offence and 33 at date of hearing, had been subjected to various sexual assault, involving rape; no weapon used. Full recovery from physical injuries within a month, but developed depression, anxiety state, phobia, personality change and skin problems and attempted suicide on five occasions. Although her condition very much improved by date of hearing, she had continuing nightmares and was still unable to lead a normal life. Slept with axe under pillow, panicked in company of men and afraid to be alone. Her vulnerability to future psychiatric injury was considered and it was found that there was a risk of psychiatric breakdown if she experienced other traumas in her life, whether or not involving men. Unlikely to be capable of forming normal relationship with a man and possibility of reconciliation with husband and chances of remarriage remote. Skin problems likely to persist for up to four years and might become established. General damages for pain and suffering and loss of amenities assessed at £12,000. (1994 figure: £18,000.)

Whitty v *London Borough of Hackney* (1987) Kemp C4–026

A woman was awarded £4,500 for depression following witnessing the electrocution of her 2 year old son and which she believed had killed him. (1994 figure: £6,480.)

Gaines August 1988, CICB, Kemp C4–012

This case concerned a female cashier who was attacked in two separate robberies within a few months. It is important to note that she suffered no physical injury, but was diagnosed as suffering from post-traumatic neurosis. At the date of the hearing (six years after the attack) she was still suffering from agoraphobia, anxiety, depression and sexual dysfunction. She was awarded a significant sum in general damages (all for psychiatric injury): £35,000. (1994 figure: £48,650.)

R v *Liverpool City Council* [1989] CLY 1255, QBD

A middle-aged man suffered psychiatric injury following an accident at work when he was struck in the face by chain. He suffered from a lot of debilitating symptoms, including depression, tiredness, poor social function, loss of appetite and sleep function. He was effectively unemployable and there was no treatment to help him. He received £15,000 for the psychiatric injury, Hodgson J commented that awards for this type of injury seemed 'surprisingly low'. (1994 figure: £19,500.)

Beattie [1989] CLY 1254, 23 May 1989, CICB, Leeds

A young single man was attacked by a single assailant as a result of which he was rendered unconscious and sustained a broken nose, two black eyes, lacerations to his face and bruising to his head and body. Prior to the attack the applicant had experienced one episode of schizophrenia in 1978 which had required admission to hospital for one month but which had resolved relatively quickly. Since the assault, he had experienced three episodes of relapse requiring in-patient treatment in December 1983, June 1985 and December 1987. Following his relapse in December 1983 remission of his symptoms proved far more difficult to achieve, his periods of in-patient care became longer and he required more intensive follow-up. Up to a few weeks before the hearing the applicant had attended psychiatric day hospital two days a week. He was diagnosed as suffering from a schizo-affective disorder. He described experiences which were probably auditory hallucinations, the content referring to scars inflicted during the assault. The assault on him in December 1982 had contributed to a relapse of his psychiatric symptoms in December 1983, and it was likely that he would remain dependent upon his family and upon receiving psychiatric treatment for the foreseeable future.

The Board awarded a sum of £40,572 which included £21,000 general damages, reduced in the light of his predisposition to schizophrenia. (1994 figure: £27,300.)

Steventon v *Cotmor Tool and Presswork Co.* [1990] CLY 1587

This young woman developed what her psychiatrist described as a 'moderate post-traumatic stress reaction' after suffering amputated fingers in an industrial accident. She was suffering enuresis once or twice weekly at the time of the trial; severe nightmares; marriage difficulties; inability to go out through fear of displaying her hand in public; severe depression. General damages for pain and suffering (including the physical injury) was £40,000. She was also awarded a sum for the future to cater for broken plates in the home. (1994 figure: £48,000.)

T, G and J [1990] CLY 1588, 12 June 1990, CICB

Infants aged respectively five, three and two at the date of witnessing their mother's murder in 1985 by their father. General Damages of £20,000, £20,000 and £5,000 respectively were awarded for their psychiatric injuries. (1994 figures: £24,200 and £6,050.)

Simpson, Re, 7 August 1990, CICB, London

In July 1985, this female was attacked by a stranger in her room at a women's hostel where she was employed as a deputy warden. She received head and facial injuries, and was also diagnosed as suffering from an anxiety state, involving panic attacks, headaches and fear of being alone. The prognosis was uncertain. Her general damages, which included a sum for handicap on the labour market were £10,000. (1994 figure: £12,100.)

C [1991] CLY 1348, 17 January 1991, CICB

Following an attack by a lesbian inmate, which included a vaginal assault, this young prison officer developed PTSD and sexual phobias. Her scores on various scales were detailed as: depression sub-scale 9, anxiety sub-scale 11, Beck Depression Inventory 12, agoraphobia score 23, total phobia score 67 and believed to be the same at the date of hearing. She had no treatment to avoid reliving incident but expected to undergo counselling. General damages (including claim for cost of cosmetic surgery): £17,500. (1994 figure: £19,425.)

W, Re January 1991, CICB, Kemp C4–013

This case concerned a female police officer who was caught in the middle of a terrorist bomb attack. She suffered only minor physical injury, but serious PTSD and had to leave the police force. Her general damages of £40,000 included a sum for loss of congenial employment and for alcohol dependency caused by PTSD. (1994 figure: £44,400.)

R, 14 February 1992, CICB, London

Female, aged 20 at date of hearing, was abused regularly by her step-father for nine years between the ages of four and 13. Abuse took the form of vaginal touching and fondling of breasts, and occurred whenever she was left alone with her step-father. Initial difficulties at age of 16 in sexual relationships with boyfriend. Nervous of older men. No psychiatric evidence obtained. General damages: the initial award of £1,000 was increased to £5,000. (1994 figure: £5,300.)

Wheatley v Cunningham [1992] PMILL March 1992, Vol. 8, No. 2
A plaintiff who suffered minimal injuries in an accident in which her husband was killed, subsequently miscarried and suffered PTSD for approximately one year and was awarded £10,000 general damages. (1994 figure: £10,600.)

JT, 5 June 1992, CICB, Leeds
Female, nine at date of trial, allegedly had been subject to sexual abuse. She was taken into local authority care, and was emotionally disturbed. Psychiatric evidence suggested a very damaged little girl who had missed out on the normal stages of development due to emotional and sexual abuse. Initial award nil; on appeal £8,500. (1994 figure: £9,010.)

The 'Marchioness' cases
A number of cases were heard in 1991–1992 resulting from the sinking of the pleasure boat, the *Marchioness* by the dredger the *Bowbelle* in the Thames on 20 August 1989 in which over 50 people died. In 1991 the case of Deborah Jane Ross was heard by Master Topley, who received £5,000 damages for PTSD (1994 figure: £5,550). She lost a friend in the tragedy, and was thrown out into the river close to the still turning propeller of the dredger. Some two years later she still suffered from a moderate depressive illness, and had experienced the classic PTSD symptoms. She became dependent upon alcohol. In addition to general damages she was awarded £1,000 for the 'trauma of the day', but which was not awarded in subsequent cases resulting from this disaster.

Higher damages were awarded to another young woman, Miss Russell, who was awarded £15,000 for her psychiatric injury (PTSD) (1994 figure: £15,900). She had also lost a friend. The severity of her case was said to be close to *Case G* of the *Herald of Free Enterprise* arbitrations, see below page 138.

M, Re 19 February 1993, CICB, London
Aged three, this boy had been found locked in a bedroom next to that in which his mother had been murdered. Evidence suggested that, although he had suffered no physical injury, he had witnessed at least part of the murder. Three years after the event he was still suffering nightmares and bed-wetting. He was aggressive and had learning difficulties. The prognosis was uncertain, the medical evidence being that the violence of the memory influenced his thought and behaviour, and the long-term effects of the trauma were difficult to assess. General damages were £20,000. (1994 figure: £20,800.)

Benn v Carnon Consolidated Tin Mines Ltd [1993] PIQR Q7

The physical injury in this case consisted of severe bruising, and the psychiatric injury consisted of a severe anxiety state and depression, but the plaintiff was likely to return to work. General damages were £18,000. (1994 figure: £18,720.)

Hale v London Underground Ltd [1993] PIQR Q30

This concerned one of the firemen involved in the King's Cross fire. He suffered little or no physical injury but received general damages for PTSD, described as of 'moderate severity' but from which he would probably never fully recover. General damages: £27,500. (1994 figure: £28,600.)

Waller and Waller v Canterbury and Thanet Health Authority (1993) Quantum, Issue 5/93, 16 September 1993

The plaintiffs alleged negligence on the part of the hospital treating their 20-year-old son. It was said that insufficient precautions had been taken to prevent him from committing suicide. The plaintiffs discovered their son's body hanging by a rope in a disused building on the hospital site. Liability was admitted. Both parents suffered from depressive disorders which caused sleep disturbance, intrusive images, uncontrolled weeping, lethargy and lack of concentration. They were each awarded general damages of £8,500. (1994 figure: £8,840.)

Anderson v Davis [1993] PIQR Q87

The plaintiff was physically injured in a road accident and also suffered from PTSD and depression. It was found that he had a genetic disposition to manic depressive illness and therefore damages for future loss of earnings were discounted by 15%. His general damages included a sum for physical injury and approximately £20,000 was awarded for the psychiatric injury. (1994 figure: £20,800.)

Murby v Derby City Transport, 8 December 1993, unreported, QBD, Nottingham

The plaintiff was a bus driver who suffered a whiplash injury and bruising after being involved in a shunt. He suffered severe PTSD, and could no longer drive. He had not worked since the accident. His symptoms included nightmares, sleep walking, palpitations, muscular tension and panic attacks. It was said that he had undergone a complete personality change as a result of the accident. Total damages were over £150,000, including £30,000 for pain, suffering and loss of amenity. (1994 figure: £30,600.)

Tredget & Tredget v Bexley Health Authority [1994] 5 Med LR 178

The facts of this case have already been mentioned (see page 66). As a result of the distress caused by the traumatic birth and subsequent death of their son, the plaintiff parents suffered psychiatric illness and a pathological grief reaction, the father being the worst affected. He was awarded £32,500 and the mother was awarded £17,500.

Vernon v *Bosley*, unreported, 30 January 1995

Finally, a case which made newspaper headlines because the total amount of damages awarded was over £1 million, and the losses all flowed from a psychiatric injury caused by the plaintiff witnessing the death of his three children when the car in which they were travelling crashed into a river. In a judgment which ran to 262 pages, Mr Justice Sedley said that this was 'every parent's nightmare become a reality'. For the psychiatric injury the plaintiff was awarded £37,500.

THE *HERALD OF FREE ENTERPRISE* ARBITRATION AWARDS

These arbitrations examined psychiatric injury in some detail and assessed damages in ten test cases. On 6 March 1987, the *Herald of Free Enterprise*, passenger and freight ferry, which had just left Zeebrugge harbour, capsized, resulting in chaos and panic. Out of the 600 or so people aboard, some 193, both passengers and crew, lost their lives. Some people witnessed the deaths and injury of loved ones, in terrible physical conditions. Many survivors spent hours in the water, not knowing whether they would be rescued. It was a traumatic event of enormous magnitude.

Many passengers entered into a compensation agreement which included an arbitration clause for the resolution of disputes arising under the agreement.

In many cases the parties were unable to agree levels of damages for 'nervous shock'. It was agreed that a selection of cases should be dealt with by arbitration before a panel of three Queen's counsel. Ten cases were chosen as a representative sample. Almost all of the claims for physical injuries and special damages in the 10 cases were resolved by agreement. The principal interest of the arbitrators in making their awards therefore related to the claims for psychiatric damage. Under the agreement each claimant received a fixed payment of £5,000 for having been involved in and having witnessed the events of the day of the disaster. This payment was disregarded by the arbitrators in assessing their awards for psychiatric damage suffered in the days after the capsize. Where survivors had also suffered the loss of relatives who died in the capsize there were fixed payments under the agreement of £5,000 to each survivor for each relative lost. Sums payable under this paragraph of the agreement were disregarded by the arbitrators when assessing damages for pathological grief. With regard to fatal accident claims there were fixed payments to the personal representatives of each deceased passenger in respect of bereavement and a further £5,000 to the estate of each deceased passenger in respect of pre-death injury, pain and suffering in addition to the usual claims for the dependants.

The arbitrators were Sir Michael Ogden QC, Michael Wright QC (now Mr Justice Michael Wright), and William Crowther QC. The award was made in February 1989.

The following passages are extracted from the reasons given by the arbitrators.

Nervous shock

The respondents have conceded that all the claimants suffered nervous shock. This rather odd legal phrase does not connote shock in the sense in which it is often used in ordinary conversation. In *McLoughlin v O'Brian* [1983] 1 AC 410 at p. 431 Lord Bridge said this of nervous shock:

The basic difficulty of the subject arises from the fact that the crucial answers to the questions which it raises lie in the difficult field of psychiatric medicine. The common law gives no damages for the emotional distress which any normal person experiences when someone he loves is killed or injured. Anxiety and depression are normal human emotions. Yet an anxiety neurosis or a reactive depression may be recognisable psychiatric illnesses, with or without psychosomatic symptoms. So, the first hurdle which a plaintiff claiming damages of the kind in question must surmount is to establish that he is suffering, not merely grief, distress or any other normal emotion, but a positive psychiatric illness.

Post-traumatic stress disorder (PTSD)

While the respondents conceded that all the claimants suffered from nervous shock, it was necessary for us to consider the nature of the illness from which each claimant suffered, mainly because identification of the nature of the illness enables conclusions to be drawn about prognosis in most cases.

The arbitrators then described the features of PTSD, and continued:

Many of the Zeebrugge victims undoubtedly suffered from PTSD; of course, some victims suffered from some other psychiatric illness, e.g., depression, at the same time.

We are asked by the claimants to make a finding that DSM III R contains a suitable guide to diagnosis of PTSD. The reason for this request is that claims from other victims are outstanding and it is desired to use findings made in this award when dealing with the outstanding cases. While we are anxious to be as helpful as possible to the parties, we do not feel able to be as dogmatic about this point as the claimants would wish us to be because points may arise in outstanding cases which have not arisen in this arbitration. Furthermore, PTSD is a very recent concept and, just as DSM III was revised in 1987, further research and experience may necessitate revision in the future. When considering the cases involved in this arbitration there did not appear to be much dispute that, in very general terms DSM III R contains a useful guide to diagnosis provided that it is not construed as a statute, but more a document which gives a guide to diagnosis. In particular, it seemed to us that passages concerning time of commencement or duration of symptoms were unduly arbitrary. We do not feel able to say more than this.

Some of the claimants lost one or more relatives in the disaster and suffered from what is termed 'pathological grief' or 'pathological mourning'. This, too, is a recognised psychiatric illness and in non-medical terms can be said to be grief the extent and duration of which is in excess of normal grief reaction.

This has posed extremely difficult problems of an obvious nature. As Lord Bridge said in the passage already quoted, a person is not to be compensated for normal grief. However, a person is to be compensated for pathological grief. 'Normal' grief varies widely between one individual and another.

Gauging the extent to which a claimant's suffering is from grief which that claimant would have suffered is a task which is enormously difficult and cannot be undertaken with any degree of precision. In each case, we have had to estimate the extent to which the claimant's grief is in excess of the normal grief which the claimant would have suffered had the death occurred in ordinary circumstances and compensate the claimant accordingly. Obviously, this can be done only in a very rough and ready fashion; the more so, since in all these cases there is another form of illness present.

The duration of the illness

The arbitrators considered the question of prognosis as follows:

Unhappily, some of the claimants continue to suffer to a significant degree. However, in all cases improvement is probable. This is not to say that the victim will ever forget the experience or that painful intrusive thoughts will cease. Plainly, that is impossible. However, in such cases the improvement will reach a point at which it can be said that, in spite of remaining intrusive thoughts etc., the victim is no longer suffering from psychiatric illness. Since compensation for nervous shock is compensation for psychiatric illness, it is the period until illness ceases which is compensatable. This has to be assessed, as is everything else, on a balance of probabilities and, for obvious reasons, the estimate approaches being the useful but nasty word a 'guesstimate'.

However, in reaching our conclusions, we have borne in mind that most, if not all, prognoses are guarded in cases in which a claimant is still *ill*. Counsel for the claimants has urged us to bear in mind that, quite apart from the guarded nature of the prognosis, very understandably, some claimants are reluctant to undergo treatment, which involves recollecting the distressing circumstances of the disaster, and may balk at undergoing such treatment. We have no hesitation in accepting this argument.

Vulnerability

The arbitrators also considered the risk of future problems:

An injury to a limb leaves it vulnerable. It is the same with psychiatric problems. All the claimants will be at risk of further illness in the face of stress which would not have affected them or would have affected them less but for their Zeebrugge experience.

This is a factor which must be taken into account when assessing compensation. Following a serious head injury, there is often a risk of epilepsy and an award of damages takes account of that risk. Our awards do likewise in respect of vulnerability to future psychiatric troubles. In our view, it is an important factor which must be borne in mind in each case, although more so in some cases than in others.

Assessment of damages

In considering their awards of damages the arbitrators said:

In 1970, in *Hinz* v *Berry* [1970] 2 QB 40, Lord Denning MR said there were only two cases in which the quantum of damages for nervous shock had been considered and Lord Pearson said that he thought it was the first case in which the Court of Appeal had considered the problem.

Although counsel have gone to great trouble in assembling a comprehensive list of reported cases of damages for nervous shock, the number of such cases is comparatively small. More important, counsel agreed that no clear guidelines can be discerned in the reported cases.

In these circumstances, our assessment must be based not upon consideration of the cases to which our attention was directed but also upon consideration of how each claimant's illness compares with cases in which damages were awarded for physical injuries.

In undertaking this task, we must record our appreciation for the very considerable help given to us by the doctors who gave evidence. It was fortunate both for us and the parties that, plainly, they are of the very highest calibre and competence.

Summary of the main findings of the arbitrators

(a) PTSD is a recognised psychiatric illness.

(b) Many Zeebrugge victims suffered PTSD.

(c) The DSM III R is a useful guide to diagnosis.

(d) Pathological grief is a recognised psychiatric illness in excess of normal grief.

(e) Some survivors suffer from other psychiatric illnesses such as depression and it is possible to suffer from more than one psychiatric illness.

(f) It may be reasonable for survivors to refuse to undergo treatment for psychiatric damage.

(g) Account should be taken in individual cases of any vulnerability to future psychiatric illness.

Case A

A 22-year-old single woman with some pre-existing fear of water. Civil servant. All her party survived. After 24 hours, reaction set in and she wept uncontrollably for two or three days. For several months she had a fear of water so intense that she could not take a bath without someone present to encourage her. She suffered PTSD for about nine months, with nightmares, loss of appetite, loss of libido, feelings of guilt and intrusive thoughts about the capsize. She constantly relived the accident in her mind. In July 1987, psychotherapy was recommended but not taken up. While her fear of water led her to cancel a trip to Sweden in 1987, in 1988 she was able to fly to Corfu and enjoy her holiday although she did not swim. She had received no treatment. The arbitrators found that for practical purposes she had entirely recovered by September 1988. Her physical injuries included bruising to her chest, back, right leg, arm, hands and left index finger. At the site of the bruising on her leg she had developed an irritable skin condition although with treatment the prognosis was good.

Total compensation £9,135.75 made up as follows:

	£	
Fixed payment	5,000.00	(1994: £6,500)
Psychiatric injuries	1,750.00	(1994: £2,275)
Physical injuries	1,250.00	
Special damages	1,135.75	

There was no award for loss of future earnings or earning capacity.

Case B

A 41-year-old married woman. All her party survived. By nine months post-accident she described symptoms of PTSD which were said by the medical experts to be 'moderately severe' and she was said to be 'moderately depressed and anxious'. She was described as 'cheerful and coping' by November 1988 and had been able to resume work as a cashier. Her principal persisting symptom was an unwillingness to be parted from her husband even for short periods to such extent that she had obtained work at the same place as him. However, treatment was advised and the arbitrators found that with treatment she should be back to normal within about 12 months. She had sustained lacerations of her left hand with damage to the tendons in the ring and little fingers and to the digital nerves, ruptured ligaments of the left thumb and multiple contusions including a probable contusion of the right kidney. The left wrist and thumb were in plaster for three weeks and in August 1987 she underwent tendon graft under general anaesthetic when her hand was put in plaster for 12 weeks. She was left with some slight scarring disability and restriction of movement in the hand.

Total compensation £20,160.82 made up as follows:

	£	
Fixed payment	5,000.00	
Psychiatric injuries	3,000.00	(1994: £3,900)
Cost of treatment for	750.00	
psychiatric injuries		
Physical injuries	8,250.00	
Special damages	3,160.82	

There was no award for loss of future earnings or earning capacity.

Case C

A 22-year-old single man. He and his travelling companion both survived. He was employed as a recreation assistant at swimming baths and was hoping to progress to a career in recreational management. He suffered from 'quite severe' PTSD in the months immediately after the incident and consumption of alcohol increased substantially. By November 1988 the symptoms were said to be of 'moderate severity' and consumption of alcohol had reverted to pre-accident level. The arbitrators approached the case on the basis that it was one of moderate psychiatric damage lasting for about three and a half years. He had to give up his job which he greatly enjoyed and was now a chauffeur for a car-hire firm which gave him very little job satisfaction. The arbitrators took into account that at present he was not suffering any loss of earnings or loss of leisure because he was working about the same hours as before and earning slightly more but he had lost his chance of promotion within his chosen career which would have brought higher earnings for shorter hours. The arbitrators thought it likely, however, that once his psychiatric symptoms had abated he would find more congenial and remunerative employment. He had no physical injuries.

Total compensation £21,728.30 made up as follows:

	£	
Fixed payment	5,000.00	
Psychiatric injuries	4,000.00	(1994: £5,200)
Loss of chance of increased leisure and potential loss of earnings	2,000.00	
Actual loss of earnings	7,309.84	
Special damages	3,418.46	

There was no award for loss of future earnings or earning capacity.

Case D

A long distance lorry driver travelling alone, married and aged 42. He suffered severe PTSD involving anxiety, sleeplessness and nightmares, sweating attacks and phobias of water and the sea. The sight of plate-glass windows or the sound of children crying caused him to think of the capsize. He had become severely depressed, irritable and aggressive. In the early stages he was drinking to excess but this problem had now resolved. His level of smoking had also greatly increased and remained high. He found his work as a long distance driver distressing because it meant he was on his own for a great deal of the time and on such occasions his mind dwelt on the capsize. He had therefore changed to work within the depot. It is highly unlikely that he will ever return to his old job. Because of his condition his marriage had come under serious strain. The doctors agreed that he would benefit from a period of regular psychiatric help for his anxiety states coupled with specific treatment for depression. Although he was naturally resistant to such treatment the arbitrators found that with the support of his wife he would undergo treatment and that over the next 12 to 18 months he is likely to make a substantial improvement. Everyone accepted that over the last two years his illness had operated at a very severe level and had greatly exacerbated his vulnerability to stress for the foreseeable future. He had also suffered bruising and whilst acting as a rescuer in the capsize he had strained both his shoulders as a result of hauling on ropes. These had caused significant discomfort for some three months and he is still having some features of painful arc syndrome in his right shoulder. He had also strained both wrists and suffered some discomfort in his back.

Total compensation £21,580.00 made up as follows:

	£	
Fixed payment	5,000.00	
Psychiatric injuries	8,500.00	(1994: £11,050)
Physical injuries	2,500.00	
Special damages	580.00	
**A loss of future earnings/ earning capacity	5,000.00	

£21,580.00—plus interest to be
————— calculated

**This was awarded because the arbitrators accepted that he now had to work longer and harder hours in less congenial employment to maintain his former level of earnings and that if he should give up or lose his present job his range of possible jobs would be restricted because he could not return to long distance driving, but that suitable alternative work could be found by his employers who were a large organisation.

Case E
A 38 year old divorced woman with a teenage daughter (who was also a survivor) living at home. She had been travelling with her mother to whom she was very close and who was killed in dramatic circumstances. The mother's body was not recovered until it was washed ashore some three weeks after the capsize. There was a difference of opinion between the doctors whether she was suffering from an abnormal grief reaction or from hysterical disassociation as a defensive mechanism. It was accepted that either she was suffering from or would suffer from pathological grief and that hysterical dissociation, if present, was designed to protect her feelings of unusually severe grief. She took a great deal of time off work, had had counselling sessions and some in-patient treatment. In addition to her grief reactions she was still suffering from 'classic and severe PTSD' which has been unremitting since the accident, and depression which had greatly improved so as no longer to be pathological. She was hoping to move home soon in which event the prognosis was that within a further year from the move she would be back at work. She would need regular counselling and treatment for depression as an outpatient for one year. She is always likely to be vulnerable to stress but she had very considerable job security as a Civil Servant so that the likelihood of her losing her job was remote in the extreme. In addition she had suffered generalised cuts and bruising.
Total compensation £30,774.07 made up as follows:

	£	
Fixed payment	5,000.00	
Psychiatric injuries	7,500.00	(1994: £9,750)
Cost of future treatment for psychiatric injuries	1,000.00	
Physical injuries	400.00	
Loss of earnings to date	4,398.89	
Future loss of earnings	4,463.43	
Fixed payment for loss of relative	5,000.00	
Special damages	3,011.75	

£30,774.07—plus interest to be
calculated

Case F

A married man aged 41 years. His wife and two friends were killed in the capsize. He had developed chronic PTSD. In particular he was hypersensitive to unexpected noises and suffered panic attacks when faced with reminders of the capsize such as a 10 minute boat trip. His sleep was frequently disturbed and he had become irritable and impatient. He had suffered a profound pathological grief reaction. The arbitrators found that 'every aspect of his everyday life has been affected by the fact that she (his wife) is no longer with him'. There was a discount in respect of the grief which he would have suffered if his wife had died in more ordinary circumstances. He was having difficulties with concentration and was thus afraid about the loss of his job in a managerial position. Out-patient treatment was recommended for 12 to 18 months after which he should have achieved a substantial degree of recovery. He would remain vulnerable to stressful incidents for the foreseeable future. By way of physical injuries he suffered a chest infection which required hospital treatment, multiple bruises and grazes, localised numbness in both heels and discomfort in the right shin. He had also suffered 40% loss of hearing in the left ear and tinnitus due to vascular damage as a result of stress. This had been diagnosed as Menieres Disease giving rise to a 10% risk of bilateral hearing loss. A 'tullio' phenomenon has also been diagnosed which is a startle reaction to veer off (in this case to the right hand side) on hearing a loud noise. He had also suffered some vertigo.

Total compensation (which does not include the fatal accident claim in respect of his wife's death) £41,042.94 made up as follows:

	£	
Fixed payment	5,000.00	
Psychiatric injuries	7,500.00	(1994: £9,750)
Cost of treatment for		
psychiatric injuries	1,000.00	
Physical injuries	20,000.00	
Further fixed payment for		
loss of relative	5,000.00	
Special damages	2,542.94	

£41,042.94—plus interest to be calculated

The arbitrators made no award for loss of earning capacity on the basis that he had managed to continue working in a sophisticated and highly competitive environment during the period since the capsize and therefore was not under any real disadvantage in respect of his earning capacity.

Case G

A divorced lady aged 34 who had been living with a man for some three years before the capsize in which he was killed. His body was not recovered until the vessel was righted on 7 April 1987. She was said to have been one of the most severely affected of the survivors with whom the doctors had been concerned and to have had a 'terrible two years'. She was subject to mood swings, being tearful, miserable and very depressed with suicidal thoughts, and she had been drinking to excess. She had become withdrawn and isolated from her friends, was very reckless about her own safety and was found to be suffering from 'a severe depressive illness'. She had occasional out-patient sessions with a psychiatrist which had not produced much improvement. She needs intensive supportive psychotherapy on a weekly basis for at least 12 months in which case there was a reasonable prospect of getting her 'on her feet' within 18 months from the arbitration. She would quite possibly find herself in stressful situations in the future and being sensitised to further disaster might well have serious problems in the future however successful the short-term treatment may be. The arbitrators found her to be one of the claimants most vulnerable to further problems both in the near and more distant future. She had been in responsible and taxing work as an international auditor which she had to give up. She was now hoping to start a small business. If all went well she would in about 4½ years be back to earning as much as she would have earned but for the accident. Her actual loss over that period would be £36,000 but there was a real risk that because of her psychiatric condition the business would fail which would cause both psychiatric and financial problems.

The arbitrators held that they had to make an appropriate allowance for the very substantial risk of unforeseen difficulties. She had also suffered bruising around her midriff and on the legs.

Total compensation (which did not include the fatal accident claim in respect of her co-habitee) £98,333.00 made up as follows:

	£	
Fixed payment	5,000.00	
Psychiatric injuries	15,000.00	(1994: £19,500)
Physical injuries	400.00	
Loss of earnings to date	21,557.00	
Loss of future earnings/ earning capacity	50,000.00	
Fixed payment for loss of relative	5,000.00	
Special damages	1,376.00	
	£98,333.00—plus interest to be calculated	

Case H

A 14-year-old boy travelling with his family. His mother and elder brother were killed. His father and sister survived. In September 1987 he was diagnosed as suffering from chronic PTSD and prolonged depressive adjustment reaction. By June 1988 he was severely depressed and at times suicidal. His schooling was disrupted by non-attendance. He was still depressed and suffering from PTSD at the time of the arbitration and the arbitrators found him to be 'severely disturbed'. The prognosis was 'quite good' in that with proper in-patient treatment for six to eight weeks with continuing outpatient care he would be 'on his feet' in 18 months to two years. The arbitrators hoped for a 'very substantial recovery' but found a significant risk that treatment would not be successful and he would still be vulnerable to relapse. Before the capsize the claimant was probably of 'A' level ability and might with very hard work have obtained university entrance. With treatment he was expected to return to full time education but there was a significant risk that he would not and would therefore have no academic qualifications. Even if he went back to his studies and recovered most of his pre-accident potential he would be a late starter with a good deal of catching up to do. He would be permanently vulnerable to stress and would have to avoid jobs of a particularly stressful nature. Even if he avoided such jobs he would be vulnerable to relapse and consequent periods of unemployment. He suffered the following physical injuries:

(a)   avulsion of the transverse processes from his first, second, third and fourth lumbar vertebrae on the right side. There was acute pain initially which subsided after about one month and thereafter continued at a reduced level for a further two months or so. He continues to have pain on stressing his back but the prognosis is good. However it is unlikely that transverse processes will fuse again at their fracture site which could create problems if he has to do a lot of lifting. His earning capacity is thus further impaired. He has been advised against participating in sports such as athletics, rugby or football. There will be permanent disability as he will tend to get aching in his lumbar spine particularly after heavy use;

(b)   severe bruising in the area of the kidneys. He had an intra-venous urogram to which he had an allergic reaction such that he almost died;

(c)   a urinary tract infection;

(d)   he developed eczema of both hands and thighs, and it is likely that stress following the disaster has been a factor in producing the disorder. Although there has been improvement, prognosis is uncertain;

(e)   generalised cuts and bruises.

Total compensation £102,453.00 made up as follows:

	£	
Fixed payment	5,000.00	
Psychiatric injuries	20,000.00	(1994: £26,000)
Cost of treatment for psychiatric injuries	8,000.00	
Physical injuries	7,500.00	
Future loss of earnings/ earning capacity	50,000.00	
Fixed payments for loss of relatives	10,000.00	
Special damages	1,953.00	

£102,453.00 — plus interest to be calculated

Case I

A married man aged 26 whose wife and four month old daughter were travelling with him. He and the baby survived but his wife was killed. He was an enlisted soldier but was discharged in July 1988 as no longer medically fit for service. He had formed an intense relationship with his wife and the army. Having lost both he was now 'on his own and totally lost'. He drinks and smokes heavily. By December 1988 he was still profoundly depressed with a high level of anxiety and instrusive obsessional thoughts. With treatment, recovery would take at least another two years and this was optimistic. He was, however, extremely resistent to treatment which was symptomatic of his condition. Without successful treatment and without regaining some motivation in life the outlook was gloomy. With successful treatment he will have had 'four to five years of severe disability'. He had suffered a contusion of the chest and two fractured ribs with some contusion of the underlying lung and one episode of haemophysis (coughing blood). He continues to experience aching in his chest when carrying out heavy work or during inclement weather.

Total compensation (excluding fatal accident claim in respect of his wife) £148,571.12 made up as follows:

	£	
Fixed payment	5,000.00	
Psychiatric injuries	15,000.00	(1994: £19,500)
Physical injuries	2,250.00	
Loss of earnings to date	8,000.00	
Loss of future earnings/ earning capacity/ Army pension rights	109,500.00	
Fixed payment for loss of relative	5,000.00	
Special damages	3,821.12	

£148,571.12—plus interest to be calculated

Case J

A 54-year-old married man working as a tractor driver at a main line railway terminal. His mother, wife, daughter and 10 month old grandchild (all of whom had lived in the same household with him) were killed. The emotional and psychological impact of the disaster had been 'catastrophic'. He is suffering from a depressive illness, pathological grief and severe PTSD. He has suicidal thoughts and had become a heavy drinker and smoker. He was receiving in-patient treatment at the time of the arbitration. The arbitrators found him to be demoralised, bitterly unhappy and depressed and at present totally unable to reconstruct his life. He would never be able to work again. The prognosis was extremely gloomy. Over a period of up to five years with treatment he may become 'more comfortable' in his daily life and may be able to take up some hobby or interest to occupy his mind. His present grief, depression and anxiety would always be with him to some extent. He was the worst of all the survivors the doctors had seen. He was suffering from a pathological grief reaction but the arbitrators 'bore in mind' that anyone who suffered the loss of four relatives would be likely to suffer considerable grief and that they had to assess the extent to which his reaction exceeded that which would be expected after the death of four relatives in other circumstances. He also suffered a hand injury, a whiplash injury of the cervical spine, an injury to the right elbow and an injury to the right middle finger. He has some continuing discomfort in his neck. His right elbow is stiff and will not straighten properly and he has intermittent triggering of the right finger. He has difficulty lifting weights such as suitcases, and stretching up and doing DIY jobs.

Total compensation (excluding fatal accident claims for deceased relatives) £151,114.27 made up as follows:

	£	
Fixed payment	5,000.00	
Psychiatric injuries	30,000.00	(1994: £39,000)
Physical injuries	5,500.00	
Loss of earnings to date	19,026.00	
Future loss of earnings	65,880.00	
Cost of DIY	2,000.00	
Fixed payment for lost		
relative	20,000.00	
Special damages	3,708.27	

£151,114.27—plus interest to be
                calculated[21]

---

[21] The *Herald of Free Enterprise* arbitrations first appeared in the *Personal and Medical Injuries Law Letter*, published by Legal Studies & Services June 1989.

SEVEN

Practical steps

Many detailed accounts are available of the intricacies of practice and procedure,[1] and the following is not intended to be a comprehensive account. Rather, it aims to deal with those issues which may possess special features in a psychiatric injury case.

LIMITATION

Time limits for bringing legal proceedings are governed by the Limitation Act 1980. The limitation period for personal injury claims is set out in s. 11. The period is three years from the accrual of the cause of action, or three years from the date of knowledge, whichever is later. According to s. 14, the date of knowledge is the time when a plaintiff first has knowledge of the following facts:

    (a)   that the injury in question was significant; and
    (b)   that the injury was attributable in whole or in part to the act or omission which is alleged to constitute negligence, nuisance or breach of duty; and
    (c)   the identity of the defendant; and
    (d)   if it is alleged that the act or omission was that of a person other than the defendant, the identity of that person and the additional facts supporting the bringing of an action against the defendant.

[1]See, for example, *Odgers on High Court Pleading and Practice*, 23rd ed. (London: Sweet & Maxwell, 1991); J. Hendy, M. Day and A. Buchan, *Personal Injury Practice* (London: Legal Action Group 1994) and J. M. Pritchard and N. Solomon, *Personal Injury Litigation*, 7th ed. (London: Longman 1992).

An injury is 'significant' if the person whose date of knowledge is in question would reasonably have considered it sufficiently serious to justify instituting proceedings for damages against a defendant who did not dispute liability and was able to satisfy judgment (s. 14(2)).

It was stated in *McCafferty* v *Metropolitan Police District Receiver* [1977] 1 WLR 1073, CA, that the test of significance is partly subjective (did this plaintiff consider it significant?), and partly objective (was it reasonable for the plaintiff not to regard it as significant?). It is clear on the test that significant does *not* mean serious, and that quite minor injuries would pass the test.

Section 14(3) provides that a person's knowledge includes knowledge which he might reasonably have been expected to acquire:

(a)   from facts observable or ascertainable by him; or
(b)   from facts ascertainable by him with the help of medical or other appropriate expert advice which it is reasonable for him to seek;
but a person shall not be fixed under this subsection with knowledge of a fact ascertainable only with the help of expert advice so long as he has taken all reasonable steps to obtain (and, where appropriate, to act on) that advice.

Though not having actual knowledge, a plaintiff may be deemed to have constructive knowledge. The word knowledge should be given its natural meaning: *Davis* v *Ministry of Health* (1985), *The Times*, 7 August 1985, CA. It has been held that the test of constructive knowledge is subjective; in other words at what date would *this plaintiff* have taken advice about his or her condition, rather than at what date would the reasonable person have taken advice.[2] Whether the particular plaintiff can pass this test will depend upon the circumstances. The knowledge concerned will only be knowledge of facts, and not law. The effect of this is that if the plaintiff does seek advice from a non-legal expert, e.g., a doctor, and is advised that he or she is not suffering from any illness, then the plaintiff cannot be said to have knowledge of the illness but advice from a lawyer that there is no claim in law would not have the same effect. Time can begin to run before the plaintiff has knowledge that is detailed enough to enable the legal advisers to draw a statement of claim. In a medical negligence case in the course of a surgical operation, a person alleging negligence is fixed with knowledge that starts the clock running when he knew or could have known, with the help of medical advice reasonably obtainable, that the injury had been caused by damage resulting from something done or not done by the surgeon concerned (*Broadley* v *Guy Clapham & Co.* [1994] 4 All ER, CA).

[2] See *Newton* v *Cammell Laird & Co. (Shipbuilders and Engineers) Ltd* [1969] 1 WLR 415.

There are many factors which may prevent a plaintiff realising that he or she is suffering from an illness, and in many cases this is entirely understandable. People are often positively discouraged from assuming they have a psychiatric injury. The doctors treating organic injuries may be full of optimism for an early and a complete recovery, and a patient who does not wish to dispute this will almost certainly be held to be reasonable.

The provision of the Act giving the court discretion to disapply the time bar is equally important. Section 33(1) states as follows (emphasis added):

> If it appears to the court that it would be *equitable* to allow an action to proceed having regard to the degree to which —
>   (a) the provisions of section 11 (personal injuries) or 12 (fatal accidents) of this Act *prejudice the plaintiff* or *any person whom he represents*; and
>   (b) any decision of the court under this subsection would *prejudice the defendant* or any *person whom he represents*;
> the court may direct that those provisions shall not apply to the action, or shall not apply to any specified cause of action to which the action relates.

It is a question, therefore, of balancing the prejudice to each of the parties. It is important for the plaintiff to show that he or she has a good arguable case, and for the defendant to show that the delay has made the defence more difficult. The court has unfettered discretion,[3] and it is *not* limited to exceptional cases.[4]

This section would be relevant in, for example, cases where the plaintiff did know of his or her illness, but through, say, fear of treatment, was unwilling to obtain the appropriate psychiatric examination, or, *because of his condition*, was unable to take the necessary steps to get proceedings off the ground.

It is important not to confuse s. 11, which is about when the plaintiff knew of a cause of action, and s. 33, which is about the court's discretion to disapply the time bar *even when there is the relevant knowledge*, as they are entirely independent of one another and apply different criteria.

There are many different circumstances in which an apparent time bar may be lifted, and it is always worth looking at the Act's provisions to see if there is a possibility of doing so. The interpretation of limitation in multi-party actions was considered by the Court of Appeal in the case of *Nash* v *Eli Lilly & Co.* [1993] 1 WLR 782. It was held that there was no difference between the court's discretion in an ordinary individual action and a multi-plaintiff action, the cases had to be considered individually. It was also held that the weakness of a case was a relevant consideration as it

---

[3] *Conry* v *Simpson* [1983] 3 All ER 369, CA.
[4] *Firman* v *Ellis* [1978] QB 886.

might be prejudicial and inequitable to allow a dilatory plaintiff to claim in settlement a sum which would reflect the risk in costs to the defendants rather than the fair value of the claim, and it was said that 'knowledge' for the purposes of s. 14 of the 1980 Act imported a state of mind of sufficient certainty that the plaintiff would be reasonably justified in embarking on the preliminaries to making a claim for compensation, and once that knowledge was gained it could not be lost. In *Dobbie* v *Medway Health Authority* [1994] 4 All ER 450, the Court of Appeal disallowed the plaintiff's application for discretion under s. 33. In 1973 she had been admitted to hospital to have a lump removed from her breast for diagnostic purposes only. When she came round from surgery, she was horrified to discover that the whole of her breast had been removed. She suffered psychiatric injury as a result of this. After surgery, the hospital tested the removed tissue and found that the lump was benign. It was not until 15 years later, in 1988, that the plaintiff discovered that her breast should not have been removed before the tissue had been tested. The court held that the plaintiff had knowledge within the meaning of s. 14(1), Sir Thomas Bingham MR said:

> The personal injury on which the plaintiff seeks to found her claim is the removal of her breast and the psychological and physical harm which followed. She knew of this injury within hours, days or months of the operation and she, at all times, reasonably considered it to be significant. She knew from the beginning that the personal injury was capable of being attributed to, or more bluntly was the clear and direct result of, an act or omission of the health authority. What she did not appreciate until later was that the health authority's act or omission was (arguably) negligent or blameworthy. But her want of that knowledge did not stop time beginning to run.

The court denied her application for discretion under s. 33, Sir Thomas Bingham MR concluding his judgment:

> I approach this aspect on the basis that the plaintiff is a grievously injured woman who has suffered much and whose claim, if allowed to proceed, might prove to be very strong. But the delay in this case, after the date of actual knowledge is very lengthy indeed. The plaintiff could have taken advice and issued proceedings before she did. Sympathetic though anyone reading these papers must be to the plaintiff, it would in my judgment (as in that of the judge) be unfair to require the health authority to face this claim arising out of events which took place so long ago.

The question of the prejudicial effect on the parties if discretion were exercised under s. 33(1), was considered in *Hartley* v *Birmingham City*

District Council [1992] 2 All ER 213. The reason for delay in issuing proceedings was the fault of the plaintiff's solicitors who issued proceedings one day out of time. The Court of Appeal held that the only proper question for the judge to ask himself in exercising his unfettered discretion under s. 33(1) was whether it would be equitable to allow the action to proceed. Where the defendant had been presented with a cast iron but windfall limitation defence, this was a factor to be taken into account along with the fact that allowing the action to proceed would not affect the defendant's ability to defend the action. It is significant that this was a case strong on its facts.

The case of *Stubbings v Webb* [1993] AC 498 concerned a plaintiff who applied to the court pursuant to s. 11(4)(b), contending that the limitation period had not begun to run until she had the requisite knowledge under the Act that the injury she had received was 'significant'. The injury was psychological caused by childhood sexual abuse by her adoptive father and brother. The Court of Appeal held that although she knew, probably within three years of her majority, and certainly knew more than three years before issuing the writ, that she had suffered a significant impairment of her mental condition, such that it would have been reasonable to issue proceedings, she did not know (nor could she reasonably be expected to know) that the impairment was attributable to the defendant's acts of sexual abuse. She had sued within three years of acquiring that knowledge. However, the House of Lords upheld the defendant's appeal, holding that the discretion afforded by s. 11 to extend or refuse to apply the limitation period in personal injury actions did not apply to actions for intentional trespass to the person. It followed, therefore, that in this case, the causes of action were subject to a six-year limitation period suspended until she attained her majority (by virtue of s. 28 of the 1980 Act). The period had expired many years before she issued her writ, and there were no provisions for extending this period. Her actions were, therefore, statute-barred. This is a most unsatisfactory decision. For example, an allegation of battery in, say, a medical negligence action where the appropriate consent was not obtained to a surgical procedure, would be subject to the fixed six-year limitation period, with no discretion to extend.

In cases of, for example, exposure to contamination which *may* result in injury on the part of the 'worried well' (see p. 71), there is no mechanism to stop the limitation clock. In a multi-party action courts may impose a cut off date by which claims should be made. Plaintiffs in such a case may have to rely on a liberal interpretation of s. 33 discretion to bring their claims at a later date. In the USA the increasing use of class actions is being developed to obtain from the court, a certified class of 'future victims' who are as yet unidentified, but for whom a compensation fund is established by the defendants (see, for example, *Re Agent Orange Product Liability Litigation* 597 F Supp 740 (EDNY 1984)).

DELAY AFTER ISSUE OF PROCEEDINGS

Once the writ has been issued, and throughout the pre-trial process, it is open to the defendant to make an application for the action to be struck out for failure to comply with procedural matters or dismissed for want of prosecution. The application to strike out can be made when there has been inexcusable delay in complying with the time limits imposed by the Rules of the Supreme Court in respect of the various steps that have to be taken, such as serving the writ or the statement of claim, complying with the automatic directions imposed by RSC, ord 25, r. 5, if appropriate, or taking out a summons for directions if not appropriate, or setting down, or any peremptory order the court may have made. There is some dispute as to whether delay will be sufficient to warrant striking out only if the limitation period has already expired. It is generally thought that striking out before the expiry of the limitation period would be fruitless as the plaintiff would merely commence a further action, but in *Janov* v *Morris* [1981] 2 WLR 1389, it was stated that if a plaintiff fails to comply with a peremptory order without explanation and the action is struck out, then it is within the court's discretion to strike out a second action on the same cause brought within the limitation period.

Dismissal for want of prosecution can take place if there has been delay which is inordinate and inexcusable or delay which gives rise to a substantial risk that it is not possible to have a fair trial. Inordinate delay is that which is materially longer than that which the courts and lawyers are accustomed to, and delay is inexcusable when it is caused by the plaintiff and/or his or her advisers. Delay which is due to the non-culpable behaviour of the plaintiff ascribable to a medical condition is not inexcusable and should be explained by reference to the opinion of medical advisers. See *Birkett* v *James* [1978] AC 297, HL.

In medical negligence cases, the court will be concerned that the hospital and/or the doctors should not have a case hanging over them for many years; this may be regarded as prejudicial in certain circumstances.[5]

It is possible for a split trial to be ordered if there is likely to be delay because prognosis is a problem, or if the plaintiff is undergoing a long course of therapy the result of which it is desirable to know before considering quantum. All that needs to be shown is that it would be just and convenient if liability were tried first, and then, if the plaintiff is successful, for quantum to be considered at a later date. This could be advantageous for the defendant in circumstances where it is felt that liability may prove difficult

[5] See *Biss* v *Lambeth, Southwark and Lewisham Area Health Authority (Teaching)* [1978] 1 WLR 382 — delay of over 11 years, action struck out. Contrast *Westaway* v *South Glamorgan Health Authority*, CA, 9 June 1986, where the action was not dismissed after 10 years because the delay, though inordinate and inexcusable, was not prejudicial.

for the plaintiff to establish, but where quantum may involve costly expert evidence. The application is made by summons in the normal way. In certain cases it may be more appropriate to ask for provisional damages (see page 106).

Striking out for failure to comply with procedural requirements can also be done in the county court, and practitioners should note the Draconian provisions of the automatic directions procedure under CCR, ord. 17, r. 11, under which, if no request for trial is made within 15 months of close of pleadings the action is automatically struck out. It may be possible to restore a case under the provisions of CCR, ord. 13, r. 4, which says:

(1) Except as otherwise provided, the period within which a person is required or authorised by these rules or by any judgment, order or direction to do any act in any proceedings may be extended or abridged by consent of all the parties or by the court on the application of any party.

(2) Any such period may be extended by the court although the application for extension is not made until after the expiration of the period.

However, good evidence in support of such an application will be required.

In *Rastin v British Steel* (1994), *The Times*, 14 February 1994, CA, it was held that on an application to reinstate an action automatically struck out, the court would consider whether the plaintiff had conducted the case with due diligence and whether there was prejudice to the defendant.

Although there is no specific power in the County Court Rules to dismiss for want of prosecution, the county court has such a power by virtue of the County Courts Act 1984, s. 76, which applies High Court practice to the county court.

DISCOVERY

Claims for psychiatric injury employ the usual mechanisms for discovery of documents. It is worth looking at discovery of medical records in some detail here as they can have great significance. There are two main areas to consider. First, there is access by the plaintiff to his or her own medical records and secondly, there is access by the defendant to the plaintiff's records.

The plaintiff will certainly require his or her own records if pursuing damages for psychiatric injury in a medical negligence claim, as, unless the negligence was blatant, it is almost impossible to assess the prospects of success without sight of the relevant medical and nursing notes, X-rays, reports and correspondence. The plaintiff may also require these documents to rebut allegations from the defendants or to substantiate or clarify susceptibility to psychiatric injury.

If discovery is required before commencement of proceedings, as in a medical negligence claim, there are two possible routes: an application to the court pursuant to the Supreme Court Act 1981, s. 33 (or the County Courts Act 1984, s. 52(2)), or reliance upon the Access to Health Records Act 1990.

An application under s. 33 or s. 52(2) is to avoid hopeless actions being commenced. The provisions restrict the power to cases involving personal injury or death. The procedure is governed by RSC, ord. 24, r. 7A, in the High Court and CCR ord. 13, r. 7(3) in the county court.

On the hearing of the application:

> ... the court, if satisfied that discovery is not necessary, or not necessary at that stage of the cause or matter, may dismiss or, as the case may be, adjourn the application and shall in any case refuse to make such an order if and so far as it is of opinion that discovery is not necessary either for disposing fairly of the cause or matter or for saving costs. (RSC, ord. 24, r. 8.)

The person against whom an order is sought must be someone who appears to the court to be likely to be a party to the proceedings, and to be likely to have possession or custody of, or power over, documents which are relevant to an issue arising or likely to arise out of that claim. It is up to the plaintiff to satisfy the court that an order for pre-action discovery is likely to assist in disposing of the matter fairly or be a saving on costs, but it is not necessary to show that the plaintiff already has a good cause of action. See *Dunning* v *United Liverpool Hospitals Board of Governors* [1973] 1 WLR 586, CA, and *Shaw* v *Vauxhall Motors Ltd* [1974] 1 WLR 1035 CA, in which latter case it was also held that before the summons is issued a letter before action should be sent to the party against whom the order is sought, setting out the documents which are required and the reasons why they are relevant.

In medical negligence cases, it is increasingly common for the health authorities to give voluntary disclosure, upon receipt of details of the allegations of negligence to be made. Department of Health Circular CH 8216 sets out the official position on disclosure. Sometimes it is not possible to give anything other than the most basic allegations, but this should not defeat an application for pre-action discovery if voluntary disclosure is not forthcoming. 'Fishing expeditions'[6] are not encouraged, but it must be remembered that the purpose of the application is to assess a case before litigation, and the plaintiff and his or her adviser will not be expected to enter into complex medical argument at that stage. It must also be understood that few medical experts will offer any opinion until they have seen the

---

[6] See *Roper* v *Slack and Parr* [1981] CLY 2165.

medical notes concerned. It is important to note that the legislation provides for disclosure to the legal advisors and any suggestion that disclosure should be made to the plaintiff's medical expert only should be strongly resisted. There are matters in all medical notes which should be checked with the plaintiff personally and this should be done before the notes are sent to the medical expert, together with any of the plaintiff's comments which are appropriate. These are such things as chronology of events, accuracy of those parts of the notes allegedly recorded from the plaintiff's own subjective accounts, advice alleged to have been given to the plaintiff, and so on.

The fact that the limitation period has expired is not a good reason on its own for refusing an order, unless it is clear that the case is doomed to failure.[7]

It is open to the defendant to raise privilege in respect of certain types of documents which may be sought, e.g., confidential reports and the like, but this should be carefully scrutinised.[8] Disclosure can be refused if it is thought that disclosure is not in the public interest, and to assist in the decision, the court can inspect the documents if necessary.

This provision is not available if the plaintiff wishes to obtain discovery from someone who is not a likely party to the action. In that case the application must be made after commencement of the action, pursuant to Supreme Court Act 1981, s. 34, or, in the county court, pursuant to the County Courts Act 1984, s. 53 (see below).

The Access to Health Records Act 1990 provides for a patient (or in appropriate cases a patient's representative) to obtain access to records made by a health professional in connection with the patient's care and treatment. There are circumstances in which the right is limited (e.g., the disclosure of the information might cause serious physical or mental harm to any person or the record would disclose information about an identifiable third party without his or her consent). The Act applies only to medical records prepared on or after 1 November 1991, unless the patient can successfully argue that, without earlier records, the later records are incomprehensible. Under the Data Protection Act 1984, a patient has access to computerised records. This is subject to limitations similar to those in the 1990 Act.

Discovery against non-parties

Discovery orders can be made against non-parties to an action. It may, for example, be necessary to obtain details of the work history of a plaintiff, particularly useful if there is any allegation of malingering, but the employer(s) may be unwilling to supply the information.

The procedure is by way of summons which should state that the application is made pursuant to the Supreme Court Act 1981, s. 34(2), and

---

[7] See *Harris* v *Newcastle-upon-Tyne Health Authority* [1989] 1 WLR 96, CA.
[8] See *Lee* v *South West Thames Regional Health Authority* [1985] 1 WLR 845.

ord. 24, r. 7A(2), and should specify the documents in respect of which the order is sought. It should be supported by an affidavit which should show how the documents are relevant to an issue arising or likely to arise, and that the person against whom the order is sought is likely to have possession or custody of, or power over, the documents.

The county court procedure is very similar, and is governed by the County Courts Act 1984, s. 53.

INTERIM PAYMENTS

In serious cases where it will take some time to assess damages, where treatment under the NHS is unavailable or unsuitable, or in cases where there is financial hardship, it may be appropriate to make an application to the court for an interim payment. Psychiatric injuries can have potentially disastrous effects upon earning capacity, and financial difficulties can delay recovery, so an application for an interim payment should be seriously considered. Similarly, it may be that, for example, psychotherapy is unavailable through the NHS and a payment to cover the cost of that could be made. The possible advantage of this to the defendant should always be kept in mind: recovery or improvement at the earliest possible stage will reduce the damages eventually payable. Although financial hardship is a factor that may be taken into account, it is not a prerequisite of entitlement to an interim payment. It is rare but not unheard of for a defendant to propose interim funding to assist the plaintiff's recovery and this is to be encouraged in the interests of all concerned.

An application can be made for an interim payment at any time after the writ has been served on the defendant and the time limit for the defendant to acknowledge service has expired. The circumstances in which the court can order an interim payment are contained within the Supreme Court Act 1981, s. 32, and RSC, ord. 29, r. 10, and are as follows:

(a)   the defendant is insured in respect of the claim, *or* is a public authority, *or* is a person whose means and resources are such as to enable him to make the interim payment; *and*

(b)   the defendant has admitted liability, or has had judgment obtained against him for damages to be assessed, *or* the court is satisfied that if the action proceeded to trial, the plaintiff would obtain judgment for substantial damages.

The admission of liability may be in the pleadings or it may be in correspondence, or even an oral admission.[9] It may be implied from

---

[9] See *Re Beeny* [1894] 1 Ch 499.

pleadings, or it may come from elsewhere, e.g., a conviction for careless driving.

The procedure is by summons which should claim a specific sum and state the grounds of the application. There should be an affidavit in support which confirms the amount of damages claimed as an interim payment, if necessary by reference to loss of earnings, expenses incurred etc. Relevant documentation should be exhibited. The ground of the application should be confirmed, together with details of any relevant financial hardship, future medical expenditure etc. If there is a relevant criminal conviction, then a memorandum of that conviction should also be exhibited. If there is financial hardship, that should be stated in the affidavit, but hardship is not a necessary prerequisite for an award to be made.[10] In the case of *Stringman* v *McArdle* (1993) *The Times*, 19 November 1993, it was held that it was not appropriate for the judge to question what will be done with the money.

In the county court, an interim payment can be awarded pursuant to CCR, ord. 13, r. 12(1).

DISCLOSURE OF MEDICAL HISTORY

In a psychiatric injury case it will be normal for both sides to require access to the plaintiff's medical history. The evaluation of the plaintiff's pre-aecident disposition is important for an understanding of the effect of the trauma experienced and its severity. The medical records may give rise to issues of causation, the reasons why the trauma may have had a (more or less) dramatic impact on the plaintiff and the prognosis for recovery.

Medical records may reveal a predisposition to mental illness; this *may* mean a reduction in damages. However, they may also reveal that the manifestation of mental illness took place a long time ago, and had not recurred until the incident which has now triggered and/or exacerbated the previous condition.

In addition to examination of the GP's records, it may also be desirable for a statement to be taken from the general practitioner who has known the plaintiff for some and who may well be able to indicate with some force and accuracy the effect of the incident upon the plaintiff. For example, in *Brice* v *Brown* [1984] 1 All ER 997, Stuart-Smith J was most impressed by the evidence of the plaintiff's general practitioner:

> I was much impressed by Dr Green. He had the great advantage of knowing the patient for a period well before this accident and has seen much of her since. He is clearly a thoughtful and intelligent man; he is not

---

[10] See *Schott Kem Ltd* v *Bentley* [1991] 1 QB 61.

a trained psychiatrist, but like many general practitioners has much experience of psychiatric problems. (At p. 1005.)

RSC, ord. 25, r. 8, provides for automatic directions in personal injury cases limiting expert witnesses to two medical experts and one expert of any other kind. Of course, there is nothing to stop a party to the action applying for different or further directions, if there is a good reason to do so. For example, in a psychiatric injury case, there may be a need for more than two medical experts, if, as will usually be the case, there is a need for an expert report on the physical injuries too. This could be because evidence of the psychiatric injury may need to be given by both psychiatrist and psychologist. In a head injury case, there would also be the evidence of a neurosurgeon if there is physical brain damage. Similarly, if there is a problem with employment or rehabilitation, consultants in both disciplines are available.

The plaintiff's report should be disclosed only on the undertaking of the defendant to forward his report in exchange. In other words exchange should normally be simultaneous, and not sequential. If reports are to be agreed then they must be agreed on all material points.

Until 1987, in medical negligence cases, medical expert evidence on the question of liability was not normally disclosed between the parties. However, RSC, ord. 38, r. 37, now provides that there shall be mutual disclosure of expert reports, unless the court considers that there are special reasons for not doing so.

MEDICAL EVIDENCE

Instructing your expert psychiatrist or psychologist

It is important to say a word or two here about the different experts that may be involved in a psychiatric injury claim. Psychiatrists are medically qualified, and can prescribe drug treatments in appropriate cases. They can also use techniques of psychotherapy, analysis and behavioural therapy, although if these become necessary, a clinical psychologist may become involved. Clinical psychologists are not usually medically qualified, but are trained in the treatment of various psychiatric and psychological disorders.

As psychiatrists are medically qualified it may, therefore, be appropriate to instruct a psychiatrist in the first instance. In addition, the plaintiff may be suffering from other physical disorders which the psychiatrist should be able to identify. If the psychiatrist believes that psychological treatment is necessary then this may either be carried out by a psychiatrist or a clinical psychologist. The extent of the medical evidence to be given at trial will then depend upon the diagnosis, treatment and prognosis.

Unlike a claim involving a physical injury, where the initial referral to the medical expert is for a report on a known injury and with emphasis on prognosis, the psychiatric injury case may involve an instruction letter that emphasises the need for careful diagnosis, possibly by reference to the criteria contained in DSM IV and ICD 10.

Where the client's degree of psychiatric injury is less clear, or where there are signs more indicative of behavioural problems rather than mental disorder, it may be sensible to instruct a psychologist as a first step. As an aid to diagnosis, psychologists often use self-assessment questionnaires which they require patients to complete (see p. 98). Such questionnaires are discoverable as part of the plaintiff's medical evidence if referred to in a subsequent medical report.

Having decided whether to instruct a psychiatrist or a psychologist, or both, it is necessary to choose the expert. In this area of personal injury law, it is particularly important for the expert to be experienced in the courtroom. Although their expertise is usually in the realm of the criminal law, forensic psychiatrists may also have a good knowledge of psychiatric injury and may be particularly useful as an expert witness. Appendix 4 lists some of the specialist clinics in this field.

The medical examination itself

By the plaintiff's doctor
It is worth mentioning again the need for sensitivity when instructing your expert(s). It is also important to give full and detailed instructions to your doctor, so he knows precisely what has happened to this plaintiff, including a copy of the plaintiff's statement. It may also help to arrange for a spouse or other close relative to attend to assist the expert about pre- and post-accident behaviour.

By the defendant
A plaintiff who sues for damages for personal injury must permit a medical examination to be carried out on behalf of the defendant, and the court will stay the action if the plaintiff unreasonably refuses to submit to an examination (*Edmeades* v *Thames Board Mills Ltd* [1969] 2 QB 67, CA). It is not reasonable to refuse examination because the doctor who is to carry it out is believed to be a 'defence doctor', although it was held reasonable to refuse if the doctor concerned had a reputation for being hostile to plaintiffs: see *Hall* v *Avon Area Health Authority (Teaching)* [1980] 1 WLR 481, CA, in which it was also held that it was reasonable to refuse if the plaintiff was in a highly nervous state, or was confused by the effects of a brain injury. In *Hall* the following was also established: the plaintiff could not insist upon the presence at the examinations of either her own doctor, or her own medical

expert, nor could she make it conditional upon a disclosure of the ensuing report. On the other hand, it was held that it may be reasonable to insist upon a doctor of the same sex carrying out the examination, or it may be reasonable for a third party to be present. Note also *Larby* v *Thurgood* [1993] ICR 66 where it was held that a plaintiff could refuse to be interviewed by the defendant's employment expert as job prospects etc. were issues of fact that could be determined by evidence at trial. The concerns of plaintiffs who are suffering from some psychiatric disorder can be given due consideration in deciding what is reasonable. On the other hand, the defence can, if it is reasonable to do so, insist upon a psychiatric examination.[11]

If the examination by the defendant's expert goes beyond pure examination and involves tests etc. then there is greater reason for refusal because of risk to health. It may be reasonable to refuse even if there is only a very slight risk.[12] In *Osman* v *British Midland Airways Limited* [1994] PMILL May 1994, Vol. 10, No. 4 an application to stay proceedings until the plaintiff agreed to be examined by the defendant's psychiatrist was refused as the plaintiff's *bona fides* were not in issue and the real reason for requesting the examination was a refusal of payment into court.

The medical report

As in any other personal injury case, the medical report should deal fully with the circumstances in which the injuries were caused and it should be clear that every aspect of the injuries has been covered in the report. Care should be taken to make sure that the medical evidence is consistent and coextensive with both the plaintiff's own evidence and witnesses. The plaintiff's lawyers should make sure that any symptoms which are cited by lay witnesses (e.g., depression, inability to concentrate, irritability) are dealt with in the report. If there is more than one medical report then inconsistencies, if any, should be noted and reconciled. The costs of private medical treatment such as psychotherapy, and, if appropriate, rehabilitation, should be clearly stated and care should be taken to avoid underestimating them.

Other evidence

The plaintiff's case is always going to be that *this* particular event produced *this* particular effect upon his or her mind. The importance of personal testimony cannot be overestimated.

In cases where proximity is the issue, full and detailed proofs of evidence are vital. If the issue is proximity to the event itself, then, as well as personal

---

[11] See *Lane* v *Willis* [1972] 1 WLR 326.
[12] See *Aspinall* v *Sterling Mansell Ltd* [1981] 3 All ER 866, CA.

evidence, the plaintiff should assemble as much external evidence as possible. This could be in the form of plans and photographs, to show exactly where the plaintiff was at the relevant times, and evidence of the timings involved. Whilst the temporal factor is not the only one in event-proximity cases, in practice it is of considerable importance; the later the plaintiff arrives on the scene, the more likely that emergency crews and hospital staff will have reduced the likelihood of a traumatic scene.

External evidence of the horror of the situation can also be of great importance. In *Brice* v *Brown* [1984] 1 All ER 997, the plaintiff (admittedly with some predisposition to mental illness) suffered dreadful psychiatric illness following a relatively minor road accident. She herself was hardly injured at all, but her daughter suffered a visually frightening, but in practice not a serious, head injury. At the trial the father of the child gave evidence as to the child's appearance, as stated by Stuart-Smith J:

> She now has a 10 cm scar running from the eye up into the hairline, and it is perhaps difficult from that to realise quite how alarming that injury must have seemed at the time. The husband, who saw her in hospital, thought that she had lost the whole of her scalp because the skin contracted upwards over the head.

Similarly, in cases where the witnessing of injury to others is in issue and the relationship of the witness to the injured person is not that of parent or spouse, evidence must be produced of the closeness of that relationship, both by personal testimony, and by statements from those who know the parties and their relationship. External evidence, such as wills or gifts, should also be obtained if available.

Since 1988 the court has had power (RSC, ord. 38, r. 2A) to direct the disclosure of written statements of the oral evidence which the party intends to lead on any issues of fact to be decided at the trial. The emphasis is now leaning heavily towards this, so careful pagination of witness statements is crucial for the optimum presentation of the case.

PLEADINGS

Plaintiff lawyers should note that the following matters should be included in the particulars of injuries on the statement of particulars of claim: the plaintiff's date of birth; the nature of the injury, details of the medical treatment already received, the continuing effect of the injury and any disability for work suffered as a result. It has also been necessary since June 1990 to serve a medical report with the statement of particulars of claim. Practitioners will be aware that the rules (RSC, ord. 18, r. 12(1A) and CCR, ord. 6, r. 1(5) and (7)) specify 'a medical report' and do not preclude the provision of further reports at a later stage in the proceedings. There is a temptation on the part of defendants to ask for further and better particulars of the plaintiff's exposure to the traumatic event, but the courts are not sympathetic to excessive or inappropriate requests (see *British Airways Pension Trustees Ltd* v *Sir Robert McAlpine & Sons Ltd*, unreported, 15 December 1994, CA).

TRIAL

The possibility of a split trial has already been considered at page 148. The more problematic situation of decisions on preliminary points was considered in *Attia* v *British Gas plc* [1988] QB 304, CA. In that case the parties asked the court to decide, as a preliminary point, whether witnessing destruction of property (as opposed to witnessing or experiencing threat of, physical injury) could give rise to a claim for damages for nervous shock. At first instance the judge found for the defendants and, on appeal, the Court of Appeal found for the plaintiff, but also commented on the suitability of the matter for decision as a preliminary point. Bingham LJ stated:

> ... one must be very cautious in determining questions of fact on assumed facts, and the risk of doing so unfairly to one side or the other is increased where, as here, the parties were by no means strangers to each other before the careless act occurred. In deciding what the defendants should reasonably have foreseen I would wish to have a much fuller picture than pleadings can give of the plaintiff's personality and circumstances as manifested to and known by the defendants.

Strain on the plaintiff

In the period coming up to trial and during the trial itself, it is important to be aware of the strain that the plaintiff will be under. Giving evidence, and anticipation thereof, may be extremely distressing for the plaintiff. The whole of the distressing events which have caused the plaintiff's injury will have to be recounted in detail. The effect this is likely to have on the plaintiff at trial and during the weeks beforehand, should be taken into consideration by the practitioners involved. The plaintiff should be reassured that his or her advisers appreciate the situation and can provide patience and sympathy. It may be necessary for the plaintiff to leave the court during parts of the trial.

Children

Special care is needed where a child is suffering from psychiatric injury, and may, for example, have suffered from violence or sexual abuse. Special care will have to be taken to ensure that the child's evidence can be given under circumstances sympathetic to the child. Unfortunately, there are no procedures in the civil courts parallel to those in the criminal courts whereby video-linked evidence can be given by children. It would be up to the child's lawyer to obtain the appropriate direction at the time of setting down.

COSTS

A plaintiff suffering from psychiatric injuries may be a time-consuming client, and plaintiff lawyers may be concerned about whether the additional time spent with the client, taking instructions, explaining procedures and preparing the client for trial, can ever be recovered. It should be possible to recover the costs reasonably incurred in dealing with such a client. We are grateful to Simon John of Cunningham John & Co. for a copy of the review of taxation in *Evason* v *Essex Health Authority* [1994] PMILL February 1994, Vol. 10, No. 1. This concerned a woman who had been wrongly diagnosed as suffering from cancer with devastating financial and psychiatric consequences. It was accepted by the court that her special and unusual needs for personal attendance should be taken into account, and the appropriate allowances were given for the additional time spent with her.

ARBITRATION

Whilst arbitration has long been a popular procedure for solving certain forms of dispute, it is not a forum usually used for the resolution of personal injury cases. However, a number of the plaintiffs in the *Herald of Free Enterprise* litigation agreed to have their cases dealt with by arbitration (see page 129), and it is worth noting the most salient features of the arbitration procedure.

The first point of note is that the parties must *agree* to refer a dispute to arbitration, and they must also agree to be legally bound by that decision. Arbitration should be distinguished from conciliation and mediation as these processes do not result in legally binding and enforceable decisions. Anyone can be an arbitrator (subject to the general rules of natural justice, and subject, of course, to the agreement of the parties). In the *Herald of Free Enterprise* arbitration, the arbitrators were three Queen's counsel, highly experienced in personal injury matters. Arbitrations are at present governed by the Arbitration Acts of 1950, 1975 and 1979, with a number of provisions in the Supreme Court Act 1981 and the Courts and Legal Services Act 1990 which are relevant to arbitrations.

The courts have limited powers under ss. 22 and 23 of the 1979 Act to set aside an award for want of jurisdiction or to remove an arbitrator for misconduct. Similarly, there is a very limited right of appeal against an arbitrator's award on the ground that it raises a question of law of general public importance (ss. 1(7) and 2(3) of the 1979 Act). Because of the nature of arbitration, there are unlikely to be enforcement problems, but if there are, then the award can be enforced in exactly the same way as if it was a court judgment.

Generally, the advantages of arbitration are said to be speed, flexibility and cheapness. Because there are no formal rules as to the conduct of an arbitration, the procedures used can be adapted by the parties to suit the particular needs of the case. The relaxed nature of the proceedings may make arbitration more attractive to parties with psychiatric problems, who may find the prospect of formal court proceedings frightening. This was a significant feature of the *Herald of Free Enterprise* arbitrations. Given the ever-present concerns about the delay and expenses within the civil justice system, it may be that increased use of arbitration will be a feature of future personal injury litigation.

EIGHT
Future developments

This chapter will examine those aspects of psychiatric injury claims which we believe are the most unsatisfactory, but will also highlight the more encouraging developments. The two areas which cause us most concern, are, firstly, the way in which psychiatric injury is regarded differently from physical injury, and, secondly, the restrictive requirements placed upon plaintiffs in 'nervous shock' cases, i.e. when the injury is the result of negligence. These latter requirements are, of course, related to the first of our concerns, inasmuch as the way in which psychiatric injury is regarded is responsible for the legal restrictions which are placed on 'nervous shock' claims.

THE PHYSICAL/PSYCHIATRIC DISTINCTION

The first concern, however, is wider than just the conceptual issues in tort: it extends to the general suspicion that psychiatric injury claims, whether in negligence or elsewhere, are open to exaggeration, and even fakery. This fear is connected with the 'floodgates' argument, which we examine in detail below. There are, tests well-known to psychiatry for investigating claims and eliminating any that may be bogus (see e.g., *Diagnostic and Statistical Manual of Mental Disorders IV*, and the 'script-driven imagery' referred to below).

There is no evidence to suggest that it is easier to fake psychiatric illness than to fake physical pain, and it seems to be an affront to the profession of psychiatry to use this argument at all. Fortunately, there is increasing awareness among lawyers, including a number of well-respected judges, of the types and degrees of severity of psychiatric illness and its consequences. It is hoped that this proper liberalisation of judicial attitudes will continue. We examine some of the more enlightened judgments in this chapter.

It is also hoped that the increasingly sophisticated methods of diagnosis and analysis in the medical field will do much to allay any remaining fears about exaggerated or fraudulent claims. For example, we have described the technique of script-driven imagery, where such things as the subject's heart rate, sweat gland activity and muscle tension are measured as the subject recalls traumatic experiences (see p. 102). There are also the developments within the assessment of PTSD and other psychiatric injuries, through such mechanisms as the administration of the Structured Clinical Interview for PTSD (SCID) and the Clinician Administered PTSD Scale (CAPS) (see p. 100). Most exciting, are the developments in the field of neurochemistry, where research has indicated that it may be possible to *physically* identify trauma-induced conditions within the brain (see p. 56).

The last point relating to physical damage within the nervous system caused by traumatic experiences, brings us to the specific requirements imposed upon a plaintiff in 'nervous shock' claims. If it becomes possible in the future to identify physical damage within the plaintiff's neurochemistry then it would be illogical to retain these requirements.

PROXIMITY

However, at present in a nervous shock case, the non-physically injured plaintiff must have either:

(a)   suffered the injury because of reasonable fear of injury to himself; or
(b)   suffered the injury because of reasonable fear of or real injury to another.

In the latter case, the injured/threatened person must stand in a special relationship to the plaintiff (what we have called 'relationship proximity'), *and* the plaintiff must have experienced the causative event itself or its immediate aftermath through his/her unaided senses ('event proximity'). Although we have some comments to make in relation to relationship proximity and the mere bystander, it is the requirement of event proximity which appears to be arbitrary and which results in injustice. It is illustrative of this that in *McLoughlin* v *O'Brian* [1983] 1 AC 410 the plaintiff recovered damages because when she arrived at the hospital her husband and surviving children were still covered in blood and dirt and in states of disorder. If the hospital had been able to clean up and sedate the accident victims before she arrived, then, despite the traumatic effect on her seeing her frightened and severely injured family, and of being informed of the death of one of her children, she would not have succeeded.

To expand further upon this point, it is interesting to look at two first instance decisions made before the House of Lords decision in *Alcock*: *Hevican v Ruane* [1991] 4 All ER 907 and *Ravenscroft v Rederiaktiebolaget Transatlantic* [1991] 3 All ER 65.

In *Hevican v Ruane*, the plaintiff's 14-year-old son had been killed when the school bus was involved in a road accident. The accident happened at 4 pm. The plaintiff, the boy's father, was told about the accident very shortly afterwards and, just before 6 pm, was told by the police that his son was dead. At 7 pm he identified his son's body in the mortuary. The plaintiff suffered a reactive depression and had to give up work. When the case came to trial, there was no dispute about the plaintiff's medical condition: the trial issue was about liability on the second limb of the proximity test — 'event proximity'.

Mantell J was the trial judge, and he acknowledged the authority of *McLoughlin v O'Brian* on 'event proximity'. He interpreted this as a recognition of the principle that there must be a causal connection between the event and the damage caused, but, using the authority of the House of Lords' cases of *Home Office v Dorset Yacht Co. Ltd* [1970] AC 1004 and *Smith v Littlewoods Organisation Ltd* [1987] AC 241, he said that as long as each link in the causal chain could be established by foreseeability, then spatio/temporal separation would not defeat a claim. Mantell J went on to say:

> So if proximity in either sense is to be used to bar this plaintiff's claim, it can only be because of an arbitrary rule special to cases of nervous shock.

The judge refused to accept such an arbitrary rule. It would have been open to him to find that the identification of the body was part of the immediate aftermath of the accident, but refused to do so, finding for the plaintiff purely and simply on the basis of foreseeability and the justified development of the common law, quoting Lord Bridge in *McLoughlin v O'Brian*:

> I have no doubt that this is an area of the law of negligence where we should resist the temptation to try yet once more to freeze the law in a rigid posture which would deny justice to some who, in the application of the classic principles of negligence derived from *Donoghue v Stevenson* [1932] AC 562, ought to succeed. . . .

In *Hevican* the judge found in favour of the plaintiff, but, following the *Alcock* decision in the House of Lords the case was successfully appealed.

In *Ravenscroft*, a woman suffered a prolonged grief reaction (classified as a depressive illness in ICD 10), following the death of her adult son in an industrial accident. She learned of his death about two hours afterwards, and, although she was at the hospital, did not see his body because her husband prevented her from doing so (the accident had been violent, and her husband feared that the body would be seriously damaged). As in *Hevican*, the trial issue concerned 'event proximity', and Ward J, sitting at Lincoln, again reviewing the cases, referred to the American case of *Dillon* v *Legg* (1968) 68 Cal 2d 728, which identified the three elements of foreseeability of injury as:

(a)   the physical proximity of the plaintiff to the scene of the accident;
(b)   whether the shock arose from the direct impact of the event, or from learning about it from others;
(c)   the proximity of relationship of the plaintiff and the victim.

This form of evaluation was approved in *McLoughlin* v *O'Brian*, as giving discretion to expand liability when the justice of the case demands it. In his judgment, Ward J saw this 'evaluation' as a way of giving the courts a discretion to weigh each of the three aspects against each other. In consequence, he saw this as giving him the discretion in this case to find in favour of the plaintiff. Unfortunately, as in *Hevican*, the House of Lords decision in *Alcock*, came very shortly afterwards, the *Ravenscroft* was also reversed on appeal.

We are impressed with this imaginative approach to the proximity tests. It would mean that *each* of the three factors would not necessarily have to be satisfied, i.e. one which weighed very heavily could mean that the requirement of another did not have to be met. This would retain flexibility, go some way towards meeting the floodgates argument, and leave discretion in the hands of the judges to provide justice in appropriate cases.

Although *McLoughlin* v *O'Brian* established the current statement of law on the 'immediate aftermath/unaided senses' point, the case (in the House of Lords) also contains judicial support for the extension of the scope of the test. For example Lord Bridge said:

... consider the plaintiff who learned after the event of the relevant accident. Take the case of a mother who knows that her husband and children are staying in a certain hotel. She reads in her morning newspaper that it has been the scene of a disastrous fire. She sees in the paper a photograph of unidentifiable victims trapped on the top floor waving for help from the windows. She learns shortly afterwards that all her family have perished. She suffers an acute psychiatric illness. That her illness in these circumstances was a reasonably foreseeable consequence of the events resulting from the fire is undeniable. Yet is the law to deny her damages as against a defendant whose negligence was responsible for the fire simply on the ground that an important link in the chain of causation ... was supplied by her imagination ... rather than by direct perception of the event? ... I have no doubt that this is an area of the law of negligence where we should resist the temptation to try yet once more to freeze the law in a rigid posture which would deny justice to some. ... ([1983] AC 410, at 442-3).

FLOODGATES

As far as the floodgates argument is concerned, again, there is some interesting judicial comment on this in *McLoughlin* v *O'Brian*. For example, Lord Edmund Davies said:

My Lords, the experiences of a long life in the law have made me very familiar with this 'floodgates' argument. I do not, of course, suggest that it can invariably be dismissed as lacking cogency; on the contrary, it has to be weighed carefully, but I have often seen it disproved by later events. It was urged when abolition of the doctrine of common employment was being canvassed, and it raised its head again when the abolition of contributory negligence as a total bar to a claim in negligence was being urged. ... (at 425 d-g.)

As we have indicated above, part of the floodgates argument appears to be concerned with the possibility of fraudulent claims. However, it seems to us that, on the contrary, the main plank of the argument, is the fear of a large number of *genuine* claims. Again in *McLoughlin* v *O'Brian* it was said by Lord Wilberforce:

The scarcity of cases which have occurred in the past, and the modest sums recovered, give some indication that fears of a flood of litigation may be exaggerated — experience in other fields suggests that such fears usually are. (at 421g.)

In *Hevican* v *Ruane*, Mantell J also disposed on the floodgates argument in a robust fashion:

That was, I think, demolished by the majority in *McLoughlin* v *O'Brian* and I shall only say that the evidence in this case would suggest that any such extension would be likely to fuel a very small number of additional claims. Nor do I consider that it would leave the door open to fraud. To sustain a claim based on nervous shock, no matter what the circumstances in which the shock was received, a plaintiff would be bound to submit himself or herself over a protracted period to the close scrutiny of psychiatrists well able to detect humbug.

A FLEXIBLE APPROACH IN NEGLIGENCE

To return to the California case of *Dillon* v *Legg* (1968) 68 Cal 2d 728, and to consider the 'just and reasonableness' requirement formulated in *Caparo Industries plc* v *Dickman* [1990] 2 AC 605 (along with the elements of foreseeability and proximity), if one *weighs* the respective *types* of proximity, then this seems to be very much in line with current judicial thinking in other areas of tort. For example in *Marc Rich & Co. AG and others* v *Bishop Rock Marine Co. Ltd and others* [1994] 3 All ER 686, CA, the question of the distinction between pure economic loss and physical damage was considered. It was held that, whether it was physical damage or pure economic loss, in both cases as the remedy is financial compensation there is no logic in seeking to draw any distinction between financial loss caused directly and financial loss resulting from physical injury or damage. What had to be considered was reasonable foreseeability, the nature of the relationship, and fairness, justice and reasonableness.

Similarly, the House of Lords has recently confirmed the Court of Appeal decision in *White* v *Jones* [1995] 1 All ER 691 that a solicitor owes a duty of care, not only to his client, but also to his client's intended beneficiary. Both Lords Browne-Wilkinson and Nolan adopted the 'incremental approach' to negligence, and emphasis was placed upon foreseeability of damage (see 714h). Lord Nolan said:

> I simply point to the facts as being relevant to the pragmatic, case by case approach which the law now adopts towards negligence claims. (at 736g.)

In *M (a minor) and another* v *Newham London Borough Council and others* [1994] 2 WLR 554 (see p. 17 for the facts of the case) Sir Thomas Bingham MR cogently argued from the point of view of the 'just and reasonableness' requirement, and in the circumstances of that case, this, in his judgment, was such as to import a duty of care. In other words, here again is emphasis on the case by case approach (see 573 B-D).

To conclude then, looking at each case and, according to the particular facts, giving different weight and emphasis to event proximity and to relationship proximity seems to us to be entirely in line with current judicial thinking. So, for example, the mere bystander can recover damages if the event proximity facts and the nature of the event itself are particularly compelling; and the loving spouse or parent can recover when the event proximity factors are more remote.

ORDINARY FORTITUDE AND EGG SHELL SKULLS

We are less happy about another recent decision: that of the Court of Appeal in *Page* v *Smith* [1994] 4 All ER 522 (see p. 14 for the facts). It was held that, in a nervous shock claim resulting from an accident in which the plaintiff suffered no physical injury, the plaintiff had to show that the psychiatric injury would be suffered by a person of ordinary fortitude and phlegm irrespective of whether he had been directly involved in the accident as opposed to being a mere bystander. It is accepted that there is a general principle of law that the *type* of injury must be foreseeable, but, we submit, it would have been better in this case not to refer to nervous shock at all, because the injury suffered (myalgic encephalomyelitis (ME)) was not a psychiatric injury. It was also held (per Ralph Gibson LJ) that causation had not been proved, i.e. that the accident had not caused or materially contributed to the condition arising, and, we submit, it would have been preferable here to treat the case as one of physical illness and to decide the case on the basis of causation only.

The result in this case was that the Court of Appeal decided what should have been a question of pure fact, i.e., was *this accident* one which was frightening to a person of ordinary fortitude. We would argue, therefore, that the ordinary fortitude test should be abolished and that the test should simply be on the basis of proximity and causation. Although the case of *Page* v *Smith* was not referred to, it appears to have influenced a recent case in Sheffield County Court: *Duncan* v *British Coal Corporation*, unreported, 4 January 1995. Judge Bruce Steven considered the case of a Colliery Deputy who went down to the coalface to deal with an accident at Rossington Colliery in 1990. One of his team had been crushed by a machine, and despite attempts at resuscitation the miner was dead. The Deputy developed a psychiatric illness, the fact of which was not disputed by the defence. The judge rejected the plaintiff's claim on the basis that the incident would not have been shocking to a person of ordinary fortitude. He said that the plaintiff had seen an inanimate body, no more harrowing than at any road accident or other incident where injury is sustained. In other words, the judge concluded that the sight of a dead body is not distressing to a person of ordinary fortitude, which seems an extraordinary conclusion to reach, and points out the inherent dangers of the ordinary fortitude requirement.

In any event, an examination of *Bourhill* v *Young* [1943] AC 92 suggests that this test *was* intended to apply only to the 'mere bystander':

The driver of a car or vehicle, even though careless, is entitled to assume that the ordinary frequenter of the streets has sufficient fortitude to endure ... the noise of a collision and the sight of injury to others, and is not to be considered towards one who does not possess the customary phlegm. (per Lord Porter at 117.)

There is also reference in that case to someone being in the area of danger (see Lord Thankerton's speech at 98-99), which again suggests that the 'normal fortitude' test was only intended to apply to the mere bystander. The implication of *Page* v *Smith* must be that the egg shell skull rule no longer applies to nervous shock cases. To avoid nervous shock cases being in an unacceptably anomalous position, the law should be clarified so that this rule, if it applies at all, only applies to the 'mere bystander'.

PSYCHIATRIC INJURY IN THE WORKPLACE

An encouraging development, however, concerns the increasing awareness of the possibility of psychiatric injury resulting from stress in the workplace, and the important decision of *Walker* v *Northumberland County Council* [1994] 1 All ER 737 (see p. 69). Although the case introduces no new principle of law (it is well established that an employer owes his employees a duty of care, inter alia, in respect of a safe system of work) the case is important in confirming that stressful working conditions can produce psychiatric injury and that damages can be recovered for this. We regard this as important in sending a clear message to employers that the debilitating effects of overwork, and stress at work can be properly compensated, and that, as far as possible, steps should be taken to eliminate unacceptable working conditions. The provisional recommendation (para. 6.20) of the Law Commission support this view (see below).

LEGISLATION

We regard the progressive development of the common law as essential, which view is supported by the provisional recommendation (para 6.21) of the Law Commission. However, in *McLoughlin* v *O'Brian* [1983] AC 410 at 431c, Lord Scarman indicated that 'nervous shock' presented a powerful case for legislation, in accordance with the statutes operative in the Australian territories such as New South Wales (Law Reform (Miscellaneous Provisions) Act 1944). These provisions regulate recovery for nervous shock regardless of whether the injury was foreseeable, i.e. there is no need to establish that a duty of care was owed. Under these provisions:

(a)   a parent (broadly defined) or husband or wife of a person killed, injured or put in peril by the defendant's (wrongful) act, neglect or default may recover damages for psychiatric injury arising out of the accident regardless of whether it occurred within the sight or hearing of the person suffering the shock;

(b)   other members of the family (broadly defined) of the victim may recover if the accident occurred within the sight or hearing of that family member. Whilst this would be a welcome development, care should perhaps be taken to assume that this will solve all the problems. These statutes do not solve the problems of methods of communication of bad news, nor do they deal with 'non-family', but intimate relationships.

LAW COMMISSION CONSULTATION PAPER NO. 137

Since writing this book, the Law Commission have produced a Consultation Paper on Liability for Psychiatric Illness (No. 137) which specifically examines the area of nervous shock and makes a number of provisional recommendations (pp. 88-92):

6.2   There should continue to be liability for negligently inflicted psychiatric illness that does not arise from a physical injury to the plaintiff.

6.3   The requirement of actual or apprehended physical injury to the plaintiff should not be reintroduced.

6.4   Special limitations over and above reasonable foreseeability should continue to be applied to claims for psychiatric illness where the defendant has negligently injured or imperilled someone other than the plaintiff.

6.7   If there is to be a list of relationships of close love and affection it should include, at least, brothers and sisters, de facto spouses and those in a stable homosexual relationship.

6.9   The requirements of closeness in time and space, and perception through one's own unaided senses, should be abandoned where there is a close tie of love and affection between the plaintiff and the primary victim.

6.12   It would be unhelpful to lay down in legislation a definition of what counts as a rescue.

6.13   There should be a rule permitting recovery for psychiatric illness by involuntary participants, i.e. someone who has become an unwilling participant in an event through the negligence of another should not have to show that the type of injury was foreseeable.

6.15   Damages for psychiatric illness should continue to be recoverable irrespective of whether the psychiatric illness is of a particular severity.

6.17   Normal principles of causation can satisfactorily resolve the question as to whether the communication of true news breaks the chain of causation between the negligence of the defendant, which caused the accident to the primary victim, and the plaintiff's psychiatric illness consequent on the communication of the news.

6.18 Where psychiatric injury is consequent on damage, or danger, to the property of someone other than the plaintiff, criteria analogous to, but no less restrictive than, those applied where human safety or injury to another is involved, should be insisted on.

6.19 The existence of a duty of care in respect of negligent communication of news causing foreseeable psychiatric illness should not rest on foreseeability alone.

6.20 Subject to standard defences, there should be liability where an employer has negligently overburdened its employee with work thereby foreseeably causing him or her to suffer a psychiatric illness.

Here is a clear indication that the law is in need of reform, and we very much welcome those recommendations which seek to do this. It is hoped that the publication of this Consultation Paper will result in an informed and stimulating debate leading to increased understanding of this important subject and the law reform that is now necessary in the areas we have suggested.

APPENDIX 1

Diagnostic criteria for post-traumatic stress disorder and acute stress disorder from DSM IV

DIAGNOSTIC CRITERIA FOR 309.81 POST-TRAUMATIC STRESS DISORDER

A.   The person has been exposed to a traumatic event in which both of the following were present:
   (1)   the person experienced, witnessed, or was confronted with an event or events that involved actual or threatened death or serious injury, or a threat to the physical integrity of self or others.
   (2)   the person's response involved intense fear, helplessness, or horror. **Note:** In children, this may be expressed instead by disorganised or agitated behaviour

B.   The traumatic event is persistently re-experienced in one (or more) of the following ways:
   (1)   recurrent and intrusive distressing recollections of the event, including images, thoughts, or perceptions. **Note:** In young children, repetitive play may occur in which themes or aspects of the trauma are expressed.
   (2)   recurrent distressing dreams of the event. **Note:** In children, there may be frightening dreams without recognisable content.
   (3)   acting or feeling as if the traumatic event were recurring (includes a sense of reliving the experience, illusions, hallucinations, and dissociative flashback episodes, including those that occur on awakening or when intoxicated). **Note:** In young children, trauma-specific re-enactment may occur.
   (4)   intense psychological distress at exposure to internal or external cues that symbolise or resemble an aspect of the traumatic event
   (5)   physiological reactivity on exposure to internal or external cues that symbolise or resemble an aspect of the traumatic event.

C.   Persistent avoidance of stimuli associated with the trauma and numbing of general responsiveness (not present before the trauma), as indicated by three (or more) of the following:
    (1)   efforts to avoid thoughts, feelings, or conversations associated with the trauma
    (2)   efforts to avoid activities, places, or people that arouse recollections of the trauma
    (3)   inability to recall an important aspect of the trauma
    (4)   markedly diminished interest or participation in significant activities
    (5)   feeling of detachment or estrangement from others
    (6)   restricted range of affect (e.g., unable to have loving feelings)
    (7)   sense of a foreshortened future (e.g., does not expect to have a career, marriage, children, or a normal life span)

D.   Persistent symptoms of increased arousal (not present before the trauma), as indicated by two (or more) of the following:
    (1)   difficulty falling or staying asleep
    (2)   irritability or outbursts of anger
    (3)   difficulty concentrating
    (4)   hypervigilance
    (5)   exaggerated startle response

E.   Duration of the disturbance (symptoms in Criteria B, C, and D) is more than 1 month.

F.   The disturbance causes clinically significant distress or impairment in social, occupational, or other important areas of functioning.

Specify if:
  Acute: if duration of symptoms is less than 3 months
  Chronic: if duration of symptoms is 3 months or more

Specify if:
  With Delayed Onset: if onset of symptoms is at least 6 months after the stressor

Specifiers

The following specifiers may be used to specify onset and duration of the symptoms of Posttraumatic Stress Disorder:

  Acute: This specifier should be used when the duration of symptoms is less than 3 months.
  Chronic: This specifier should be used when the symptoms last 3 months or longer.
  With Delayed Onset: This specifier indicates that at least 6 months have passed between the traumatic event and the onset of the symptoms.

Associated features and disorders

Associated descriptive features and mental disorders.   Individuals with Posttraumatic Stress Disorder may describe painful guilt feelings about surviving when others did not survive or about the things they had to do to survive. Phobic avoidance of situations or activities that resemble or symbolise the original trauma may interfere with interpersonal relationships and lead to marital conflict, divorce, or loss of job. The following associated constellation of symptoms may occur and are more commonly seen in association with an interpersonal stressor (e.g., childhood sexual or physical abuse, domestic battering, being taken hostage, incarceration as a prisoner of war or in a concentration camp, torture): impaired affect modulation; self-destructive and impulsive behaviour; dissociative symptoms; somatic complaints; feelings of ineffectiveness, shame, despair, or hopelessness; feeling permanently damaged; a loss of previously sustained beliefs; hostility; social withdrawal; feeling constantly threatened; impaired relationships with others; or a change from the individual's previous personality characteristics.

There may be increased risk of Panic Disorder, Agoraphobia, Obsessive-Compulsive Disorder, Social Phobia, Specific Phobia, Major Depressive Disorder, Somatisation Disorder, and Substance-Related Disorders. It is not known to what extent these disorders precede or follow the onset of Posttraumatic Stress Disorder.

Associated laboratory findings.   Increased arousal may be measured through studies of autonomic functioning (e.g., heart rate, electromyography, sweat gland activity).

Associated physical examination findings and general medical conditions.   General medical conditions may occur as a consequence of the trauma (e.g., head injury, burns).

Specific culture and age features

Individuals who have recently emigrated from areas of considerable social unrest and civil conflict may have elevated rates of Posttraumatic Stress Disorder. Such individuals may be especially reluctant to divulge experiences of torture and trauma due to their vulnerable political immigrant status. Specific assessments of traumatic experiences and concomitant symptoms are needed for such individuals.

In younger children, distressing dreams of the event may, within several weeks, change into generalised nightmares of monsters, of rescuing others, or of threats to self or others. Young children usually do not have the sense that they are reliving the past; rather, the reliving of the trauma may occur through repetitive play (e.g., a child who was involved in a serious automobile accident repeatedly re-enacts car crashes with toy cars). Because it may be difficult for children to report diminished interest in significant activities and construction of affect, these symptoms should be carefully evaluated with reports from parents, teachers, and other observers. In children, the sense of a foreshortened future may be evidenced by the belief that life will be too short to include becoming an adult. There may also be 'omen formation' — that is, belief in an ability to foresee future untoward events. Children may also exhibit various physical symptoms, such as stomachaches and headaches.

Prevalence

Community-based studies reveal a lifetime prevalence for Posttraumatic Stress Disorder ranging from 1% to 14%, with the variability related to methods of ascertainment and the population sampled. Studies of at-risk individuals (e.g., combat veterans, victims of volcanic eruptions or criminal violence) have yielded prevalence rates ranging from 3% to 58%.

Course

Posttraumatic Stress Disorder can occur at any age, including childhood. Symptoms usually begin within the first 3 months after the trauma, although there may be a delay of months, or even years, before symptoms appear. Frequently, the disturbance initially meets criteria for Acute Stress Disorder (see p. 429) in the immediate aftermath of the trauma. The symptoms of the disorder and the relative predominance of re-experiencing avoidance, and hyperarousal symptoms may vary over time. Duration of the symptoms varies, with complete recovery occurring within 3 months in approximately half of cases with many others having persisting symptoms for longer than 12 months after the trauma.

The severity, duration, and proximity of an individual's exposure to the traumatic event are the most important factors affecting the likelihood of developing this disorder. There is some evidence that social supports, family history, childhood experiences, personality variables, and pre-existing mental disorders may influence the development of Posttraumatic Stress Disorder. This disorder can develop in individuals without any predisposing conditions, particularly if the stressor is especially extreme.

Differential diagnosis

In Posttraumatic Stress Disorder, the stressor must be of an extreme (i.e., life-threatening) nature. In contrast, in **Adjustment Disorder**, the stressor can be of any severity. The disgnosis of Adjustment Disorder is appropriate both for situations in which the response to an extreme stressor does not meet the criteria for Posttraumatic Stress Disorder (or another specific mental disorder) and for situations in which the symptom pattern of Posttraumatic Stress Disorder occurs in response to a stressor that is not extreme (e.g., spouse leaving, being fired).

Not all psychopathology that occurs in individuals exposed to an extreme stressor should necessarily be attributed to Posttraumatic Stress Disorder. **Symptoms of avoidance, numbing, and increased arousal that are present before exposure to the stressor** do not meet criteria for the diagnosis of Posttraumatic Stress Disorder and require consideration of other diagnoses (e.g., a Mood Disorder or another Anxiety Disorder). Moreover, if the symptom response pattern to the extreme stressor meets criteria for **another mental disorder** (e.g., Brief Psychotic Disorder, Conversion Disorder, Major Depressive Disorder), these diagnoses should be given instead of, or in addition to, Posttraumatic Stress Disorder.

Acute Stress Disorder is distinguished from Posttraumatic Stress Disorder because the symptom pattern in Acute Stress Disorder must occur within 4 weeks of the traumatic event and resolve within the 4-week period. If the symptoms persist for more than 1 month and meet criteria for Posttraumatic Stress Disorder, the diagnosis is changed from Acute Stress Disorder to Posttraumatic Stress Disorder.

In **Obsessive-Compulsive Disorder**, there are recurrent intrusive thoughts, but these are experienced as inappropriate and are not related to an experienced traumatic event. Flashbacks in Posttraumatic Stress Disorder must be distinguished from illusions, hallucinations, and other perceptual disturbances that may occur in **Schizophrenia, other Psychotic Disorders, Mood Disorder With Psychotic**

Features, a delirium, Substance-Induced Disorders, and **Psychotic Disorders Due to a General Medical Condition.**

Malingering should be ruled out in those situations in which financial remuneration, benefit eligibility, and forensic determinations play a role.

DIAGNOSTIC CRITERIA FOR 308.3 ACUTE STRESS DISORDER

A.   The person has been exposed to a traumatic event in which both of the following were present:

(1)   the person experienced, witnessed, or was confronted with an event or events that involved actual or threatened death or serious injury, or a threat to the physical integrity of self or others
(2)   the person's response involved intense fear, helplessness, or horror

B.   Either while experiencing or after experiencing the distressing event, the individual has three (or more) of the following dissociative symptoms:

(1)   a subjective sense of numbing, detachment, or absence of emotional responsiveness
(2)   a reduction in awareness of his or her surroundings (e.g., 'being in a daze')
(3)   derealisation
(4)   depersonalisation
(5)   dissociative amnesia (i.e., inability to recall an important aspect of the trauma)

C.   The traumatic event is persistently re-experienced in at least one of the following ways: recurrent images, thoughts, dreams, illusions, flashback episodes, or a sense of reliving the experience; or distress on exposure to reminders of the traumatic event.

D.   Marked avoidance of stimuli that arouse recollections of the trauma (e.g., thoughts, feelings, conversations, activities, places, people).

E.   Marked symptoms of anxiety or increased arousal (e.g., difficulty sleeping, irritability, poor concentration, hypervigilance, exaggerated startle response, motor restlessness).

F.   The disturbance causes clinically significant distress or impairment in social, occupational, or other important areas of functioning or impairs the individual's ability to pursue some necessary task, such as obtaining necessary assistance or mobilising personal resources by telling family members about the traumatic experience.

G.   The disturbance lasts for a minimum of 2 days and a maximum of 4 weeks and occurs within 4 weeks of the traumatic event.

H.   The disturbance is not due to the direct physiological effects of a substance (e.g., a drug of abuse, a medication) or a general medical condition, is not better accounted for by Brief Psychotic Disorder, and is not merely an exacerbation of a pre-existing Axis I or Axis II disorder.

APPENDIX 2

The criminal injuries compensation tariff scheme

Effective from 1 April 1994.

THE TARIFF FOR PSYCHIATRIC INJURY

Shock

Shock is specifically stated to include conditions attributed to post-traumatic stress disorder, depression and similar generic terms covering such psychological symptoms as anxiety, tension, insomnia, irritability, loss of confidence, agoraphobia, preoccupation with thoughts of self-harm or guilt, and related physical symptoms such as alopecia, asthma, eczema, enuresis and psoriasis. Disability in this context will include impaired work (or school) performance, significant adverse effects on social relationships and sexual dysfunction.

Disabling mental disorder where the psychological and/or physical symptoms AND disability persist for more than six weeks from the incident:

	Band	£
moderate — lasting for over 6 to 16 weeks	1	1,000
serious — lasting for over 16 weeks to 26 weeks	9	4,000
severe — lasting over 26 weeks but not permanent	12	7,500
very severe — permanent disability (excluding physical symptoms alone for which the maximum award is band 12)	17	20,000

APPENDIX 3

Leaflet produced by Westminster Social Services on coping with a major personal crisis

COPING WITH A MAJOR PERSONAL CRISIS

This leaflet has been produced to help people affected by the Thames Riverboat Disaster.

We hope it will also help anyone facing a major personal crisis.

Somebody you know may have died or been involved in the Riverboat Disaster on 20 August 1989.

Your experience was a very personal one but this pamphlet will help you to know how others have reacted in similar situations. It will also show how you can help normal healing to occur and to avoid some pitfalls.

Normal feelings and emotions you may experience

Fear
- of damage to oneself and those we love.
- of being left alone, of having to leave loved ones.
- of *breaking down* or *losing control*.
- of a similar event happening again.

Helplessness
- Crises show up human weakness, as well as strength.

Sadness
- for deaths and losses of every kind.

Longing
- for all that has gone.

Guilt
- for being better off than others, i.e., for surviving, for being alive, for still having material things.
- regrets for things not done.

Shame
- for having been exposed as helpless, emotional and needing others.

- for not having reacted as one would have wished.

Anger
- at what has happened, at whoever caused it or allowed it to happen.
- at the injustice and senselessness of it all.
- at the shame and indignities.
- at the lack of proper understanding by others and their inefficiencies.
- Why Me?

Memories
- of feelings, of loss or of love for other people in your life who have died at other times.

Disappointed
- for all the plans that can now never be fulfilled.

Hope
- for the future and better times.

Every one may have these feelings. Experience has shown that they may vary in intensity according to circumstances. Nature heals through allowing these feelings to come out. This will not lead to loss of control but stopping these feelings may lead to other and possibly more complicated problems.

Do remember; crying can give relief.

Physical and mental sensations

Some common sensations are tiredness, sleeplessness, bad dreams, fuzziness of the mind including loss of memory and concentration, dizziness, palpitations, shakes, difficulty in breathing, choking in the throat and chest, nausea, diarrhoea, muscular tension which may lead to pain, e.g., headaches, neck and backaches, abdominal pain/tummy ache, menstrual disorders, change in sexual interest.

Numbness
Your mind may allow the misfortune to be felt only slowly. At first you may feel numb. The event may seem unreal, like a dream, something that has not really happened. People often see this wrongly either as *being strong*, or *uncaring*.

Activity
Helping others may give you some relief.

Reality
Facing the reality, by attending funerals, inspecting losses, returning to the scene, will all help you to come to terms with the event.

As you allow the disaster more into your mind, there is a need to *think* about it, to *talk* about it, and at night to *dream* about it over and over again. Children play and draw about the event.

Support
It can be a relief to receive other people's physical and emotional support. Sharing with others who have had similar experiences can help.

Privacy
In order to deal with feelings, you may find it necessary at times to be alone, or just with family and close friends.

Family and social relationships

New friendships and relationships may develop. On the other hand, strains in existing relationships may appear. The good feelings in giving and receiving may be replaced by conflict. You may feel that too little or the wrong things are offered, or that you cannot give as much as is expected. Accidents are more frequent after severe stress. Alcohol and drug intake may increase due to the extra tension.

SOME DOS AND DON'TS

Don't bottle up feelings. *Do* express your emotions and let children share in the grief.

Don't avoid talking about what happened. *Do* take every opportunity to review the experience. *Do* allow yourself to be part of a group of people who care.

Don't expect the memories to go away — the feelings will stay with you for a long time to come.

Don't forget that children experience similar feelings.

Do take time out to sleep, rest, think and be with those important to you.

Do express your needs clearly and honestly.

Do try to keep your life as normal as possible after the acute grief.

Do let children talk about their emotions and express themselves in games and drawings.

Do send children back to school and let them keep up with their activities.

Do drive more carefully.

Do be more careful around the home.

Warning: accidents are more common after severe stress.

WHEN TO SEEK PROFESSIONAL HELP

1. If you feel that your emotions are not falling into place over a period of time, you feel tension, confusion, emptiness or exhaustion.
2. If after a month you continue to feel numb.
3. If you continue to have nightmares and poor sleep.
4. If you have no one with whom to share your feelings and you feel the need to do so.
5. If your *relationships* seem to be suffering badly, or *sexual problems develop.*
6. If you have *accidents.*
7. If you continue to *smoke, drink* or take *drugs to excess.*
8. If your *work* performance suffers.
9. If you are worried that those around you are particularly vulnerable or are not healing satisfactorily.
10. If as a helper you are suffering *exhaustion.*

Do remember that you are basically the same person that you were before the disaster. *Do remember* that there is a light at the end of the tunnel. *Do remember* that if you suffer too much or too long, help is available.

WHERE TO SEEK PROFESSIONAL HELP

Riverboat Helpline, Westminster Social Services, Charlwood House, Lillington Gardens Estate, Vauxhall Bridge Road, London SW1V 2SY. Phone 930 5262/3.

Westminster City Council Social Services
Issued by Westminster Social Services but based on leaflets produced by the Australian Red Cross 1983 and Kent Social Services.

APPENDIX 4

Providers of counselling treatment and medico-legal reports

Set out below is a list of the professionals and clinics who are known to provide counselling and treatment for patients as well as producing medico-legal reports for solicitors.

The list is included not as an approved list of accredited experts but only as an informed guide to assist practitioners for the purposes of client referrals and/or expert reports. The authors therefore disclaim any responsibility.

The list is compiled in alphabetical order according to town or city.

Dr D. A. Bennett, 'Courtlands', Elms Road, Hook, Basingstoke, Hants RG27 9DP. Tel: 01256 762677. Fax: 01256 765348.

Dr David C. Muss, Director of the PTSD Unit, Birmingham Nuffield Hospital, 22 Somerset Road, Edgbaston, Birmingham B15 2QQ. Tel: 0121 456 2000. Fax: 0121 454 5293.

The Woodbourne Clinic, 21 Woodbourne Road, Harbourne, Birmingham B17 8BY. Tel: 0121 434 4343. Fax: 0121 434 3270.

Mr Bill McKinley, Chartered Clinical Psychologist, c/o Case Management Services, 17a Main Street, Balerno, Edinburgh. Tel: 0131 451 5265. Fax: 0131 449 5158.

Dr Derek Chiswick, Consultant Forensic Psychiatrist, Royal Edinburgh Hospital, Morningside Place, Edinburgh EH10 5HF. Tel: 0131 537 6000.

Dr Martin G. Livingstone, Senior Lecturer in Psychological Medicine and Honorary Consultant Psychiatrist (adults) and Ms Christine Puckering, Lecturer in Clinical Psychology (children), University of Glasgow, Academic Centre, Gartnavel Royal Hospital, 1055 Great Western Road, Glasgow G12 0HX. Tel: 0141 211 3920. Fax: 0141 357 4899.

Dr Morgan O'Connell, Royal Naval Hospital, Haslar, Gosport, Hants. PO12 2AA. Tel: 01705 584255. Fax: 01705 762205.

Professor M. P. Feldman, Partner in REACH Personal Injury Services, 5 Wigton Grove, Leeds LS17 7DZ. Tel: 0113 268 0059

Professor John Gunn CBE, Consultant Forensic Psychiatrist; Professor W. Yule, Consultant Clinical Psychologist; and Mr W. P. De Silva, Consultant Clinical Psychologist, Institute of Psychiatry, De Crespigny Park, Denmark Hill, London SE5 8EF. Tel: 0171 919 3123 (forensic psychiatry) or 0171 919 3242, 0171 919 3243, 0171 919 3217 (psychology). Fax: 0171 708 3497.

Dr Leopold Henry Field, 152 Harley Street, London W1N 1HH. Tel: 0171 935 0444.

Mr Alan Hackworth, Marketing Director, The Priory Hospitals Group, Priory Lane, London SW15 5JJ. Tel: 0181 878 9559. Fax: 0181 878 8491.

Mr Ken Baddley, Disability Services Co-Ordinator, The Royal Hospital for Neuro-disability, West Hill, Putney, London SW15 3SW. Tel: 0181 788 4511. Fax: 0181 780 1883.

Professor M. R. Trimble MD, BSc, MPhil, FRCP, FRCPsych, Professor of Behavioural Neurology and Consultant Physician in Psychological Medicine, National Hospital for Neurology and Neurosurgery, 23 Queen Square, London WC1N 3BG. Tel: 0171 829 8743. Fax: 0171 833 8658.

Dr J. Thompson, Chartered Clinical Psychologist and Senior Lecturer in Psychology, Department of Academic Psychiatry, University College London Medical School, Wolfson Building, 48 Riding House Street, London W1N 8AA. Tel: 0171 380 9470. Fax: 0171 352 2035.

Dr Nigel Eastman, Head of Section and Senior Lecturer, St George's Hospital Medical School, Department of Mental Health Services, Jenner Wing, Cranmer Terrace, Tooting, London SW17 0RE. Tel: 0181 682 0033. Fax: 0181 682 3450.

Dr Stephen O'Brien, Consultant Psychiatrist, Huntercombe Manor Hospital, Huntercombe Lane South, Taplow, Maidenhead, Berkshire SL6 0PQ. Tel: 01628 667881. Fax: 01628 666989.

The Unit Manager, Adolescent Forensic Service, Salford Mental Health Trust, Bury New Road, Prestwich, Manchester M25 3BL. Tel: 0161 772 3666. Fax: 0161 772 3443.

Dr Peter Hodgkinson (Director) Chartered Psychologist and Mr Michael Stewart (Director), The Centre for Crisis Psychology, Four Arches, Broughton Hall, Nr Skipton, North Yorkshire BD23 3AE. Tel: 01756 796383. Fax: 01756 796384.

Dr Margaret Oates, Honorary Consultant Psychiatrist, Department of Psychiatry, University Hospital, Queen's Medical Centre, Clifton Boulevard, Nottingham NG7 2UH. Tel: 0115 9249924 ext. 41339. Fax: 0115 970167.

Dr Ian Matson, Consultant Psychiatrist, Dyke Bar Hospital, Grahamstone Road, Paisley, Renfrewshire PA2 7DE. Tel: 0141 884 5122. Fax: 0141 884 7162.

Mrs M. A. Preston, Consultant Clinical Psychologist, TEAM Health Care, Lyons Court, 1666 High Street, Knowle, Solihull, West Midlands B93 0LY. Tel: 01564 730101. Fax: 01564 778755.

Dr J. Guy Edwards, Consultant Psychiatrist & Honorary Clinical Senior Lecturer, University Department of Psychiatry, Royal South Hants Hospital, Southampton, Hants SO14 0YG. Tel: 01703 550118.

Dr Gordon Turnbull, Consultant Psychiatrist, Clinical Director of the Traumatic Stress Treatment Unit, Ticehurst House Hospital, Ticehurst, Wadhurst, East Sussex TN5 7HU. Tel: 01580 200391. Fax: 01580 201006.

Dr Keith Rix, Consultant Psychiatrist, High Royds Hospital, Menston, Ilkley, West Yorkshire LS9 6AQ. Tel: 01943 876151. Fax: 01943 870471.

Dr Gerald Bridge, 'The Retreat', Heslington Road, York. Tel: 01904 412551.

APPENDIX 5
Selected further reading

LAW

Books

N. J. Mullany and P. R. Handford, *Tort Liability for Psychiatric Damage* (Sweet & Maxwell, 1993).

W. A. Barton, *Recovering for Psychological Injuries*, 2nd ed. (American Trial Lawyers Association, 1990).

Articles — in addition to those cited in the text

M. Davie, 'Negligently Inflicted Psychiatric Illness: The Hillsborough Case in the House of Lords' (1992) 43 NILQ 237.

R. English, 'Nervous Shock: Before the Aftermath' [1993] CLJ 204.

T. K. Feng, 'Nervous Shock: Bystander Witnessing a Catastrophe' (1995) 111 LQR 48.

B. Lynch, 'A Victory for Pragmatism? Nervous Shock Reconsidered' (1992) 108 LQR 367.

B. McKenna, 'Stress injuries at work' (1994) 144 NLJ 1652.

K. J. Nasir, 'Nervous Shock and Alcock: The Judicial Buck Stops Here' (1992) 55 MLR 705.

A. Ritchie, 'Damages for psychiatric injuries' (1994) 144 NLJ 1690.

H. Teff, 'The Hillsborough Football Disaster and Claims for Nervous Shock' (1992) vol. 32 Med Sci Law No. 3 252.

LEGAL PRACTICE

Books

J. Hendy, M. Day and A. Buchan, *Personal Injury Practice*, 2nd ed. (Legal Action Group, 1994)

J. M. Pritchard and N. Soloman, *Personal Injury Litigation*, 7th ed. (Longmans, 1992).

D. Brennan, *Provisional Damages* (Legal Studies and Services, 1986).

MEDICINE

Books

R. Bluglass and P. Bowden (eds), *Principles and Practice of Forensic Psychiatry* (Churchill-Livingstone, 1990).

J. Davidson and E. Foa (eds), *Post-traumatic Stress Disorder: DSM IV and Beyond* (American Psychiatric Publishers, 1993).

J. Gunn and P. J. Taylor (eds), *Forensic Psychiatry, Clinical, Legal and Ethical Issues* (Butterworth-Heinemann, 1993).

C. B. Scrignar, *Post-traumatic Stress Disorder*, 2nd ed. (New Orleans LA: Bruno Press, 1988).

Articles — in addition to those cited in the text

N. Breslau and G. Davis, 'Post-traumatic Stress Disorder: The Stressor Criterion' (1987) 175 *Journal of Nervous and Mental Disease* 255, 262.

S. Joseph et al, 'Crisis support and psychiatric symptomatology in adult survivors of the Jupiter cruise ship disaster' (1992) *British Journal of Clinical Psychology*, 31, 63.

A. McFarlane and P. Papay, 'Multiple Diagnosis in Post-traumatic Stress Disorder in the Victims of a Natural Disaster' (1992) 176 *Journal of Nervous and Mental Disease* 498, 502.

R. Mayou et al, 'Psychiatric consequences of road traffic accidents' (1993) 307 BMJ 647.

C. Pugh and M. Trimble, 'Psychiatric Injury after Hillsborough' (1993) 163 *British Journal of Psychiatry* 425.

M. Weller, 'Post-traumatic stress disorder' (1993) 143 NLJ 878.

W. Yule et al, 'The Jupiter sinking: Effects on children's fears, depression and anxiety', J Child Psychol. Psychiat, 31, 1051.

W. Yule, 'Post-traumatic stress disorders in children' (1992) *Current Opinion in Paediatrics*, 4(4), Aug 1992.

POPULAR ACCOUNTS OF TRAUMA

Books

D. Muss, *The Trauma Trap* (Doubleday, 1991). (A self-help book.)

G. Sheridan and T. Kenning, *Survivors* (Pan, 1993). (An account of the experiences of those who have survived trauma.)

Index